A FINE VIEW
OF THE SHOW

A FINE VIEW
OF THE SHOW

Letters from the Western Front

Andrew Jackson

ଌ

First published in the United States in 2009

Copyright ©2009 Andrew Jackson

Library of Congress Control Number: 2009903718

ISBN 978-0-557-06225-6

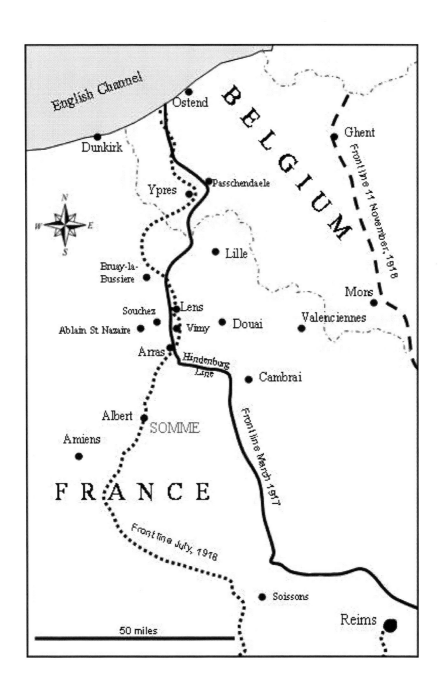

Contents

Foreword

Written between May 1915 and January 1920, the wartime letters of Captain Hector Jackson offer intriguing insights into the life and times of an idealistic young man swept up in the greatest conflict the world had ever seen. Born in 1892 to English parents then living in Karachi, Hector Jackson was sent to boarding schools in England, receiving his secondary school education at Charterhouse, one of the country's most eminent public schools. Although bright, Hector was anything but bookish, excelling at "games," as team sports were then generally known. Popular, good natured, and cheerful, Hector earned the respect and loyalty of both faculty and schoolmates. Indeed, it is tempting to conjecture that the friendships the young man made at Charterhouse became just as important to him as his relationships with his more distant blood relations.

Hector's family background – which helped to shape his highly appealing character – is capably covered in Andrew Jackson's introductory chapter. As Jackson explains, Hector's parents were members of the English upper middle class, well educated, but sometimes financially challenged. His father, Dr. Moses Jackson, had shared rooms at Oxford with the poet and classicist A.E. Housman, a figure who had a continuing interest in the Jackson family's welfare. Though not part of the main story, Housman's unrequited love for Moses and his interest in his family recurs as fascinating subtext at various points in the Jackson family's story.

In 1911, the Jackson family's destiny took a sharp turn as Hector, his parents, and two of his three brothers left England for a new life on an isolated dairy farm in a remote corner of Langley, a rural municipality located near Vancouver, in Canada's westernmost province of British Columbia. It was an odd move for the Jacksons and undoubtedly a difficult one for Hector. When acquired by the Jacksons,

i

Applegarth (as the family named their property) was 160 acres of woodland, floodplain, and pasture, its only buildings being a very modest wood frame farmhouse and unsubstantial barn. For the once privileged young man, life at Applegarth was the very antithesis of what he had known at Charterhouse.

At the time of the Jacksons' emigration, Canada's westernmost province was the most British part of the nation, 52.2 percent of its residents having been born in the United Kingdom or its numerous possessions. An even larger percentage – 67.8 percent – could claim British roots. It was an environment in which Hector and his family might well have felt at home. The area around Applegarth, however, was home not to genteel, well-educated Britons, but rather, to numerous Scandinavian and Canadian-born settlers, none of whom could claim the pedigrees or rarefied experiences of Moses and his family.

The outbreak of the First World War in August 1914 brought change to Hector's life once again. Aged 22 at the time and inculcated with the patriotic values of the British upper middle class, Hector may well have been torn between the duties he owed to his family and those owed to the King. The war had been raging for just twelve months when, like thousands of other British-born Canadians, he determined to enlist in the army, not as an officer, as befitted his social standing and education, but in the ranks, becoming a sapper in the Canadian Engineers.

Leaving for Britain in March 1916, Hector began to write to family members to describe his experiences. His early letters home reveal a certain class-consciousness as he lamented the general lack of "decent fellows" amongst his fellow engineers, save for a few who had been educated in schools such as his. On reaching Ottawa, however, Hector happily socialized with the daughters of the capital's upper crust. Once back in England, as his letters note, the pattern would continue as he visited old haunts, looked up relatives and schoolmates, and made many new acquaintances. His genial nature, dashing good looks, and inherent social skills earned him many invitations, quickly forged new friendships, and, apparently, created a host of female admirers. The list of ladies to whom he owed letters would eventually become unmanageable.

FOREWORD

While a student at Charterhouse, Hector had developed attributes of leadership, including self-confidence, resourcefulness, and selflessness. His natural charisma, energy, and ability to inspire and command respect had been recognized even while he was training as a sapper. Little more than a month after leaving Canada, Hector received an officer's commission, the combined result of recognition of talent and familial influence in Canada's corridors of power. The army's trust was not misplaced. As Andrew Jackson documents, despite his affinity for social recreation, Hector was hardworking, studious, and utterly devoted to his duties. While in England, Hector acquired much of the technical knowledge he would later use when posted to the Western Front, but he also experienced some frustration, for as his letters disclose, his salary was less than adequate for a lifestyle filled with tennis, dances, concerts, and parties. Further, as Hector lamented, some of his training was repetitive and lacked apparent purpose.

Posted to France in October 1916, Hector's life changed once again. The grim reality of trench life that he had only glimpsed as hospital trains arrived at railway stations in London hit him squarely in the face. His letters, formerly filled with images of a post-Edwardian society attempting to preserve the vigour of a former age, assumed a slightly darker tone. During the next two years Hector experienced the repulsive reality of the Western Front, serving on the Somme, at Vimy Ridge, and in the dreaded Ypres Salient. Although he attempted to make light of the dangers he often faced, many of those who served at his side were felled by machine gun bullets, ripped apart by shells, or had their lungs destroyed by gas.

The exhilaration that Hector experienced in England and which would heighten in the face of battle, contrasted sharply with the social suffocation and lack of opportunity he had experienced in rural Canada. Though he may have been a loyal and loving son, his letters revealed a love of high adventure far from the constraints of home. "Canada," he wrote, "is all very well but you don't live." As time went on, however, Hector took pride in the Canadian Corps' achievements, referring to their capture of Vimy Ridge as "our own show," observing how the victory had placed the dominion's troops in good stead in London, and noting how his experiences working on and off his parents' farm had prepared him well for his duties in the field. Hector's divided loyalties were indicative of many with his background and his observations shed further light on the question of how a sense of Canadian national identity began to develop as a result of the war.

Hector's letters to his mother and aunt were often circumspect, with potentially worrying details downplayed as he projected a carefree attitude that denied the constant threat of artillery bombardments, landmines, and snipers. While belittling the depth and extent of the mud of Passchendaele to his mother, however, Hector was more forthcoming in his correspondence with his teenaged brother, Gerald. Perhaps emboldened by his younger sibling's curiosity, Hector's descriptions of battle conditions were somewhat more graphic. His accounts of combat are spontaneous and clear. As we follow Hector in his journey in the last hundred days of the war, the suspense and excitement build. Hector repeatedly put his own life on the line during his time on the Western Front, earning several nominations for the Military Cross for gallantry under fire. When the award was finally made, Hector was typically self-effacing, urging his correspondents *not* to place its initials after his name.

Hector's is a life that deserves to be remembered. His letters to his family, coupled with other correspondence in this compendium of letters, further our understanding young officers' lives during the First World War. I leave it to Andrew Jackson, who has breathed fresh life into the story of a Canadian war hero and placed it well within the context of the time, to take up the tale and bring it to its startling conclusion.

Warren Sommer
Fort Langley, British Columbia

Preface

This is a collection of letters, written by a young man thrown into one of the most horrific wars ever fought, the First World War. The Great War. The War to End All Wars. And of all the theatres of that dreadful war, the Western Front stands out as perhaps the most desolate and most wasteful of human life.

The Somme, Flanders Fields, Passchendaele. The names alone conjure up gut-wrenching images. Scarred skeletons of trees standing in shell-churned landscapes of scorched dust or mud. Long ragged lines of exhausted men, launched from the relatively safety of their sodden trenches by the blast of a whistle, to run the gauntlet of merciless machine gun fire across no mans land, only to be clawed to a deadly standstill just a few yards later by rusted barbed wire entanglements. Dully reflecting flooded shell craters littered with putrefying corpses of soldiers, too numerous or too exposed to enemy fire to be collected by their brothers in arms. Lines of khaki figures, their gas-blinded eyes swathed in filthy bandages, one hand on the shoulder of the man in front, blindly following in his footsteps.

The young man who wrote these letters was Hector John Roderick Jackson. Hector volunteered for the Canadian Expeditionary Force in Vancouver in 1915 and arrived on the Western Front at the height of the Battle of the Somme in October 1916.

It would be four long years before Hector was finally released from the military to return to British Columbia. During that time he would receive a commission in the Canadian Engineers, climb Vimy Ridge, be awarded the Military Cross for bravery under fire at Passchendaele, and be part of the final offensive that routed the German Army and forced its surrender. He would join the stream of wounded flowing from the front in the last days of the war, poisoned by mustard gas.

Hector's travels and travails over these four long years were recorded in his letters to his mother, Rosa and his youngest brother Gerald, back on their farm in British Columbia, and to his aunt, Margaret, who lived near London. His writing brings to life the day-to-day business of trench warfare and provides a fascinating insight into the live-for-the-moment attitude that young men develop to counter the stress of warfare (the life expectancy of a 2nd lieutenant on the Western Front was reduced to just two weeks at one stage of the war).

These letters were collected by Hector's brother Gerald, who typed them out in the 1970s to preserve them. They are reproduced here completely unedited apart from a few very minor typing errors. I haven't attempted to change Hector's style of writing, which is probably much as he spoke - an enthusiastic stream of consciousness, with long sentences, separated only by commas.

Andrew Jackson
December, 2008

Acknowledgements

A number of people have played critical parts in the writing of this book. I would like to acknowledge my brothers, Martin and Brian Jackson who supported the idea of putting the compiled letters, including selected correspondence with A.E. Housman from the family collection, into a single document for posterity and to reach a wider audience.

Dr. Mary Rubio, Professor Emeritus in English, University of Guelph, and Dr. Jonathan Vance, Professor and Canada Research Chair, Department of History, University of Western Ontario, were kind enough to read an early version of the manuscript. They both played a pivotal role by recommending that I look into publishing the letters. They also suggested that I expand the linking text considerably, putting the letters into their wider historical context, and filling in the background picture of what was happening in Canada during the war years.

Through a serendipitous internet connection and common research interests, Warren Sommer, principal of Legacy Heritage Consultants, got in touch with me and proved a veritable font of information on the Langley and Greater Vancouver area during the years of the First World War. He also helped enormously by taking me to a number of the sites in British Columbia that featured in Hector Jackson's letters, including a visit to the family farm in Aldergrove. Just as importantly, he selflessly offered to act as copy editor of the manuscript, suggesting numerous improvements. Without his help there would have been some gaping holes in the story.

Nona Lambert, the current owner of the Jackson's old family farm, Applegarth, kindly allowed me to visit her and provided useful material on Moses Jackson's life in British Columbia.

Information from Library and Archives Canada was used extensively during research. In particular, the digitized copies of the unit war diaries proved invaluable in tying the letters to locations and activities as, due to military censorship, most letters lacked any locality information.

I would also like to acknowledge the tolerance of my wife, Jackie, during the many months of weekends and evenings that I spent researching and writing the book. A lesser woman would probably have divorced me by now.

Finally I must acknowledge my father, Dr. Gerald Jackson, who was responsible for collecting the letters and painstakingly transcribing them into a typed document so many years ago. Without this work, no book would have been possible and the letters, and the valuable resource they represent, would have been lost forever.

Chapter 1

Sons of the Empire

One afternoon in early March 1917, young Lieutenant Hector Jackson's well-earned rest was interrupted when the ruined village in which he was billeted just west of Vimy Ridge in northern France, was again pummelled by heavy artillery from just behind the German-held crest to the east. Two days later Hector wrote one of his regular letters home to his mother:

> We had some 'Heavies'[1] in here a few days ago pretty close to us; the nearest was 40 yds. and plastered us with mud and bricks, blew the door open and tore the canvas windows; we were lucky as one billet got a direct hit, killed 3 and wounded 7. I had a fine view of the whole show from our place 200 yds. away.

Hector had a "fine view" of the minor shelling incident he described that afternoon, but he also had a close-up view of a much larger part of the war on the Western Front, from his baptism of fire in the Battle of the Somme, through the Canadian nation-building capture of Vimy Ridge, to the hollow, mud-mired victory at Passchendaele and the final rout of the exhausted German armies that led to their unconditional surrender on November 11, 1918.

In the first week of August 1914, the German Army had stormed through Luxembourg and Belgium into northern France. It swept before it the French Army and the small poorly-prepared British

---

[1] Heavy artillery shells.

Expeditionary Force that had come to France's aid, rapidly advancing southwards, with the objective of capturing Paris and forcing the French to surrender. But a month later, in early September 1914, when the German forces were almost within sight of Paris, the Allied Forces rallied to repulse the Germans thirty miles towards the Belgian border. There, both sides bogged down. With winter looming, the opposing armies dug two lines of defensive trenches; the trench lines rapidly extended westwards in a "race to the sea," as each force tried to outflank the other. The line of trenches soon reached the beaches of the English Channel to complete a 300-mile front that snaked from the coast, across France, to the Swiss border. The two opposing forces then churned up the line with barrages of artillery during a series of battles at Ypres, Artois and Champagne. Some of these artillery duels lasted many weeks, periodically exploding into full-blown battles throughout the early part of the winter before the armies settled into their cheerless frozen trenches to wait for spring, when both sides hoped to sweep the other away.

Britain's declaration of war against Germany in August 1914, was not legally binding on Canada. However, Canada, as part of the British Empire, enthusiastically supported Britain. The Canadian Prime Minister, Sir Robert Borden, announced in the House of Commons that "When Britain is at war, Canada is at war. There is no distinction."

Although Canada had just over 3,000 regular troops in its army when the war broke out, she could draw on an additional 55,000 members of the "militia," civilians who served on a part-time basis on weekends and in the summer. The first troops of the Canadian Expeditionary Force left for Britain in October 1914, barely two months after the declarations of war between Britain and Germany, en-route to joining the Allied front line.

The opposing armies in France found that their plans to win an early and decisive victory in the spring of 1915 did not materialize. The stalemate continued long after spring had come and gone. In fact, the line that had been established in 1914 did not move more than ten miles in either direction during the next two years. The defensive lines of both sides were so strong that attempts by either army to break through the barbed wire and massed machine guns of the enemy's trench lines were beaten back with huge loss of life, in offensives such as the First Battle of Ypres. Even when a breakthrough did occur, poor communications generally resulted in the opposing side forcing the enemy back to their original positions.

In April 1915, the Germans attempted to break the deadlock, using poisonous chlorine gas for the first time. In a series of battles, some involving the use of gas, 300,000 soldiers on both sides were killed. Both sides realized that they needed more men if they were to achieve a breakthrough. Recruiting drives were stepped up in Britain and throughout the British Empire, including Canada. In June the British War Office requested the Canadian Government to provide additional troops. Canada committed to raise two additional Divisions to support the pair that were already in Europe. Hector Jackson was one of the many who volunteered to swell the ranks.

Hector Jackson was born in the city of Karachi in India on March 27 1892. [1] His father, Dr. Moses John Jackson, was the principal of the D.J Sind College in Karachi at the time. A description of his father's background helps one understand how Hector's character was shaped by Moses' influence.

Moses Jackson had been born in Ramsgate, England, in 1858 into a family of professional educators and had shown himself to be a very intelligent student with a talent in the sciences. He was accepted by the University College of London at the age of 17, where he was awarded the Neil Arnott Medal in Experimental Physics. Moses developed a well-rounded character, excelling in academics as well as in athletics and rugby. Two years after entering university he was offered a scholarship to St. John's College at Oxford which he took up in 1877. There he continued to be a natural sportsman who excelled, with little apparent effort, in his studies, athletics and in the college rowing team.

While in his third year at Oxford, Moses was assigned a room on the same staircase as two other undergraduates of the same age: Alfred W. Pollard and Alfred Edward Housman. Housman was to become one of the best known British poets of his time. Moses and Housman initially had little in common. Athletic Moses was a science student, described by E.W. Watson as "a vigorous rowing man, quite unliterary and outspoken in his want of any such interest." This latter

---

[1] Karachi is now in Pakistan.

characteristic, however, appears to have been used largely in jest against his literary friends, as Housman said that he much admired Moses' command of the English language. Another acquaintance later described him as "good looking with a taste for literature." [1] Pollard described Moses as "a delightful science scholar."

In contrast, the quiet, retiring Housman was studying Latin and Greek and limited his exercise to long country walks. However, as he got to know him, Housman was attracted

Hector's father, Moses Jackson, aged about 20
| Family album

by Moses' charisma, his straightforward character and kindly manner and the three young men developed a strong friendship. [2]

In 1881 Moses sailed though his final examinations, or "Greats" as they were known, achieving a First Class Science Pass. Housman, scornful of many of his lecturers and possibly influenced by Moses' apparent lack of need for long hours of study, did not put in the required preparation and failed his Greats in Classics dismally.

After completing his degree at Oxford, Moses moved to London, putting his degree to work as examiner of electrical specifications at the London Patent Office, a position he held for the next six years. In addition to working at the Patent Office, Moses began part-time studies for a doctorate at the University of London, where he had originally begun his university studies. He maintained his interest in athletics and

---

[1] Addler.
[2] Graves R.P. (1979) A.E. Housman *The Scholar-Poet*.

won the Quarter Mile Members Challenge cup at the London Athletics Club. Moses was awarded a Doctor of Science in Physics in 1883.

A year after Moses moved to London and while he was occupied with his part time studies, Housman followed him to the Patent Office in London, obtaining a low-paid job as a clerk. Housman joined Moses and the Moses' brother, Adalbert, who was studying for his undergraduate degree at the University of London, in rented rooms in Talbot Road, Bayswater.

Over the next three years, Housman's feelings for Moses deepened from friendship to one-sided adoration. Housman came to realise that his attraction had grown beyond mere friendship and that he was in fact homosexual. This fact only became public knowledge in 1967 when an essay by Housman's brother, Laurence, was published. Moses on the other hand, was unswervingly heterosexual. In 1885, Housman realized that his love would never be reciprocated and, with

Alfred Housman, aged 18 | Archival photo.

a broken heart, he moved out of his shared lodgings into his own accommodation.

Moses and Housman remained friends but Moses "kept him at a greater emotional distance, treating him with kindness and consideration, but making it clear that their relationship would not advance in the direction that Alfred longed for."[1] Although he had begun writing poetry years before, Housman fervently channelled his personal loss into his writing, penning many of the poems that were later to be published in his best-known volume of poetry, *A Shropshire Lad*.

---

[1] Graves R.P., *A.E. Housman: The Scholar Poet*, 1979.

Moses also found new accommodation.[1] The landlord was a retired coachman, Philip Kingston, whose daughter, Rosa Chambers, had attended university, possibly also at the University of London. In May 1885 she married a young man named John Chambers, but he died tragically just nine months later.

Moses and the recently widowed Rosa soon fell in love. Moses, however, felt that his job at the Patent Office was not sufficiently well paid if they were to be married. He therefore

Rosa Chambers, the young university-educated widow with whom Moses Jackson fell in love. |
Family album

applied for a teaching position with the Colonial Service in India, a position that offered better chances of promotion. He was offered a post as principal of the newly established Dayaram Jethmal Sind Science College in Karachi, which he accepted.

At the end of 1887 Moses bade farewell to both Rosa and Housman. Housman's biographers refer to the parting of Housman and Moses as "stiff," with Moses asking Housman to forget him. Housman's feeling of devastating personal loss was reflected in later poems.[2]

---

[1] In Bloomfield Street, nearer the Patent Office than his earlier accommodation.

[2] Laurence Housman, ed., *A.E.H., Poems VII,* 1937.

He would not stay for me; and who can wonder?
  He would not stay for me to stand and gaze.
I shook his hand and tore my heart in sunder
  And went with half my life about my ways.

And again:[1]

Shake hands, we shall never be friends, all's over;
  I only vex you the more I try.
Alls wrong that ever I've done or said,
  And nought to help it in this dull head:
Shake hands, here's luck, goodbye.

But if you come to a road where danger
  Or guilt or anguish or shame's to share,
Be good to the lad that loves you true
  And the soul that was born to die for you,
And whistle and I'll be there.

Moses sailed from England to India via Gibraltar, Italy and Egypt, arriving in Karachi in early 1888. He threw himself into his new profession as a teacher like his father. Over the next twenty years, Moses built up the college from two small back-street bungalows to a well-regarded national institution with several hundred students. Today the college counts judges, a Speaker of the Indian Legislative Assembly, government ministers and Dr. Abdul Qadeer Khan, father of India's nuclear programme, amongst its alumni. The college still operates, some 120 years after Moses took up his post. One alumnus, Dr. Mohanlal Sonpar, reminisced in a book published to celebrate the 50th anniversary of the founding of the college.[2]

> The College's atmosphere was conducive to initiative, freedom and independence. It emphasized character more than bookish studies. It had been created by teachers like Dr. Jackson. Dr. Jackson concealed a simple kindly heart under a rough and austere exterior.

---

[1] *More Poems, 30.*

[2] Prof. L.H.Ajwani, ed., *An Account of the Golden Jubilee of the Dayaram Jethmal Sind College, Karachi 17-23 January 1937,* 1939.

Dr. Jackson generally wore clothes made of white drill or 'zeen'. His necktie was also made of white washable cloth. He did not mind wearing clothes that were mended or patched. He rode a bicycle and did not bother about the show of a four wheeler. I have had the experience of many colleges but I never saw a principal with even half his simple tastes.

The outstanding feature of his character that struck everyone was his love of discipline. He would not allow even a pencil to fall down during his lecture. It would therefore be no exaggeration to say that Discipline was synonymous with Dr. Jackson.

When as a schoolboy I came to Karachi in 1901, I wished to see the college. It was closed on the day I visited it. It was closed for the students and professors, but not for Dr. Jackson. I saw him standing in the Chemical Laboratory, working away with the sleeves of his shirt tucked up and a towel on his shoulder. My first impression of him, therefore, was that to him work was worship. Later on as a college student, I learnt that he did not believe in genius as such. He believed that hard work made geniuses of men. He was a fine example of it – a self made genius.

As with many Victorians, Moses put great store in the value of engineering. Another of his old students, G.J. Butani, recalled:

I was an engineering student of the D.J. Sind College in the years 1900 to 1905. Our Principal during this time was Dr. Jackson. No doubt, he was a 'man amongst men'. 'My Engineers' he used to call us. We had several classes jointly with . . . students of the Arts Class and he would not begin his lectures till 'his Engineers' came in.

Moses Jackson in Karachi wearing his habitual white drill clothing. | *Family album.*

8

For two years after arriving in India, Moses maintained a long-distance romance with Rosa, but towards the end of 1889, he returned to England on two months' leave to marry his fiancée.

In spite of their earlier "stiff farewell," Moses paid Housman a surprise visit at the Patent Office soon after his return, but refrained from mentioning his imminent marriage to avoid upsetting his friend. Moses and Rosa were married on December 9 at St Saviour's Church in Paddington. Housman only found out about his friend's marriage after Moses had returned to India with his new bride. Housman's diary contains a single heart-rending entry: "Tuesday Jan: 7 - I heard he was married." Housman later wrote a poem about Moses' marriage, including the lines:

> So the groomsman quits your side
>   And the bridegroom seeks the bride:
> Friend and comrade yield you over
>   To her that hardly loves you more.[1]

In spite of this devastating disappointment, Housman and Moses began to patch up their friendship, Housman still hoping against hope that he could build a deeper relationship with Moses.

In 1886, three years before Moses had married Rosa, Housman had published *A Shropshire Lad*. This collection of poems that he had worked on in the dark years after his separation from Moses included many oblique references to his love for his friend; it became an immediate publishing success. Four years after Moses' marriage, in an amazing turn of fortune, Housman, who had failed his final exams at Oxford, was offered the Latin Chair at the University College of London. His fame as both a classics scholar and poet was cemented.

Until his marriage, Moses had lived on the college premises in Karachi, but on his return with Rosa, or Rosie, as he affectionately called her, he rented a bungalow with a view to starting a family.[2]

---

[1] Epithalamium - Last Poems XXIV.
[2] Known as Hassanally's Bungalow.

Hector was the second of the four sons of Moses and Rosa: Rupert (born 1890), Hector (1892), Oscar (1895), and Gerald (1900). Moses invited Housman to become Gerald's godfather, a role he gladly accepted. All Moses and Rosa's sons were born in India, except for Oscar, who was born during a long leave in England.

In the 1890s, Karachi was a dangerous place to bring up young children, with endemic malaria and cholera during the hot, wet monsoon season, and annual outbreaks of bubonic plague. Moses was forced to close the College in March and April of most years owing to the plague, and to move the students ninety miles inland to drier Hyderabad.

As was usually the case with British civil servants based in India, each of Moses' and Rosa's four sons was sent to England to be educated once they reached school age. Moses chose a school in the small town of Godalming in Surrey. There they began their schooling at Branksome Preparatory School.

Once in England, Hector never returned to India and had only limited face-to-face contact with his father during his occasional leave periods back in England. In contrast,

The house in Karachi that Moses and Rosa moved to a number of years after starting their family, after the college expanded. | Family album

Five-year-old Hector in England showing the cheerful and mischievous side of his character. | Family album

Rosa spent many months at a time in Godalming with her children, living in a house in Peperharow Road, adjacent to Charterhouse School. From about 1906, she remained in Godalming, providing a stable home for her sons. Moses and Rosa reverted to their loving, but long distance relationship. Paternal influence on Hector and his brothers was mostly through weekly, or more frequent, letters and Hector became a prolific letter writer. Moses' diary for that period shows that he did not let distance soften his disciplinary control over his sons – "Hector badly reported on . . . must be severely treated" he records in one entry. This distant parenting caused Hector to develop an independent and self-reliant character that became apparent as he grew older.

In late 1907 Moses had a disagreement with the board of directors at the D.J. Sind College over two students whom he believed had cheated during their exams. Moses felt that the board failed to give him the support a principal needed and, in the words of one of his past students, Dr. Mohanlal Sonpar:

> He was a man of principle. When persons and principles stood in opposition he was no respecter of persons; but he would go to any length to save his principles. When disagreement occurred between the Board of the College and himself, he did not care to bow to the Board, but bent his knee before the alter of his principles. He quietly resigned the post and severed connection with the institution which he had reared with his own hands.

And so Moses left D.J. Sind College and moved from Karachi to Baroda (now called Vadodara) 450 miles east of Karachi. The city of Baroda was the seat of Maharaja Sayajirao III. The Maharaja was a member of the Gaekwar dynasty, which had ruled the Princely State of Baroda since conquering the city of Baroda in 1721. He had ascended to the throne in 1875 at the tender age of 12, and was educated largely by British teachers in an especially built school in the palace grounds.

By the time he took over running the state from his advisors, the Gaekwar, as the Maharajah was commonly known, had become a great admirer of the British and in particular their education system; he was also among the wealthiest men in the world. Each year he travelled to

Britain and other parts of the world to recruit talented people to help develop Baroda.

During his sixty-four years on the throne, the Gaekwar revolutionised the State of Baroda with numerous far-sighted social changes, such as free and compulsory education. He imported new technology, initiating the construction of a large railway network, revolutionizing the water supply for Baroda, and founding the Bank of Baroda, all of which still operate today.

One of his most memorable achievements was to found the Baroda College of Science, which was later expanded and renamed after his death, the Maharajah Sayajirao University of Baroda. In 1907, the Baroda College of Science required an Acting Principal, and the Gaekwar offered Moses the position as he was in the process of resigning from Sind College.

When Moses accepted the position on December 19, 1907, the college had some 900 science students. Unlike most of the rest of India, the Gaekwar had banned any caste discrimination in education, and the university catered for students from all castes and both Hindu and Islamic students. Today the University of Baroda is still one of the premier universities in India.

In addition to his position as Acting Principal of the College of Science, Moses also held the post of director of science studies for the State of Baroda. Whilst all the Gaekwar's sons were educated in England and the United

The Gaekwar of Baroda and his only daughter Indiraja, to whom Moses acted as tutor. This silver framed photo was given to him by the Gaekwar on his departure from Baroda. | *Original held by Roslyn Jackson*

12

States, his only daughter, Indiraja, was instead schooled in Baroda with the best private tutors available. For much of his time at Baroda, Moses was also responsible for teenaged Indiraja's education to prepare her for her matriculation exam.

The Baroda College of Science fell under the auspices of the Faculty of Science at the University of Bombay. But in November 1908, less than a year after becoming principal, Moses initiated his vision for a full university, the Baroda Science Institute, completely independent of the Science Faculty at the University of Bombay. He put forward a detailed proposal, complete with building plans, which was strongly supported by the Gaekwar, and tried to persuade the Baroda Education Commission to fund it. But the following year the commission rejected the idea, saying that the state could not afford the luxury.

With his vision for the future of the institution shattered, Moses became frustrated. In 1910, after only three years in Baroda but more than twenty years in India, and disillusioned with the political direction that India was moving in, Moses retired from the Indian Civil Service and turned his back on India, sailing from Bombay on April 7, 1910.

Forty years later, after continual battles with its governing body, the University of Baroda finally came into being, independent and along the lines that Moses Jackson had charted and argued for so passionately.

Moses was a strict disciplinarian in the Victorian mould, but with a kindly nature. | Family album

Once back in England, Moses rejoined Rosa and their sons in their house in Godalming. Moses then travelled extensively in England, visitng numerous institutions whilst looking at possible positions. He applied for at least two of these, one as professor of physics at London University, the other as director of education to the Borough of Bradford. By this time the rift between Moses and Housman had fully healed. Early in 1911, Housman moved from the University College of London to take up the prestigious Kennedy Chair of Latin at Cambridge and his star was shining brightly. In this position at Cambridge he became acknowledged as the greatest Latin scholar in the English-speaking world. He was later offered the poet laureateship but, as with all other proffered honours, he declined. Housman provided a letter of referral in support of Moses' application to the Borough of Bradford:[1]

The Jackson family in England in about 1907. From L to R: Gerald, Moses, Rupert, Rosa, Hector, Oscar. | *Family album*

---

[1] The original of this letter is held by Hugh Jackson.

1 Garborough Villas
Woodridings
Pinner
6 Feb. 1911

It is more than thirty years since Dr M.J. Jackson and I were undergraduates together and during the whole of that time I have held his character and intellect in the highest admiration; indeed there is no one to whose example I owe so much. His mind is eminently practical and his long tenure in the office of Principal of the Sind College at Karachi has given him an intimate acquaintance with the work of education and administration. I think him excellently qualified both by gifts and by experience, for the Directorship of Education at Bradford.
A.E. Housman

It appears that Moses was not offered either post, or he decided not to accept the positions. He had no desire to return to India, where political unrest was increasing, and he cast about for a new challenge elsewhere in the British Empire, somewhere where he could have control over his own destiny, not beholden to a fickle board of governors or a ream of petty bureaucrats.

A.E. Housman, Classics scholar and poet. |
Archival photo

At that time, western Canada was still a new frontier, hungry for skilled and well-educated settlers. Since his return to England at the end of April, 1910, Moses had been considering a move to Canada as one of his options. He felt that the country was a place where he could make his mark and raise his sons. About a year after returning from India, after failing to find a suitable position in England, and at the relatively advanced age of 52, he made the bold decision to move to British Columbia to take up farming.

While Moses was in India, Hector had continued his schooling in England. Towards the end of 1906, 14 year-old Hector completed his junior schooling at Branksome and moved to nearby Charterhouse School. The school was situated just up the hill from the Jackson's house in Godalming, and Hector was assigned to Verites House (one of three school houses at that time).

Charterhouse was part of the English public school system (independent schools relying on private sources for their funding). The school had been founded in London in 1611 and moved to its current site on a low hill, less than a mile north of the centre of Godalming in 1872. Its graceful stone buildings were set among extensive wooded grounds and sports fields. In addition to the excellent academic reputation that it had built up over the previous 250 years, the school had also contributed to the writing of the rules of football in the 19th Century, and contributed many players in the early days of the Football Association (FA) Cup. The school's stated mission is the same today as it was when Hector was admitted, namely "to stimulate independent enquiry and intellectual curiosity, to enrich spiritual awareness, to match physical fitness with love of the arts, and to promote individuality together with a sense of duty to friends and society." In short, the school's goals embodied a philosophy that Moses would have thoroughly approved of.

Charterhouse School in about 1910. | *Archival photo*

Like his father, Hector had developed into a keen sportsman, and seems to have thrived in the British public school environment. School records show him representing Charterhouse in - gymnastics and football. Whereas Hector's brothers were all highly academic, Hector appears to have been less intellectual, but with a very practical bent. He selected "modern" classes in his last two years at Charterhouse, which de-emphasised Latin and Greek studies and concentrated more on sciences. During this period he was in the "Army Class" which prepared students for the entrance exams for officer training at Sandhurst or Woolwich and a subsequent military career.

Hector Jackson at Charterhouse. |
Family album

According to Charterhouse records, he "finished high in his class" in each of his annual exams. While at Charterhouse, Hector appears to have become a charismatic individual with his father's gift of attracting a circle of friends with his straightforward and open character and sporting ability.

By 1910, when Moses returned from India for the last time, Hector had entered his final year at Charterhouse. With a latent sense of adventure, he applied to join the Indian Police. He awaited the outcome of his school final exams before deciding whether to go to take up a position in India or move with his parents to Canada. His elder brother, Rupert, was already in his second year at Cambridge studying medicine, and was committed to remaining in England to complete his degree. Oscar was 15 years old and attending Oundle School,[1] and 11 year-old Gerald was near the end of his time at Branksome in Godalming.

---

[1] Near Peterborough, 80 miles north of London. Rupert had also attended Oundle.

Hector (front left) in a school gymnastics team photo | *Charterhouse Archives*

Leaving the family in England once again, Moses travelled to British Columbia in the spring of 1911 to find a suitable property on which to start his new venture. Initially basing himself in accommodation on Hornby Street in downtown Vancouver, Moses began to search for suitable land in the Fraser Valley, about fifty miles southeast of Vancouver and just a few miles north of the American border. By April 1911, he had selected a secluded 160 acre quarter section, about two miles southwest of the newly built village of Aldergrove.[1] The property had a perennial stream[2] to provide a water supply and a wonderful view of the snow-capped volcanic peak of Mount Baker. Moses boarded with the property's owners, the Grysons[3], while waiting for the sale to be completed.

---

[1] To the southeast of the intersection of 24th Avenue and 256th Street.

[2] Bertrand Creek.

[3] Spelt 'Griegson' in the 1911 Census of Canada.

In June of that year Housman wrote a letter to Moses, which is reproduced in part below.[1]

1 Garborough Villas
Woodridings
Pinner
12 June 1911

My Dear Mo,

I hear from Godalming that you have fixed on an estate of 160 acres, but I do not know where precisely, nor what the main crops are to be. I got your long and instructive letter while I was at Cambridge, where the term is now over, so that I am back here until October. I had no official duties to perform, but I gave them an inaugural lecture, which they wanted me to print, but I did not.[2] Everyone is very amiable, but dinners, calls, garden parties, the climate and the hot weather made me rather tired . . .

I do not want to make investments on my own account in the wild-cat colony you now inhabit, where you have to put Angleterre on your letters to get them to England; but if you happen to want extra capital you might just as well have it from me and prevent it from eating its head off in a current account at a bank . . .

Moses accepted Housman's offer of a loan, and purchased the Gryson's farm which he named Applegarth.[3] In August 1911, while the sale of the farm was being finalised, he wrote to his family in England, asking Rosa and his three youngest sons to join him.

641, Hornby St.,
Vancouver, B.C.
11 Aug., 1911

My dear Rupert and Hector and Oscar and Gerald,

I don't think there will be many more omnibus letters from you, as the little flock of fine old men is on the way to be a bit scattered. I have letters from all of you up at Aldergrove, but only one from Oscar here at this moment. You must all be tough and steadfast wherever you are, and

---

[1] Letter held by Jackson family.

[2] This highly regarded and much-quoted inaugural lecture was finally published by Cambridge University in 1969, long after Housman's death.

[3] The name may have come from a family connection in Ayrshire, Scotland, where his grandfather had lived.

some time we will arrange to meet again at once, perhaps in a nice home here.

I hope you are all having a good time at home. No doubt you are helping Mamma well, as she says you are. Next month will be an exciting time for all of you, but you are all young and elastic enough to like some excitement. I shall be very glad to see those of you who come out here. And you will like to be in the wild bush, and yet in a comfortable house to keep you dry and warm.

Rupert. You know your course well enough. You will have a fine third year at Cambridge. The following two years in London is the part I don't like. You must ascertain how you will do best there, in the way of scholarships, locality to live in, and interesting work. You will often see Housman at Cambridge and Ward in London[1]. Ward will be very good, but don't take too much of him, and of course you will appreciate anything he is able to do, which a lot of the raw Colonial cubs that he has sometimes taken an interest in don't always do. Make a budget and keep accounts. Keep up your exercise, and don't waste money in other ways. Get all you can out of the money, without stinting yourself on food or appearance. Let us know what difficulties you find.

Hector. I suppose we shall soon hear your result. One will be glad to hear that you did well, but it will not distress me if you don't get in. India isn't all you suppose, and it is an unconscious struggle to live in a hot climate like that. You will have to be very firm in every way. We will provide enough for the start, but you must save money almost from the first. You must be at pains to find out all regulations affecting you, and must be very careful in regard to ordinary laws of health. If you come out here you will not get so much money at first, but you will have a better life. And of course clever people make much more money here than there.

Oscar. I shall hope to see you in six weeks or so. You gave Mamma a good account of your Coronation proceedings, but I can hardly read your execrable writing.[2] Get a little more size and firm character on to it.

---

[1] A.E.N. Ward was a London solicitor and a close friend of both Moses and Housman; he lived at 51 Chepstow Place, in Kensington, London, and appears to have acted as both Moses' and Housman's solicitor.
[2] The coronation of King George V took place at Westminster Abbey on June 22, 1911. Presumably Oscar visited London as part of an Oundle School outing.

Postcard of the Coronation procession for King George V and Queen Mary in London.
| *Archival photo*

I shall be glad to see a good report as to your school work. And get some good strong flesh on your body to come out with. You will grow sturdy out here, and enjoy the life.

Gerald. What a fine lot of new things you will see on the journey. Take good care of yourself. I wonder how old Chummie will get on.[1] He will be getting nearer the land of his origin. You will be sorry to leave Branksome and all the boys there, but I daresay some of them will be envying you. I shall hope to meet you on the train a little before you get here, and you will think the country fine. I hope you will not get too tired. You will become quite an experienced traveller.

Now goodbye. God bless you, good boys all. I am going back to Aldergrove today.
Much love from
Your affectionate
PAPA

---

[1] Gerald's pet Chow.

Hector was either not accepted for the position with the Indian Police, or he decided not to go. Instead he travelled with his mother, brothers and his aunt Agnes to Canada.[1] The family boarded the *Empress of Ireland* in Liverpool and sailed to Quebec City, where they arrived on September 14, 1911. They reached their new home in Aldergrove a week or so later, just as summer was drawing to a close and the leaves on the alders were turning yellow.

In 1911 Aldergrove was a tiny settlement on the road that led east from New Westminster[2] to Abbotsford, and onward to the interior of British Columbia. The rutted Yale Road, as it was generally known, wound its way around the stumps of trees too big to remove during its construction and was a mix of gravel, mud and wooden corduroy sections. The Aldergrove area had a population of less than one hundred people. The village of Aldergrove itself possessed a bakery, butchery, machine shop, blacksmith and harness shop, hotel, two churches and a branch of the Bank of Toronto. Planked sidewalks flanking the road linked some of the commercial buildings. A single telephone had recently been installed in the settlement. Access to the area had been improved enormously the previous year by the completion of the British Columbia Electric Railway (BCER), running from the city of New Westminster to Chilliwack, a rural community in the eastern Fraser Valley. The journey from Aldergrove to New Westminster took only one to two hours by train.

Land promoters in the Applegarth area took advantage of the construction of the railway to paint an enticing picture for prospective settlers. Aldergrove was portrayed as a farmer's paradise with rich soils, a mild climate and ready access to nearby markets for their products. A promotional brochure put out by New Westminster promoters F.J. Hart & Co proclaimed:

---

[1] Agnes Katherine Jackson was one of Moses' younger sisters. She was 25 at the time. She subsequently settled in Mission, B.C., near Moses' new farm, where she was later joined by Moses' youngest sister, Irene Phoebe Jackson.

[2] New Westminster was named by Queen Victoria as the first capital of British Columbia; it was a port for international sea traffic, the heart of the lumber and salmon industries, and a spur line for the Canadian Pacific Railway.

22

There is no more favorable region for a small farm nor is there a land under the sun which shows such examples of health. We do not yet know the possibilities of an acre, in spite of all the market gardener has done.

True, the climate around Aldergrove was milder than that inland and the new railway that connected the Fraser Valley with New Westminster and Vancouver offered considerable promise but, not surprisingly, reality was not nearly as rosy as the promoters' pamphlets suggested. Much of the soil around Aldergrove was glacial clay and gravel which was very difficult to plough and poor in nutrients. Further the climate was much wetter than suggested. Moses, however, had chosen his farm with care and the soils over at least part of the farm, along Bertrand Creek, were better than most.

Despite the mediocre soils, parts of the area were suited to dairy farming. There were already a number of small dairies in the Aldergrove area when the family arrived. Moses decided to develop Applegarth along similar lines, using a system that was being developed whereby a truck came daily to collect his ten-gallon cans of milk and deliver them to a railway station for transport into New Westminster. Moses also planned to develop hayfields for winter fodder and to plant a small apple orchard and vegetable garden, largely for the family's own consumption. The

Hector (front left), Oscar (back left), Gerald, Rosa, Moses and Moses' sister Agnes or Irene at Applegarth, soon after the family arrived in British Columbia (c.1912). | *Family album*

creek that ran through his property would provide water, as well as salmon and trout for the family's table.[1] All in all, Moses felt he had the raw materials with which to build an appealing vision for a new life, reminiscent of Housman's idyllic picture of rural life in *A Shropshire Lad*.

When the Jackson family arrived to join Moses at Applegarth, they found that its farm buildings were primitive, consisting of a small wooden house with a cramped attic, a narrow porch along the front and back, the latter overlooking the creek, and a small single-storey barn. The home lacked electricity. Heat came from a wood-burning stove in the kitchen and light was probably provided by kerosene lamps and candles. Water had to be drawn from a well and wood cut and carried into the house for heating and cooking. The contrast with the large and comfortable houses in Karachi, complete with a score of servants, and Godalming must have come as a rude shock to Rosa.

A sketch of the Applegarth farmhouse by Hector's aunt, Agnes. | *Family collection*

---

[1] The last remnants of the apple orchard that Moses planted are still in existence on the farm today.

Applegarth was some two miles from the nearest stores and post office in the small settlement of Aldergrove. The family apparently lacked a car, at least to begin with, and Rosa had a daily five-mile heavily-laden walk, along a narrow track that quickly became muddy in wet weather.[1] Not surprisingly, it was a life style that Rosa never fully embraced. A local resident remembered her regularly collecting large bags of English magazines from the post office to keep in touch with life at "home."[2]

When the family first settled on the farm, a large part of it was still covered with thick, bleak forest of Douglas fir, alder and western red cedar, and the family spent much of their first years clearing fields and chopping wood to feed the kitchen stove and keep the house warm in winter. Hector's army medical records show that he had lost part of his left index finger, quite possibly from the slip of an axe. Clearing advanced slowly as new-growth had to be continually cut back, limiting the advances made each year. Nonetheless, in contrast to Rosa, Moses delighted with his new life on the land, applying his fundamental scientific and engineering skills to building the farm and business and, together with Rosa, acting as tutors to Hector's younger brothers, Oscar and Gerald.

Hector's younger brother, Gerald, as a teenager on the family farm at Aldergrove in the Fraser Valley, B.C. | *Family album*

---

[1] The direct road to the farm was only built after 1945.
[2] Mrs Jessie Boston quoted in *The Place Between*, Aldergrove Heritage Society (1993).

For the first time in many years, Hector found himself in his father's company for an extended period. In spite of the separation he had experienced while he was being schooled in England when his parents were in India, Hector had developed many of his father's characteristics. In line with the values instilled by the British public school system, he was a hard worker with strong self-discipline and belief in his principles. Moses, who had loved lecturing to "his Engineers" in Karachi, must have relished being able to pass this interest on to his son, teaching him to apply scientific theories to a practical end. Hector had shown no sign of wanting to emulate his father's university education and, as his oldest son in Canada, Moses groomed him to take over the family farm in due course.

Hector dedicated himself fully to whatever projects he undertook. He became a highly competent builder and mechanic, comfortable in the saddle, and able to control a team of horses hitched to a plough. His somewhat rarified British public school education was now balanced by hard physical work and practical application of theory.

But Hector also had a lighter side to his personality. His demeanour radiated good humour and self-confidence. In his free time he continued playing sports in the nearby community of Aldergrove, as well as further afield in Vancouver. He was also a member of the

Applegarth circa 1920. The building on the right was the primitive farmhouse. All the original farm buildings were replaced in the late 1940s. | *Family album*

choir at the church in the nearby settlement of Patricia.[1] Hector's photographs and letters indicate that he developed a wide circle of friends in Patricia, Abbotsford and Vancouver.

In 1913, barely eighteen months after Moses had bought Applegarth, the western world, including Canada, slipped into a severe economic recession. This must have been a terrible setback to Applegarth, which Moses was struggling to turn into a viable business. The market for produce shrank and the Jackson family had to work hard just to make ends meet, let alone increase production. Clothes and shoes were repaired continuously, by family members with little previous experience in such tasks.[2]

The farm suffered a further blow in the summer of 1914 when a severe drought caused crops and wells to fail; Bertrand Creek, which flowed through Applegarth, dried up almost completely.[3] In spite of this, one of the local papers reported in September that Moses' produce was exhibited at the Aldergrove Fair and, along with others, was described by an observer as comparing favorably with anything he had seen exhibited in the best markets that year. In spite of strenuous efforts, with his income faltering, Moses found himself unable to repay Housman's loan, nonetheless he remained optimistic that the family's fortunes would turn when the economy recovered from the recession.

The outbreak of the war between the British Empire and Germany on August 4 put paid to these hopes and piled on still more financial woe. Prior to the war, Germany had been the world's sole producer of potash, an essential ingredient in fertilizers. This supply was cut off at the outbreak of hostilities and the price of potash in Canada rose from $35 per ton to $500 per ton, putting a huge burden on farmers' costs.

Most Canadians expected that the British Expeditionary Force would quickly repulse the Germans in Europe and that the war would

---

[1] The church in Patricia, near Aldergrove, was nominally Lutheran, with a dominantly Scandinavian settler congregation, but the Jacksons appeared to have been regular attendees.

[2] Hector's younger brother, Oscar, continued to mend his own shoes throughout his life, even when he was in his seventies and comfortably well off.

[3] Report dated September 1, 1914, in the *British Columbian*.

be over by Christmas. Spirits were high and "Patriotic Societies" and "Patriotic Sewing Circles" organized numerous fund-raising events for the war effort. The Jackson family took an active part in these endeavours. A newspaper article in the *British Columbian*, dated November 17, 1914, reported on a patriotic concert that took place in Patricia, near Aldergrove:

> Mr. Hector Jackson sang "It's a Long Way to Tipperary". Most enjoyable was the singing by the Patricia Patriotic Choir, composed of Mrs. Jack Murdoch, Miss Helen McIntyre, Miss Vera McIntyre, Mr. Jones, Mr. Sid Kirkby, Mr. Hector Jackson and Mr. Oscar Jackson, of "Rule Britannia", "The British Grenadiers" and that great battle song of the ages, "Men of Harlech".

By early 1915, however, pure patriotic spirit had been overlain by the realization that the war was going badly for the Allies.[1] Clearly there was an urgent need to recruit men to augment the troops already in France. Recruiting officers, accompanied by crisply turned out

Recruiting advertisement in the North Shore Press in 1916. | *Archival photo*

---

[1] The Gallipoli campaign in Turkey was floundering and the German Army was making a breakthrough on the Russian front.

military bands, began to tour the towns and villages of the Fraser Valley, urging young men to volunteer for the armed forces. A local newspaper reported:

> Thursday was a red letter day for the people of Aldergrove when they had the pleasure of seeing and welcoming the 131st Battalion. The band which preceded the soldiers and played on the stand, arrived an hour before the advertised time . . . When the children appeared they were delighted with the men who cheered and sang military ditties of their own composing.

With Canada still in recession and the farm struggling financially, Hector and Oscar started working on other farms and doing piece-work on road construction to earn additional income. In May 1915, nine months after the start of the war, Hector wrote a note to his mother from the farm of Charles Hill-Tout in Abbotsford, not far from the Jackson farm in Aldergrove.[1]

Abbotsford,
18. 5. 15.

Dear Mamma,

    I got over here at about 6 O'clock, and have left the cow at Wells place. I will go down in a day or so to see about anyone buying it, so far she is pasturing down here for her milk. We have been quite busy just lately, putting up a fence, and planting a 3 acre field of barley. I was harrowing all yesterday afternoon. This morning as it is raining I have been putting bee hives together and arranging the honey trays.

    Please send off clothes as soon as possible if they have not left already, as I have to clean up for supper and wear a collar. I have spoken to Agnes[2] about money, as I don't expect to need any just yet, but as soon as I get enough I am going to Sumas for my teeth. Charlie will be getting plenty of work in a few days, I expect, and if Willie can't pay me I am going to work for a few days with him each month to raise something. I must stop now as I have to get out to my bee hives.

    Your affectionate,
    HECTOR

---

[1] Charles Hill-Tout was a pioneer settler at Abbotsford who, like Moses, had previously been an educationist, founding Buckland College on Burrard Street in Vancouver. He devoted many years to anthropological work among the Salish people of the west coast.
[2] Hector's aunt who had settled nearby in Mission, B.C, with her younger sister, Irene.

During the months that the war had been raging in Europe, Hector's thoughts had apparently been evolving. Although he was born in India and lived in Canada, he had spent most of his formative years in England and, like many young men of similar background, he considered himself British first and foremost, and a citizen of his adopted country in a distant second place. Britain's war was his war.

Moses and the British public school system had combined to instill a Victorian sense of discipline, duty and a strong work ethic in all the Jackson boys, and Hector may well have had a deep-seated desire to prove himself in his father's eyes. Moses had never had to fight a war, and fighting on behalf of the Empire would help Hector to gain his father's respect.

Hector's irrepressible sense of optimism and a taste for social life was also influencing his thoughts. After experiencing the sophistication and variety of life in southern England, and having glimpsed what the social life in Vancouver offered, Hector was apparently becoming frustrated with the limitations of farm life in rural British Columbia. In contrast, from a distance and through the filter of the popular press, the war was a heroic and exciting adventure - a battle of good against evil. The disfigured war-wounded had not yet begun to flood back from the front, suggesting that the conflict was glorious rather than ghastly. Measured against this romantic and patriotic image, the prospect of spending the rest of his life eking out a living on a marginal farm in the backwoods of British Columbia must have had little appeal.

Canadian War Poster circa 1915. |
National Archives of Canada

By the middle of 1915, Hector had decided to volunteer for the Canadian Expeditionary Force. His first two attempts to enlist were unsuccessful, not because of his injured finger, but owing to sub-standard vision in one eye. Hector, however, was determined. In August 1915 he wrote home from the Hill-Touts' farm.

Abbotsford.

12. 8. 15.

Dear Mamma,

I am afraid I have not written for an awful long time and I have a fair amount of news.

We have finished the threshing which was quite a big job, we had Billie Swanson and 12 other men, and got the job done in two days. Margaret Owen[1] came down to spend the week here for her holiday and she asked me up for a weekend last week, we had lots of tennis. I met a Dulwich boy called Hoyle from Victoria who is awfully good at tennis, and we went out to see 2 cricket matches at Brockton Point.[2] Burrard XI against a picked team. I had lunch with Noel, Buckley and two other fellows on the Saturday.[3] While I was up I tried again for enlistment, but my eye put me out. Pulleston and Harry Burnett came down this week end, and we took a holiday Saturday afternoon and played tennis, also today. I am going up to Vancouver next weekend to try again at the 104th and taking lunch with Pulleston; he is taking me out to the Dennison tennis club.[4]

We had a fire here last Saturday week which burned the Jap shack completely.[5] Luckily it was insured for $700 so there was no loss. Helen had a new baby boy called Edward Alan.

I have been taking photos lately, I am sending a few prints. I am taking up Latin again, or rather I help Mildred with her work most evenings; it does me quite a lot of good.

---

[1] Margaret Owen was the daughter of Rev. C.C. Owen, Dean of Christ Church Anglican Cathedral in Vancouver.

[2] Brockton Point is in Stanley Park, Vancouver.

[3] Noel Robinson was on of the Jacksons's neighbours. The Buckleys were neighbours of the Hill-Touts near Abbotsford. Eric Buckley was a year younger than Hector.

[4] Dennison was a BC Electric Railway station in Abbotsford, with a lumber mill nearby, run by the King family.

[5] The Hill Touts are likely to have had one or two Japanese or Chinese workers on the farm to do some of the hardest manual labour.

We have been having venison for some time now. Willie and I each shot a deer, mine was rather small, but it tasted awfully nice.

Is it true that Tom McIntyre[1] has got Summer's job at the Customs? He hardly seems the kind of man for the place. I shall have to stop in a few minutes as I am going to help Mildred with some Algebra. I have got a chance of making $10 in some road work with any luck. I am sure I need it.

What is Oscar doing about the bike? We have been building a very elaborate chicken house where the old shack used to be.

The jerkiness of this letter is caused by a superabundance of Hill Tout spirits. I can't think consecutively for 2 mins.

Your loving,

HECTOR

A week later, Hector walked up the hill from the New Westminster train station to the recruiting centre that had been set up at the 104th Westminster Fusiliers Drill Hall and attempted to enlist for the third time.

This time Hector took a slightly different tack. He filled in the application form, listing his occupation as "driver and bridge carpenter." Following the instructions from the recruiting sergeant, he covered his bad eye and, using his good eye, rapidly read off the first few lines of letters from the eye chart on the wall. He then covered the other eye and repeated the performance, working mainly from memory. The recruiting officer stated that everything seemed in order and that Hector should report for basic training with the Duke of Connaught's Own Rifles (D.C.O.R.) in Vancouver.[2]

On the morning of Monday August 16, 1915, less than forty-eight hours after his fudged eye examination and acceptance, Hector reported to the D.C.O.R. drill hall in Beatty Street in Vancouver, and took the first step on his journey to the Western Front.

---

[1] The McIntyres were neighbours at Applegarth.

[2] Named after then Governor General of Canada, Field-Marshal H.R.H. the Duke of Connaught, Queen Victoria's son.

N. Vancouver.
21. 8. 15.

Dear Oscar,

I have been up here at the D.C.O.R. Drill Hall[1] since Monday and am getting into the way of things, though everything is awfully rough and unsettled. This hall has members of the D.C.O.R. and is also a drafting station for the 62nd and 72nd, so all the rooms are full up, and we sleep around the drill shed with two blankets and a waterproof sheet; luckily I have my overcoat. We get up at 6.30, and have what is called "Jerks" or rather physical marching from 7.00 to 7.30, when it is fine we go across Georgia Bridge for ½ a mile partly at the double.[2] If wet, it is [indecipherable] . . . kind of business inside; at eight we have breakfast, all of us line up at the call and pass by, with our mug plate fork and spoon and get our meal on the installment plan, meat or bacon from one man, beans from the next, fried bread and a kind of butter, and then tea. The bread is on a table when we get into the dining shed (Clarence Shortreed is one of the cooks).[3] 9.30 is parade with a short break till 12, dinner at 1. Parade at 2.30 till 4 and tea at 5. We are then off till 7 next morning, which means we can sleep out. The Owens have told me I can sleep at their place if I like any time, but I don't intend to wear out my welcome too soon. I went over to see them Tuesday night and stayed for an hour or so, and am going out to a show with them in a few days. I am patronising the Movies now in the evenings; I have nothing much to do most evenings and have not received my pay yet. They pay us $5 on the 7th, 14th and 21st of each month and make up the rest on the 1st. I won't be in with this lot much longer as I have been down to N. Vancouver today to get a transfer to the 6th Engineers.[4] I believe the pay is 1.25 instead of 1.10 and it is a much more interesting drill. Also Noel and his lot with Eric Buckley have joined. I passed the eyesight test by means of my memory as before, and will get my transfer as soon as there is a vacancy.

There are scarcely any decent fellows here, it is almost like the steerage. I have found a fellow called Saker who is Army Policeman and stands around the barrack room doors. He was at Bedford[5] and his wife

---

[1] The DCOR Drill Hall is still situated in Beatty St., just southeast of Vancouver's city centre.

[2] The bridge no longer exists as this part of False Creek has been filled in.

[3] The Shortreed family owned the General Store in Aldergrove.

[4] The original 6th Field Company Canadian Engineers Drill Hall is still standing at the corner of Forbes Avenue and 15th Street W in North Vancouver.

[5] A British public school, fifty miles north of London.

knows Agnes and Irene quite well as he has a farm at Hatzic.[1] He himself knows Joe Brealey. I found another Bedford & Oxford man at the Engineers. There is no one here I greatly admire though the whole lot are quite decent as far as they go. I am writing this sitting on my blankets on the floor of the drill hall just before going to bed.

22. 8. 15. We have just had Reveillé, I get up a bit early so as to avoid the rush, it was not cold last night and I slept pretty well. We have just had fall in for "Jerks" so I have to close. I will write again soon and let you know my whereabouts.

Your affectionate,
HECTOR

Hector transferred to the 6th Field Company Canadian Engineers as planned in October and then spent four or five months based at the Engineers' Drill Hall in North Vancouver, undergoing basic military

Hector (3rd from right) soon after transferring to the 6th Field Comapny Canadian Engineers in North Vancouver, learning to construct brushwood revetting to support the side of trenches with a group of fellow recruits. |
Family album

---

[1] Hatzic is a small settlement eight miles upstream of Mission on the Fraser River.

and engineering training.

Hector's commanding officer approved his Attestation papers at the end of his basic training, on January 29, 1916. The papers stated that Hector agreed to serve "for the period of one year or during the war now existing between Great Britain and Germany should that war last longer than one year . . ." Hector was to leave for Ottawa on the first leg of his trip to the Western Front by train within weeks, as part of a draft of 150 men. He typed a letter to his brother, 21-year-old Oscar, confirming his imminent departure for Ottawa.

N.Vancouver

31. 1. 16

Dear Oscar,

I have got the Orderly Corporal again, and cannot go out so I am trying my hand at typewriting in the orderly room.

The date has been changed again as you have heard and 150 are going instead of 100, 50 to a coach.

I will let you know when we are going and if you can get off you might call up Muriel and see if she wants to come and see us off.[1] I had a letter from Mamma today, the Applebys are all ill and she has decided to come up to Vancouver, I hope that does not mean a general gloom.

I am fully booked up for the rest of our stay so I will not be able to see your works; if you had been on day shift I would have come out by Jitney.[2] When you have any money to spare you might send Gerald what you owe me.

I am feeling rather sleepy now so don't suppose I will last out much longer.

I tried my hand at drilling a squad this afternoon, it is awfully hard on the voice, as we had 3 lots going at once and the Hall is full of echoes; also the squads kept running into each other unless we were very careful.

Your affectionate,

HECTOR

---

[1] Muriel Sprott was the daughter of Charles Frederick Sprott who had previously been the Reeve (Mayor) of Burnaby, now part of Greater Vancouver. Charles Sprott was, like Moses, a native of Mayfield, Sussex, and moved from Burnaby to Aldergrove a year before the Jacksons settled there. Muriel was two years younger than Hector.

[2] Originally an American slang word for a five cent coin, but then used for a small vehicle that carried passengers along a regular route, since the fare was five cents. The jitney that served Aldergrove was run by Goodman Hamre and was established in 1914.

From Vancouver, Hector boarded a troop train to Ottawa with his fellow recruits. There is a six week gap in Hector's letter writing while he travelled across Canada.

Once his group of recruits arrived in Ottawa, it was assembled and kitted out for departure to Europe. While they waited for additional recruits to arrive, the men's training continued.

Hector apparently already knew people in Ottawa and he enlarged this circle of acquaintances. In spite of the army's call on his time, he managed to fit in a busy social schedule.

Hector outside the Parliament buildings in Ottawa, immediately before leaving for Europe.
| *Family album*

When the time came for his unit to depart, it again travelled by troop train, from Ottawa to St. John on the Bay of Fundy, New Brunswick. There, Hector and his fellow recruits, each with a cylindrical kit bag and rifle slung over their shoulders, boarded the troop ship T.S.S. *Metagama*, bound for England.

Restrictions were in place on writing letters to avoid sensitive information about the sailing dates of convoys leaking out to the German submarines that were already prowling the North Atlantic. In fact, on March 24, just as the T.S.S *Metagama* with Hector on board, reached southern England, the French passenger ship *Sussex* was torpedoed in the English Channel with the loss of fifty lives. Hector's next letter was therefore written only after boarding the troop ship in New Brunswick for the voyage to England.

T.S.S. *Metagama*,
11. 3. 16. 5.30 p.m.

Dear Mamma,

We are off at last. I have just come down from the deck seeing the last of St. Johns Harbour.

I am in 1st Sitting for meals and had just got up from supper when the Donkeys began working and we heard the whistles of a tug, there was a general movement to the deck. We were pulled out stern first by the Lord Kitchener, and then turned around and made for the open sea under our own power.

We passed the gun boat *Canada*, all the sailors came up on deck and climbed up the rigging to wave and cheer. The sun was too low to get a decent photo so I left it as I have only 6 films left.

I have the very front cabin, with 3 others, of course there are other decks lower who share the same doubtful privilege, but I am going to get the full benefit on any swell that happens; there is a slight motion already and I am rather curious to know how I will stand the trip. The last crossing was no test.[1]

I got into St. Johns at 8. a.m. yesterday and shunted around for three hours till we got to the Docks, then we were marched on board and given out Berths, slept the night in the harbour and pulled out today. We

T.S.S. Metagama. | *Archival photo*

---

[1] In 1911, when Hector first immigrated to Canada with his mother and brothers.

are liable to stay around Halifax for several days till we get in touch with the rest of the Convoy and transports; I don't expect to be in England for my birthday.

I spend most of my time in my cabin, sleeping or writing as there are 4 sittings for meals so we can't use the dining room, and the smoking room draws the worst element.[1] We had a simply splendid send off from Ottawa, almost all the various girls came down to say Goodbye. The Bostocks and the Senator himself,[2] the Misses Gwynne, Cassels, Bell, Brown, Godwin and some others and we were loaded with cakes and candies. I am having a party in my cabin again tonight to finish up some of the cake.

I am sending a photo of a group taken with Lambart's camera by Jessie Harris who gave the party. I took one myself but have not developed it yet, and some others as well.

Roy Kinmond has stayed behind for a Commission, if I had wanted one it would have been the easiest thing to have got one through Bostock and Colonel Gwynne, but I don't know if it was worth while.

I have got another firework from Tiger about the mine thing, she . . .[3]
(Remainder of letter missing)

Hector (front row, centre) during life boat drill on T.S.S. Metagama. | *Family album*

---

[1] In spite of four years of farm life and social mixing with farm labourers, Hector obviously still maintained his English public school class-consciousness.

[2] The Hon. Hewitt Bostock, a senator from British Columbia, who held various cabinet posts at provincial and federal levels in Canada. Hector had been at Charterhouse with his son.

[3] "Tiger" was the nickname of one of Moses' younger sisters, Ida Caroline Jackson, who was known in the family for a fiery temperament. At this time she was in her mid-forties.

A boxing match on board T.S.S. Metagama *en route from Canada to England.* | *Family album*

Chapter 2

ENGLAND

Hector's troopship arrived safely in England after a cramped, but uneventful two-week voyage. The T.S.S. *Metagama* docked at Liverpool, and the recruits boarded the inevitable troop train again and travelled south to Bordon Camp, about 45 miles southwest of London. The camp was the base for many of the new troops arriving fresh from Canada and other parts of the British Empire.

On arrival, Hector was reassigned to the 7th Field Company, 4th Divisional Engineers.[1] The 4th Canadian Division was to undergo its preliminary divisional training in the Bramshott area.

Bordon Camp was a better camp than many as it had been constructed only five or ten years earlier. Most of the barracks were constructed of wood, but others were merely canvas stretched over a wooden frame, hastily built for the flood of arriving troops. In spite of its drawbacks, the camp at Bordon was a big improvement on the camps on Salisbury Plain where the first Canadian Division had done its training in abysmal weather that had resulted in high rates of illness.

Luckily for Hector, Bordon Camp was only about twelve miles west of Godalming, where he had spent his school days at Branksome

---

[1] This was an administrative error and the unit was soon renamed the 10th Field Company Canadian Engineers, 4th Canadian Division.

Bordon Camp, Hampshire. | *Courtesy of www.roll-of-honour.com, © Martin Edwards 2008.*

and Charterhouse. He therefore knew the area well and had relatives, friends and acquaintances within easy reach. In spite of military restrictions, he found England a breath of fresh air, after what he felt was the backward environment and claustrophobic life of a struggling farm in rural British Columbia. He threw himself into the training and social life with enthusiasm.

> Hants.
> 28. 3. 16   8.15 p.m.

Dear Oscar,

I don't know whether you recognise the name of this camp; I did not myself when we landed at the station, but coming down the road I ran across a sign board "Frensham 3 miles" and began to look around me. We are 7 miles from Aldershot and 14 from Godalming, and quite near Liphook and Liss. I am writing this in the Guard Room, and am on guard tonight and have just come off my first turn; it is quite a farce here, I just hang around one of the entrances to the Camp with a swagger stick, and bugger around for 2 hours. We got into camp on the 26th and have not settled down yet, but luckily except for yesterday the weather has been good and it certainly looks good after B.C. everything is neat and green and houses and trees all around.

Today we went for a route march through Stanford, Headley and quite near Bramshott and in the afternoon I played in a match for No.7 Coy against the A.S.C.[1] We lost 5:3 but the ground was filthy and we had ordinary boots. They put me captain, but I would hate to play as badly again.

There are 4 South African regiments here; one is a Highland one and they look quite smart.

I phoned up Ward and he wants me to stay up at Chepstow Place when I get leave;[2] the rumour of going to France seems to have gone the usual way. We are due to stay here for 2 months, I believe, I am taking 2nd leave which will not be for 2 weeks anyway.

I intend to get hold of a bike and chase around the country.

29th 8.30 a.m. I have just come in from my 2nd shift and have one more from noon till 2. Luckily last night was clear except at 1 o'clock and then the rain soon stopped. As soon as it got dark my post changed to the officer's quarters. The only excitement seems to have been a mule which got loose, but it was nowhere near my beat so I missed even that. They chased it into a shack because it was impossible to catch, and that raised a fine old row, as it happened to be full of engineers. We have just this moment turned out to the Major and as usual were complimented on smartness.

The Orderly Officer will be around at 9.30 on visiting rounds and then we should be free for a time.

I have just finished a film pack which ought to have some interesting pictures. 6 were taken at the Golf Club skiing, 3 groups on the ship, one between here and Liverpool and 2 in Camp.

I phoned up Ward a few days ago, and have an invitation to stay with him whenever I get leave, so my stay in London ought not to cost too much. We have a wet Canteen here which sells very good beer, we usually call in at night and get a pint, but the place is crowded so I believe we will go farther afield in future.

I am going to walk out to some of the villages around and pay calls on the Rideals and Knowles. Our rations are less here than in Canada and we are putting in 2½d. a day for extra food.

31. 3. 16 We have just been paid and there seems to be a fearful muddle; I raised £2 for the whole month, so they must be keeping back a

---

[1] Coy.: abbreviation for company. A.S.C.: Army Service Corps, also stationed at Bordon.
[2] Ward's home, just northwest of Hyde Park.

whole lot to give later. Last night after guard I went out for a walk through the S.African lines to Stanford village; it was crowded with a mixture of S.A. and Canadian soldiers and they have a circus working over time. I went out to find a tailor, cycle shop and a photographic store, and was successful all along, except that they want to charge 3/6[1] for a bike for the weekend, so I let them know what I thought. I have put in for a weekend pass and mean to get around and see what is going on. Of course the roads are fine, even in spite of floods and plenty of rain.

The whining voices of the village shop keepers rather get on my nerves, but the girls voices are a change for the better. We had a medical exam which was a simple farce. We went in stripped of course, and were asked about our feet, eyes, ears and throat, and that was all. All they could have been looking for was skin diseases. No. 9 Coy is due to leave here at any time for Shorncliffe,[2] I don't know why they were picked on, but it suits me perfectly, as I can see we ought to get a good time here with any luck; there has been absolutely no attempt at drill or training except squad drill, and I don't see when it is to start.

4th I am going to finish this up and post it tonight, we have just come in from a short march through Headley and around by various byways; the marching does a whole lot of good after the long journey, but everyone is fearfully soft. Send this letter on to Aldergrove as it will save me repeating anything. So far I have had no Canadian mail, it does not seem to have arrived yet. Next week I ought to have some films done. I will send some, but I have promised a lot, and they may become expensive. The food has improved an enormous amount, in fact everyone was satisfied, so we don't have to go round and buy meals. Canada certainly seems a thing of the past, I must find the various people I know and see how I like them.

Goodbye from,
(Sapper) HECTOR.[3] 502765.
C/o. A.E.N. Ward.

---

[1] Three shillings and sixpence.

[2] Shorncliffe was a large military camp, just west of Folkestone, in southeast England. Hector was sent there a month later.

[3] The lowest rank in Engineer units.

The first Zeppelin bombing raid on England took place on January 19, 1915. Only four people were killed, but the public reaction was one of total shock and outrage. Until then, the war was something that happened in other countries, and Britain had been separated from harm by the English Channel. That the war had come to them, and that civilians had been targeted, hardened public attitudes considerably. There were a further nineteen air raids on Britain during 1915 and by 1916, when Hector arrived in England, Zeppelin raids were occurring regularly. In that year, twenty-three raids resulted in 293 deaths. During a raid on the night of September 2, 1916, a Zeppelin was shot down over London by Second Lieutenent W. Leef-Robinson, for which he was awarded the Victoria Cross. A London newspaper reporter described the scene:

> I saw high in the sky a concentrated blaze of searchlights, and in its centre, a ruddy glow, which rapidly spread into the outline of a blazing airship. Then the searchlights were turned off and the Zeppelin drifted perpendicularly in the darkened sky, a gigantic pyramid of flames, red and orange, like a ruined star falling slowly to earth. Its glare lit up the streets and gave a ruddy tint, even to the waters of the Thames. The spectacle lasted two or three minutes. It was so horribly fascinating that I felt spellbound – almost suffocated with emotion, ready hysterically to laugh or cry.

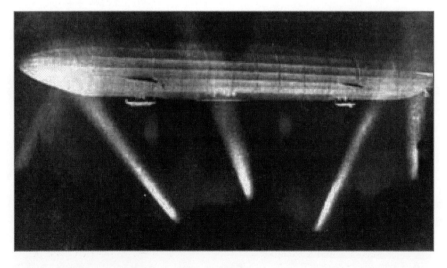

A Zeppelin on a night raid over London is caught in the searchlights. | *Archival photo*

When, at last, the doomed airship vanished from sight, there arose a shout the like of which I never heard in London before - a swelling shout, that appeared to be rising from all parts of the metropolis, ever increasing in force and intensity.

The crash site became quite an attraction. Hector mentioned it in a letter home dated December 15, 1916, and he sent a piece of wire from this Zeppelin home to British Columbia as a souvenir.

But in spite of this more tangible evidence of the battles raging across the channel in France, the English were determined not to let the war disrupt daily life more than necessary.

> Bordon Camp,
> Hants.
> 3. 4. 16.

Dear Gerald,

I am starting a kind of serial letter which may finish any time. We are having grand weather just now, it is almost Summer and the dust is getting vile; and to finish this off we still have our thick Ottawa Stanfield underwear.[1]

We have had two Zepp scares, one on Friday night and we expect another tonight. On Friday night at about 11 a sergeant stuck his head in our room (there are 34 in it) and told us all to dress and get out on parade grounds as Zepps had been sighted about 60 miles off.

This was our first scare so everyone was fairly excited and hurried out. It was a perfect night without a moon, in a few minutes the lieutenant sent us back to our bunks and we lay down in all our clothes. There was nothing to be heard except motor despatch riders flying up and down the road, and a few sarcastic words about the Kaiser and Germans in general, then we all fell asleep as we were . . . [idecipherable section]   The second scare was last night, but no one seemed to care; we just dressed and fell asleep and scarcely took any notice.

I have taken the film pack to be developed and will get them tonight or tomorrow, they ought to be fairly decent. This morning 7 and 8 marched down to see No. 9 off for Shorncliffe, they had a drum and fife band to play them down and it was fearfully hot and dusty and we had to stand in the sun for nearly an hour.

---

[1] Stanfield's, a men's underwear company, was established in Nova Scotia in 1870. One of its founders, Robert N. Stanfield, served as leader of the Progressive Conservative Party from 1967 to 1974.

Eight of us went for a walk to Frensham Ponds[1] and had tea at the hotel, it was of course quite expensive as we had expected, but it was very good eating and the place was the first I had recognised since I landed. The first leave starts tomorrow, and everything will be in a muddle for about two weeks. As soon as both leaves have got back, and if the weather permits, we leave for Shorncliffe and go under canvas for our real training.

Collecting cigarette cards of war scenes or heroes was popular during the war. | Archival photo

But I take this all with a grain of salt as we have waited a fearful time, and had no real training, in fact we have just wasted our time as far as I can see.

I am sending a collection of cigarette pictures which may be if interest; just now I am collecting army badges, a new series, but I have only just begun.

I heard from Marg[2] today but have got no Canadian mail, it seems to me that there has been a colossal muddle about our whole journey. We are not really the 7th Coy. but the 10th Coy. 4th Divisional Engineers. Someone has been creating companies and Ottawa knew nothing about it. Nothing has come out on Orders about changing our number, so I am still No.7 but anyhow Bordon Camp will find me, as Tiger has been addressing me as 6th Field Coy. and the letters arrived.

10. 4. 16. I am writing this in the guard room as I am doing another guard. We have almost finished as our Orderly Officer has been round and I have only one more shift from 12 to 2 p.m. and then must pack up as I am on leave tomorrow for 6 days. I want to look up Mr. Ward and Mrs. McClellan and then beat it down to Deal and see Tiger.

I phoned up the Rideals on Saturday when I was out at Grayshott and was asked out to lunch Sunday but could not go because of the Guard.[3]

---

[1] Ten miles southwest of Bordon Camp.

[2] Margaret Adelaide Jackson, Hector's aunt was about 50 years old at the time and became a regular correspondent with Hector throughout the war. Her occupation is not clear from her letters, but she may have been a private governess.

[3] Greyshott is three miles southeast of Bordon Camp.

Has any assigned pay arrived yet?[1] We are kept short here because of keeping back a certain amount for uniform and $16 in hand.

Yours affectionately,

HECTOR

Bordon Camp,
Hants.
3. 4. 16.

Dear Marg,

Thanks for the letter, I hope Tiger let you know in time that I am not getting leave till the middle of the month.

We had a pretty fierce journey across. I have come to the conclusion that I am no sailor; of course it might have been a whole lot worse as it was a calm crossing except for one day.

I was not seasick but was dizzy most of the time. We have two Zeppelin scares which means getting up and dressing, they have never been near yet but were close last night and tonight they are due overhead.

Unfortunately I have had to sign over $16 a month as otherwise the Govt would take it, so I go fairly slow. I am looking forward for a weekend pass to see Ch'house next week and various Godalming friends, but all leave has to go to Headquarters and takes some getting. Weather is great and we are feeling fairly happy, we have only had one bad day and that was as bad as I want.

I hope everything goes well

Your affectionate,

502765 (Sapper) HECTOR
7th Coy.

"Marg", Margaret Adelaide Jackson, Hector's aunt who corresponded with Hector throughout the war. | *Family album*

---

[1] Assigned pay was a portion of a soldier's pay which was directly paid into his savings account at home so that he would have something to live on when discharged after the war. It could also be directed to the account of a relative, to provide income in the soldier's absence.

Bordon Camp
Hants.
7. 4. 16.

Dear Marg,

Thanks very much for the letter and note. I am taking my leave next Tuesday till Sunday, it has been suddenly sprung upon us without warning, and I have had to write a few hurried notes.

I intend to get down to Deal about Thursday if Tiger can put me up. Have had no more Zepp scares lately and things have been generally slow, but I suppose we will settle down to work when we are all back from leave.

Your affectionate,
HECTOR

———————

51, Chepstow Place,
Pembridge Square, W
13. 4. 16.

Dear Mamma,

I have had my leave at last and am staying up here with Mr. Ward; he has been awfully decent about everything and I have used his house just whenever I happened to be around.

I came up to Town[1] Tuesday morning with several others and we had lunch at Lyons and separated.[2] I phoned up the office and went around at 1.30 and we went to Inwoods Chop House and had the first decent meal since I left the parties at Ottawa. Then I beat it for this house, secured a key and, started a lone voyage of discovery finishing up with the Adelphi Tina.[3] Yesterday was raining on and off, and I came in for dinner and got off to bed at 10, with a hot bath. I am going to the Gaiety tonight and leaving for Deal tomorrow morning.[4] There are a tremendous lot of soldiers on the streets, and saluting is an absolute nuisance especially for the officers, all the parks are full of wounded, in different stages of convalescence, some are frightfully battered about, but absolutely cheerful. At all times of the day the soldiers straight from the trenches come out in small parties from the various stations and attract very little attention.

———————

[1] London.

[2] Lyons' Corner House was a chain of restaurants established in London in 1909.

[3] Possibly the Adelphi Theatre in the Strand.

[4] Gaiety was s West End theatre that specialized in musical entertainment.

I was down at the Public Schools Club today but it has all gone to pot for lack of funds and no longer exists as a club.

It is awfully amusing how the word Charterhouse acts as a charm especially in conjunction with Canada on my uniform; I have not yet quite decided how Canadians are looked upon, of course it depends on what part of the country you are in. But altogether they seem to have a fairly good name.

'Tiger' - Ida Caroline Jackson, another of Hector's aunts, lived in Deal on the southeast coast of England. Her nickname was derived from her name, Ida, and her fiery temperament. | *Family album*

Tiger was at Knepp Castle till just lately but I could not get down there though it was only at Horsham.[1] Lady Burrell asked me down, but it was so soon before leave that I could not get a pass.

Trench life may have its charms, but it feels great to get back to old times;[2] lying in bed till 8, and have someone draw the blinds and bring hot water.

Your last letter crossed mine, and is still at Bordon waiting for me.

Your affectionate,

HECTOR

During the First World War, commissions were often awarded to men based on their family's social standing, rather than by selection of those with leadership ability. Some officers even bought their commissions. After Hector left Vancouver, Rosa had apparently been talking to influential acquaintances, possibly Senator Bostock, to have Hector awarded a commission. Her efforts apparently bore fruit.

---

[1] Twenty-five miles east of Bordon Camp, Knepp Castle was the ancestral stately home of Sir Merrick and Lady Burrell.

[2] Bordon Camp provided training in trench construction and warfare.

Bordon,
24. 4. 16.

My dear Mamma,

Your wish has come true, I have been given a Commission in the Canadian Engineers and am to report at Shorncliffe to the Training Depot; that shows what a little pull will do if put into the right hands. Nothing has been said about any recommendation of course but I was given notice to appear at the Orderly Room the morning after I got your letters; they had been delayed at Ottawa and got muddled up in the change of numbers of the Company. I only got them 22.4.16.

I had no idea what it was for, but expected it to be about forming a Divisional football team, as it seems left to me. When I heard I nearly refused but have decided to try it, and Capt. Watt has promised to take me back in the Coy if I decided at any time to give it up. Thanks very much for your efforts.

I hired a bicycle for last weekend and biked over to Godalming, through Headley, Grayshott, Hindhead and Witley Camp. The roads were fine till just about Milford and Moushill. From the Hammer Ponds into Milford village the whole place is changed, you would not recognise the old picnic grounds; they are a mass of trenches and huts. The roads are bumpy for fast riding but are still 1st class according to B.C. standards. Godalming itself has not changed all the shops are the same. Pitchers as usual are having a bankruptcy imminent and Church Street has been repaved. I don't care for the Phillips memorial but they say it was worse when new.[1]

I first called at Branksome and saw both of the Sylvesters;[2] his hair is quite white, but Mrs. has not changed much. Charterhouse is the same as ever except they are building a Memorial Arch facing the bridge on the Charterhouse side, just in front of Hall. It makes a fine entrance and they are putting Brooke Hall there. They are also building a new Armoury.

I called at the Crisps and saw a few and was asked to come in again as soon as I get leave, but I have too many people to be certain of getting anywhere.[3] Then I went back and had tea at Branksome and walked across and saw the Lovejoys; Mrs. Annie was away at Clifton. Neither of the Newmans were in so I biked back. Sunday I went over to the Rideals. Mr. and Ione were the only ones at home except Oliver the small boy. Ione is

---

[1] John Phillips was the Senior Wireless Operator on the *Titanic*.

[2] Charles Sylvester was a schoolmaster at Charterhouse.

[3] Mr. and Mrs. F.A. Crisp were a wealthy couple who lived at the Manor House in Godalming and had five daughters. They regularly invited Charterhouse boys and Priorsfield School girls over for Sunday afternoon tea.

awfully pretty and must be quite a handful to manage. She is just full of fun; about 19 now and spends most of her time in Town.

I believe I get a week's leave when I report to settle about kit, and then I suppose I settle down again. The whole Division is under orders to go to Shorncliffe so I am staying here with them till they go. I have signed my Transfer papers and been passed medically fit so there should be very little trouble. I get about $2.60 a day and $1 field allowance and so I can live on my pay. I don't suppose I will draw on any money that I signed over. Has it come yet? This is war time, and as nothing lasts any time, I have decided to get as much fun out of life as is possible, of course consistent with the usual standards. I have completely changed my views since I left for a place where you see new faces occasionally. I believe Aldergrove would have finished me, and I don't quite understand myself. Luckily so far I have had a splendid mail and am doing my share to keep it up, but it will soon get out of hand as it has a habit of increasing at every fresh place we stay at.

Ione Rideal, one of Hector's many female friends, was the daughter of family friends, and an aspiring actress in London. | *Family album*

I have been asked down to lunch any time at the Burrells at Knepp Castle and want to work that in if it is possible; it really pays to know the nicest people around, wherever you go. I know that no one would think I had come out here to fight for my country etc. by the stuff I am writing about, but I will get all I want of that without any poking into the future.

I am sorry I forgot Gerald's birthday letter but we were in a hopeless muddle around that time and I forgot Oscar's as well.[1]

---

[1] Gerald had turned 16 on March 13.

McNair got his V.C. just lately and Branksome got an extra half.[1] He and his platoon were mined by the Germans in their trench but it must have been set too deep and lifted them up. The German idea was to storm and hold the crater formed, but McNair came down to earth again only shaken, and collected as many men as possible holding the place and then got reinforcements under fire.

In the Cloisters there are four framed Casualty Lists, about 300 altogether. I was studying them when a fellow Sparrow (in Duckites in my time) happened along with his sister; it was quite a chance meeting but seemed very fitting.

Must close now,

Your affectionate,

HECTOR

Went down to Deal and stayed 3 days. Marg, Tiger and Miss Cooper were there. Will send photos.

A few days after Hector wrote this letter, the 4th Canadian Division moved to Shorncliffe in southeastern England, where Hector was to receive officer's training at the Engineers Training School. Shorncliffe was a major training establishment for Canadian troops and its pre-existing wood and stone barracks had been hurriedly augmented by a small city of tents a few months before Hector arrived. By April, 1916 approximately 40,000 Canadians were stationed in the camp. In addition to the Engineers Training School, the camp also accommodated a Machine Gun School and the Canadian Army Medical Corps Training Depot.

The camp was situated on high ground just southwest of Folkestone and from the surrounding open fields, the troops could easily see the coast of France on a clear day and even hear the distant boom of heavy artillery from the killing fields of the Western Front if an easterly wind was blowing.

Hector wrote to his brother, Oscar, shortly after arriving. Oscar was in the process of volunteering for the Canadian Expeditionary

---

[1] Lieutenant Eric A. McNair was two years younger than Hector, and like him was born in India, and went to school at Charterhouse, where the two met. He was awarded the Victoria Cross for his actions on Valentine's Day, 1916.

Force, back in Vancouver. Like Hector he was initially assigned to the Duke of Connaught's Own Regiment. His Attestation Papers were dated May 26, 1916.

Hector's letter suggests that, having returned to England, Aldergrove would hold little appeal to him after the war.

Shorncliffe
1. 5. 16.

Dear Oscar,

We have shifted once more and are now under canvas here 5 miles from Folkestone and the weather is just great. We are in just as great a muddle as ever as witness the pay parade today which is two days overdue. We all marched up and stood around the Pay Office by Companies; after twenty minutes wait we all marched back again as there was no pay for our Company from Bordon. My Commission is hanging fire but should materialise this month.

Last Monday at Bordon I was called up to Orderly Room and told about a commission. Captain Watt had orders to send me down to report at Training School here right away. I asked for leave to get up to Town and arrange about money and kit, but he said his orders were explicit, I had to report right away. This was changed to Wednesday as the whole Division left that day, and for the first 4 days I used to be called out regularly to see about my transfer. At last I signed 3 more sheets and Major Hill let me know that I might get an appointment any time within the month.

I went down to Rideals last Sunday before leaving and found Dr. Rideal, alone and the small boy Oliver at home. Their place is looking fine and Ione is just splendid, we had the greatest time and stayed at home while the others went to church. She certainly is pretty and knows how to enjoy life.

As soon as I raise my stars[1] and get leave and sensible pay I can see far ahead, because I have absolutely changed my views on life in the last few months. N.V.[2] started it, Ottawa pretty near completely finished it and London has fixed it absolutely. By the time I get to France I ought to be alright; of course there is nothing serious, but Life is too short and the Aldergrove safety valve compressor has come off with a vengeance.

I have managed to get along fairly well with the 2/6 a day that we get, so I should get through with the $2.60 and $1 field allowance that I

---

[1] Achieves promotion to lieutenant.
[2] North Vancouver.

am allowed. I have to pay 75c mess fund and 10c to a Batman or valet, and after a few more extras this leaves me with about 2.50 a day clear.[1] I went out with a few fellows yesterday on to the Leas and listened to the band for an hour, and then took in a Sunday Concert at the Pleasure Gardens;[2] Lady Tree recited and the Deal Marines String Band played 2nd.[3] It is raining with the sun shining at intervals. I have been up once more and done a little more signing of papers, but can get no definite answer as to when I get my appointment.

I believe I am going once more to see Tonight's the Night,[4] I saw it in Town, and it is coming down here all this week.

We had a fine Church parade on Sunday with De Pencier preaching and two bands.[5] There were 3,000 troops present.

Two drafts have left for France since we arrived; it seems the Engineers are getting it pretty badly just now. A Company which left last week has had 80 returned already in Casualties.[6]

I had 8 letters today and a pair of socks, also one photo, so I am feeling fairly cheerful. Just go right ahead and find as many decent families as you can; it is what makes life worthwhile and helps an awful lot. I have developed a cheek now which surprises me. I took a rather decent girl to the theatre and to Gattis when I was up in Town;[7] I had not met her till the night before, coming back in the Tube.

Well so long,
Yours,
HECTOR

Pass on photos.

----

[1] A batman was a soldier assigned to one or more officer as their personal servant. The position was sought-after as it exempted the soldier from many of the more onerous duties.

[2] The Leas was a main promenade running along the sea front in Folkestone. Pleasure Gardens was a grand Victorian theatre on Bouverie Road in Folkestone; it opened in 1888 and was demolished in 1964.

[3] Helen (Holt) Tree, wife of the famous actor Sir Herbert Beerbohm Tree.

[4] A musical comedy that opened in London in April 1915.

[5] Rt. Rev. Adam Urias de Pencier, Bishop of Cariboo with New Westminster. De Pencier served with the 62nd Canadian Overseas Infantry Battalion as a chaplain and was later awarded the O.B.E.

[6] A Company consists of about 100 men. War casualties were mounting at a terrible rate.

[7] Gattis was a music hall.

Church of England
Soldiers Club,
Woodward Hall,
Folkestone.
8. 5. 16.

Dear Mamma,

This is a birthday letter in case it takes especially long to reach:
Many happy returns of the day.[1]

I have just got back from another weekend leave, and had a good
time. It was the cheapest I have spent so far and was a great relief after
Camp. I got up at 2.15 and went to Mrs. McLellan and found her in. Edie
Edwards was out at her War Work so we went out and had tea and left the
latch key inside; this meant getting through a window with a ladder.

In the evening Edie Edwards and I had dinner at "Arthurs" and left
Mrs. McLellan indoors; she is an invalid just now, and has grown a lot
thinner but she is awfully jolly. We went to see the Brintons in the evening
and stayed for about an hour. They have a small flat at 36 Kanelagh
Gardens, Stamford Brook Ave. W in case you don't have their address.
They want me to call in any time I am in Town.

I have not got a transfer yet, and the rest of the Company are going
back to Bordon if the latest rumour can be believed. Rupert is lending me
£50 which he in turn is borrowing, I believe.[2] I have had no pay now for
some time, I must have about £5 in hand, so won't want to touch the
Assigned: I suppose it has arrived at last.

9th. We are all in tents this morning because of especially bad rain,
so I am going on with this letter. I have just heard that my transfer is
liable to hang around yet. I have had another medical exam here and got
the signature of more assorted officers.

I had the misfortune of losing the camera, and what is worse some
undeveloped photos I especially wanted to see. I left it in the train on
Saturday night, and there is no trace of it at the Lost Property Office.

---

[1] Her 56th birthday. Rosa was born in Ramsgate, Kent on June 10, 1860.

[2] Hector's elder brother, Rupert, had completed his Natural Sciences Tripos at Clare
College, Cambridge, and his clinical training at Guy's Hospital where he had qualified as
a Member of the Royal College of Surgeons and Licentiate of the Royal College of
Physicians of London in 1914. He volunteered for the Royal Army Medical Corps in 1914,
though in what capacity is not quite clear as his commission as a Temporary Lieutenant
RAMC was only effective from November 8, 1915. In the interim he worked with the
French Red Cross at a convalescent hospital at Lannion, on the Brittany coast, perhaps as
a volunteer civilian doctor. He left there in November 1915 when he was commissioned
and moved east to take part in the Battle of the Somme in mid-1916.

I have not discovered any friends in Folkestone, and it is quite time I did, as if I get stationed here and the others move on, I don't intend to flock by myself. I find that knowing decent people makes all the difference as just now I can't seem to take any interest in my work: it is all absolutely useless and only kept up just to keep us busy; we are back at the kind of work I had in the first few weeks. When I get started on the new course I will have all kinds of things to keep me busy, and I hope to get back my enthusiasm, because I hate working when I don't see the use. I was in the Sergeants' Mess yesterday with the rest of our tent and got very good feeding and not at all a hard job. Washing up and cleaning pans, we had about 4 hours to ourselves.

They have given us our full kit at last, it is webbing and not leather. We also have rifles which are completely useless except for drill; they have been returned from the front and condemned but the bayonets are fine and sharp. Just now I am B3 Coy. but we shift around the whole time and it is only my number which saves me.

When I was up in Town I rode around quite a lot on busses and got a fairly good idea of London; before that I used the Tube and saw nothing. On Sunday I paid my first visit to Golders Green and Hampstead Heath with a very decent girl Phyllis Pressley. I met her the last time I went up, we discovered quite a lot of places and had a fine time. Her sister is engaged to a War Officer in the Sherwoods.[1] He worked up from a private at the beginning of the war, but he had been in the Harrow O.T.C. and had the Training.[2] I don't believe we are going on parade this morning as the rain is simply fierce and anyhow there is nothing to do, and absolutely no chance of drying anything until the sun comes out. Will you take the Birthday Money out of the assigned pay as I am broke and even behindhand till Pay Day when I should be a rich man. I know how useful $5 can be on the farm for small things.

If no pay arrives it might be just as well to write Ottawa, there seems to be a muddle there as in most branches.

This letter matches the weather, but it will be more cheerful next time. I am annoyed about the camera.

(Address to 65 London Wall)[3]

Your affectionate,

HECTOR

---

[1] The Sherwood Foresters Regiment from Nottingham.

[2] Officers' Training Corps.

[3] London Wall is a street just northeast of St Paul's Cathedral. This address was probably Ward's legal offices.

56

Shorncliffe, C. I. E. D.
14. 5. 16.

Dear Marg,

I just got your letter as I came in this evening, I had an idea I had answered your last addressed to Bordon and must apologise. My appointment was up in Orders Friday night dated 9. 5. 16 and this is Sunday. I am getting myself paraded tomorrow morning to see where and when I am to report, I want to stay till Tuesday morning, as we are paid Monday night, and I know the trouble if I get out, also I have an idea that I am drawing both my Lieutenant's pay of $6.60 and my sapper's $1.10 so I don't want to hurry. We have had fearful rain for 5 days and it looks like another spell tonight; tent life is no joke when there is 3 inches of mud everywhere outside, and ½ inch on the tent floor.

Eric Buckley and I went to the 'Count of Luxembourg' last night and I saw 'Tonight's the Night' again last week at Folkestone, it was not at all bad.

I took a weekend in Town last Saturday and stayed with Mr. McLellan, came back Sunday night. It looks as though I can get a week or 10 days leave next week so I am not doing badly; if some kind person would give me $1000 I would feel a whole lot happier.

My mail comes in spurts like arterial bleeding, and is very welcome, but it keeps me busy returning so as to keep the pot boiling. I heard from Nan Bostock, her mother and little sister are coming over here for a summer holiday, and must have started by now. Also a girl I knew in Vanc. is at Bexhill[1] so Canada is doing its best to come to me as I can't go there; not that I want to in the least just now. Captain Otter seems to have been Old Carthusian,[2] I saw his name on some of our Casualty Lists in Cloisters at School. Did you happen to know Priolean at Norwich? He is a Captain now and engaged. Also - which shows how I look for coming marriages in the Sketch - I see Mary Lodge is engaged to a Lieutenant. [3]

Must stop now,
Your affectionate,
HECTOR

P.S. I believe Bodgers Oundle are the people for ties, but Fosters at Oxford and Cambridge are sure to have them.

---

[1] Thirty miles southwest of Shorncliffe.
[2] Old boy from Charterhouse School.
[3] The *Daily Sketch* was a tabloid newspaper published from 1909 to 1971.

Officers' Mess,
R.E.Barracks,
Shorncliffe
25. 5. 16.

Dear Mamma,

I have got back from leave at last, and I suppose I have to settle down to work now. Yesterday was Empire Day so there was nothing to do here. I went down to Ramsgate and saw the Cole family except Dulcie who was at school. They were awfully nice and gave me a very good day. I went around most of the places I knew and finished up at the new tennis club, but did not play. When we got back Vera and I played singles in the play-ground and I am sorry to say she won 6-2 2-6 7-5 which was rather disgraceful, but she is quite good and has played all winter. I missed my connection at Ashford late at night, and had a five hour wait, which meant getting up here at about 6.30 and a hurried shave and change before breakfast.

I have to report at Orderly Room at 10 today to see what is going to happen to me, as so far I don't know whether I am to go on a Course or be attached here.

We eat well here and it is fairly comfortable but of course I am pretty well lost at present. Just at this moment 2 fellows have come back

The Cole family circa 1910. Elizabeth Jackson (centre) was Moses' elder sister. She married Frederick Cole, a teacher at her father's school in Ramsgate. Dulcie was the youngest of their three children (2nd from right) and Vera (left) was the middle child. The woman on the extreme right was probably another of Moses' sisters, possibly Ida, "Tiger". | Family album

on leave and are full of experiences.

My kit cost me about £40 so far and there is more to come I am afraid, I have my allowance in the Bank of Montreal. Mr. Ward has paid so far, and I am paying him back by degrees, so as to keep a decent balance. I have paid £25 so far and today is pay day which means another £15. Rupert talks of getting leave this week but I am afraid he will have to come to me as I can't get leave just now for any time worth while.

6.30   I have been attached to B. Coy. and have spent today as supernumerary Orderly Officer inspecting Rations and all the small duties around Camp. I am taking it on again tomorrow which means 5 o'clock in the morning, but I don't intend to make a fool of myself if possible when I get on my own. I have just procured a batman to myself and am settling down but the process as usual to begin with is costly. I saw Mrs. McClellan and Edie Edwards for an hour or so just before I left Town, but could not stay. I am afraid my trips have to be curtailed now, as travelling 1st costs an awful amount and I want to keep within bounds just now. Rupert is supposed to get leave in a few days, but someone says there is a general order stopping leave just now.[1]

I know you like small details, so here is tonight's dinner: soup, fish, beef with potatoes and green French beans, a college or plum pudding, ices and desert. Wines are extra and not up to much.

All the Vancouver bunch have been transferred to A. Coy. which means France shortly. No 9 Coy. and a draft left on Saturday and 3 battalions this morning, so a general change around the camp is taking place. I believe I have had all your letters now; always address to 65 London Wall, it is safer.

I have bought a fine trench coat, a double thickness of waterproof material, and oiled silk liner between, with huge collar flaps and storm cuffs. It has a detachable lining and makes it two coats in one and only comes to the knees to keep out of mud. Everything was from Thresher and Glenny.[2]

I have to stop now but will write to someone in a little while.
Your affectionate,
HECTOR

---

[1] The Allies were gearing up for the first offensive of the Battle of the Somme.
[2] A well-known London-based outfitter.

Officers Mess,
R.E.Barracks,
Shorncliffe.
4. 6. 16.

Dear Mamma,

I have just got back from seeing Rupert off at the station, he came down here yesterday as I could not get leave to go up to Town. I went down to Folkestone in the evening and then took dinner at the Metropole, getting out in time for the Revue at the Pleasure Gardens Theatre which was not bad.

Rupert stayed at a small hotel in town, and I came down to him at 9.30 a.m. (Sun) and watched him eat breakfast. We took a Bus out towards Hythe, and walked from there about 5 miles to Lym, had a good lunch and got a lift back in a car to the hotel which finished the day nicely. He has not changed, except for a small moustache, and his face looks thinner. I took a photo with the new camera, which might be decent and will send prints out, though he is getting some taken in Town.

I have been in charge of a party of markers at the Ranges since Wednesday, which is not very exciting work. We each have targets to look after and keep scores; they put 2 men to a target for marking purposes.

I am having my teeth seen to free of charge by the Depot dentist except I pay for any extra material such as gold or porcelain for fillings; it won't cost £1 for all my teeth so I am lucky.

I have discovered a Mrs. Wood at Hythe whom I helped to carry some cakes for the hospital; she wants me to come for dinner some time this next week, and I see signs of tennis. I have a racquet and am going to see about a 2nd hand bike.

Hector's elder brother, Rupert, as an acting major in the Royal Army Medical Corps. | *Family album*

There is a fearful wind blowing which nearly upsets the whole tent, and a cold rain, in fact we have a large fire up at the Mess, and I have lighted my oil stove to keep things cheerful.

I have joined at the right time as usual, 15 more officers landed from Ottawa and I am senior to the bunch by 1 week.

Your affectionate,
HECTOR

Officers Mess,
R.E.Barracks,
Shorncliffe.
14. 6. 16.

Dear Mamma,

Thanks very much for your letter which I got when I came in this afternoon. We were out around Lympne and Etchinghill[1] supposed to be putting it in a state of defence for a rearguard action against troops advancing up the Eltham valley railway from Folkestone. You can see it all

1915 Premier motorcycle similar to the one that Hector bought. | *Archival photo*

---

[1] Five miles west and north of Folkestone respectively.

on a map. They gave us 5 hours, two battalions and 8 machine guns. My job was acting Staff Officer which merely meant riding round, and would have been criticising, except I am in the learning stage. Rupert and I were over almost the same ground a week ago, and I was out there myself 2 days ago. I have a motorcycle now and have to go slow in the expenditure. Arthur, who shares my tent, and I went shares but as I am leaving on Sunday for an 8 weeks course at Brightlingsea, Essex[1] near Clacton, I have decided to take it over and pay installments on it. I get my gasoline free from the A.S.C.[2] which is good, as it is 2/4 a gallon.

Vera's fiancé is a private in the Liverpool Rifles whom she met at the tennis club; all I know is that his first name is Gerald, and they seem quite happy; he has left for France.[3] I can't afford a photo yet so you will have to be content with snaps. All my pay is in the Bank of Montreal, and is deposited there at the beginning of each month. I have an idea they have been paying me Sapper's pay as well, so if you get full assigned pay, just hang on to it. I have notified them here, so it should only be a half month.

There is a very nice band playing outside the Mess, they have just finished "Poet and Peasant."[4] Everyone I have come across in my travels is very good about writing and I am getting a crowd of congratulations which ought to keep my ears burning, also socks, so I should worry. Mrs. and Ruth Bostock are in England now, I must see if I can get in touch with them. Also Muriel Attwood is down here somewhere and wants me to look her up. Jessie Dale-Harris has been especially good at sending photos and good wishes, her aunt is Lady Buckmaster, and I am to look her up and present her card, but I have so many things I am supposed to do that I don't. I will write to Gerald very soon, and let him know anything interesting. Oscar can always pass on letters to you if you remind him. I sent the cigarette pictures.

Tonight is our last night of mourning for Lord Kitchener[5] and it will seem strange to go around without the crêpe.[6] I don't know if I told you about a Mrs. Wood at Hythe whose basket of cakes for the hospital I carried. I was at dinner there last night, they are quite decent and I wish I was not leaving just now. Mrs. Wood has promised me tennis and it will have

---

[1] A Royal Engineers base on the coast, northeast of London.

[2] Army Services Corps.

[3] Vera Cole married James Gerald Crawford, and they had two sons.

[4] *Poet and Peasant Overture* by Franz von Suppe (1819-1895).

[5] Lord Kitchener, British Secretary of State for War, was killed on June 5, 1916, when the British cruiser HMS *Hampshire*, on which he was travelling to Russia, was sunk by a German mine west of the Orkney Islands.

[6] Black mourning ribbon.

ENGLAND

to wait. I must get up to the Mess for dinner, and then scribble off various letters to catch the Canadian mail; my stamp bill is about 2/6 a week, and my fountain pen needs plenty of refilling. It is rotten luck for Bill McIntyre. I must write to Vera and see how things are progressing.
      Till next time'
      HECTOR

Hector left Shorncliffe for his eight week course at the School of Military Engineering in Brightlingsea, Essex, on Saturday June 17. He travelled by train via London and took his motorcycle with him. He spent the night at A.E.N. Ward's house and relaxed with a friend, taking advantage of a weekend away from the military environment. The following afternoon, he caught the train to Colchester and then rode the last ten miles down to the small coastal town of Brightlingsea on his motorcycle. Brightlingsea lies at the mouth of the River Colne, north of the Thames estuary. At that time, its economy was centred on oyster fisheries and ship building, although these industries were dwarfed by its importance as a defensive area. Hector was billeted in the town where social life was probably limited. While at Brightlingsea, Hector's class received advanced training in bridge and other defence construction.

R.E. Mess,
School of Military
Engineering,
Brightlingsea, Essex.
23. 6. 16.

Dear Mamma,
      Six of us are down here on an 8 weeks course in Engineering under Majors Stewart and Gregson. I wonder if you know Gregson, he is a delightful old gentleman, over 60 and knows Karachi fairly well; must have been in India a long time. There are 18 of us altogether and about 50 N.C.O.s;[1] most of the others are Highland or Lowland R.E.s[2] and a very decent lot.
      I have discovered Lieut. Lownie who knew Aitken and especially his twin sons. He has been around India and Ceylon for 5 years.

[1] Non-commissioned officers, i.e. sergeants and corporals.
[2] Royal Engineers.

63

Also an awfully decent boy Davies from Bradfield and Caius,[1] just about 22. I have the key of his billet and we get on famously, and work our notes together. So far the lectures are all old work as I have all the notes and more from the N.V. class.[2]

My old "Bus" is working in fine style. We have 4 motor cycles altogether in the class and I am getting a photo of the 4 of us with one each on the carrier, it should be interesting.

We have done various works during the

Hector's group practising bridge construction at the School of Military Engineering at Brightlingsea, Essex. | *Family album*

week, digging and fortifying positions; on Wednesday we put an old cottage in a state of defense, loopholing[3] and sandbagging the walls. I have the whole afternoon off as we were set a task to get finished in the regulation 4 hours. We actually did 9'x3'x3' and started at 11.15. All the N.C.O.s and Officers had their tasks staked out along the line and we just raced. Canada in the shape of me won, as I got finished by lunch 12.50 thanks to gravel pit practice in B.C.[4]

I am having a simply splendid supply of letters just now, five this morning including one from Ags.[5] Also Vera who seems to have got one from Oscar.

I find it rather handy to get to an Imperial Mess,[6] as we get Canadian allowance and can make 1/3d a day with care. The motorcycle has

---

[1] Bradfield College, a public school in Berkshire, and Caius College at Cambridge University.

[2] The 6th Field Company Canadian Engineers in North Vancouver.

[3] Making holes in walls and trench parapets for firing through.

[4] Presumably shoveling gravel for roads or concrete construction on Applegarth.

[5] Agnes Jackson, Hector's aunt in Mission, B.C.

[6] British army officers' mess.

made me most fearfully hard up of course and I am learning to live on a pittance, but it is good practice, and anyway there is nothing to spend it on here except gasoline and an occasional minor Bust. But even those seem a waste of time once the novelty wears off. When I move off I will sell the machine, and it will be like a Bank account to help out with extra kit.

I hear we are going to have a trip up to London to go over the defense scheme, and pick holes in it. This will be by one of the motor busses placed at our disposal by the A.S.C., it will end up with a Theatre party and all kinds of fun. So I must allow for it in my expenditure. I went up to Chepstow Place on my way down here and stayed Saturday night. Among other things I went out to Hendon and saw Graham White go up, also ran into the back wheel of a bicycle opposite the Marble Arch coming down the Edgware Road. I made an awful mess of the rim but was really his fault, though it cost me 4/6d in repairs. Sunday I went up with Mr. Ward to the Temple for the morning service; the singing was an absolute treat.[1] After the service we went into the Dining Halls of the Inner and Middle Temple. Lord Mersey was showing a few friends around.[2] He looks old.

I caught the 4.29 from Liverpool St. after lunching at the Bath Club and bicycled from Colchester. Tennis is out of the question here, so amusements are limited to a fine point. I am going to a Whist Drive on Tuesday if all goes well.

I heard from Nan Bostock; Mrs. is staying with the Romanis's for some time.

I owe Gerald a letter,
Your affectionate,
HECTOR

P.S. I believe I can get Gerald a piece of shell from the Lowestoft bombardment.[3] Davies was O.C.[4] the work of digging up and disposing of live shells.

---

[1] Temple Church in London was built in the 12th Century as the headquarters of the Knights Templar.

[2] Lord Mersey, Sir John Charles Bigham, was regarded as the grand old man of the English legal profession and presided over the *Lusitania* and *Titanic* enquiries. He died in 1929.

[3] Gerald had obviously asked Hector to send back any souvenirs he could. Early on the morning of April 25, 1916, German Navel forces shelled the town of Lowestoft, Sussex, fifty miles from Brightlingsea, Essex, for twenty minutes, killing four civilians. The Royal Navy forced the German force to break off the shelling but it suffered damage to two cruisers and a destroyer.

[4] Officer Commanding.

Temple Church, London by Augustus Pugin & Thomas Rowlandson. | *Archival photo*

Chapter 3

The Battle of the Somme

By the summer of 1916, when Hector was on his engineering course at Brightlingsea, Essex, the Battle of Verdun had been raging northeast of Paris for six long months. The Allies had planned to stretch the Germans to the breaking point by attacking simultaneously on the Eastern Front with Russia, the Southern Front with Italy and the Western Front in France. However, the Germans forced their hand by attacking at Verdun with the aim of "bleeding the Allies to death" in a battle from which they could not afford to withdraw.

Because of the need to funnel all available supplies and men into the Verdun area, the rest of the front line bogged down. The French Army was bearing the brunt of the attack and its high command urged the British to open another front to divert some of the German Army's efforts away from Verdun. In response to this plea, and in spite of the shortage of supplies and troops, the Allies began a massive attack on the German lines, well to the west of Verdun. The campaign became known as the Battle of the Somme, named after the River Somme, which wound its way over the flat low-lying area. The British offensive was launched on July 1, 1916. The objective was to pierce the enemy lines and pour cavalry through the gap to attack the German back areas and outflank a larger portion of the enemy's defences.

As with most of the offensives of the war, the attack was preceded by days of shelling that aimed to soften up the enemy by destroying their bunkers and breaching their defensive barbed wire entanglements. Unfortunately for the British, the German concrete bunkers proved remarkably resistant to the shelling and protected their occupants well. Critically, the shelling also failed to break the barbed wire. As a result, when the Allies finally attacked over a twenty-mile front in the early morning, the German troops were well warned, and they emerged from their bunkers and used their machine guns very effectively. The Allied troops, laden with the equipment needed to defend the new line they hoped to establish, were easy targets for the enemy machine guns and artillery as they advanced slowly through the churned-mud approaches to the German lines. The slaughter was horrendous. The British and Commonwealth forces received almost 58,000 casualties on the first day of the battle. These included some 20,000 dead, the vast majority of whom were British.

Hector's elder brother, Rupert, was in the Somme area during the attack and subsequent battle. He was with the 91st Field Ambulance Company, R.A.M.C.,[1] attached to the 32nd Division, and was probably somewhere in the French-held southeastern part of the line. France subsequently awarded him the Croix de Guerre for gallantry under

Delville Wood, the Somme, 1916. | *Archival photo*

---

[1] Royal Army Medical Corps.

fire, evacuating French wounded from the front.[1] The Battle of the Somme continued interminably, with each side convinced that the other was about to collapse.

While the battle was raging, Hector continued his training in England, champing at the bit to join Rupert in France. It would be only a matter of time before the slaughter of the Somme necessitated reinforcements from England and Hector was soon to be one of the thousands sent over to fill the gaps in the ranks.

The new 4th Canadian Division had nearly completed its training in England and its phased move across the Channel to France was planned to begin in August to relieve the exhausted Australian and New Zealand troops at the Somme. After a short period of acclimatization, they were designated to form the core of a strong attack in the middle of September.

R.E.Mess,
School of Military
Engineering,
3. 7. 16.

Dear Mamma,

I have two letters to thank you for, and goodness knows how many other people. The class work is getting strenuous and time limited. I feel more or less sure I get all your mail, there are no long waits and I expect by now you have got my acknowledgement of the Assigned pay. Also both birthday letters arrived. I have kept fairly well in touch with Vera, but I can't say I call her awfully pretty; she is fairly amusing and lively.

I also heard from Oscar since he joined and must answer it when I have waded through. I must have 2 letters to answer to get even, and it looks a pretty hopeless task even for me. Now for your 2nd letter which came this morning when I was out pontooning. We all went into mourning for Kitchener for the week. It is most unfortunate about your teeth and must be uncomfortable. Mine are going to trouble me again soon, I must get started on them when I get back to Folkestone. Tell Oscar, I will do so myself, that as soon as he gets a commission, not before, to transfer to the Engineers. There is absolutely no comparison in the life, especially at the Front.

I will get a regulation R.A.M.C. badge and send it.

We are pontooning all today and yesterday, and continue different

---

[1] Croix de Guerre awarded on April 7, 1917.

bridges all the week and next. I got a few photos strictly against orders, as the place is of tactical importance. Rupert must have been in all this last fighting. I have not heard from him for some time; he must be pretty busy. Davis and I are getting fun out this place in spite of a rather unpromising outlook.

I was over at Dedham again last Sunday, and saw the Ashwins again and we are going over to them on Saturday for tennis or a boating party.[1]

Later: Davis and I are taking a weekend in Town and I am putting up at his Place at Hampstead.

I heard of your visit from Muriel and Mrs. Schou.[2] I suppose it must have been a change for Gerald, but he ought to get a whole lot more, as I can't help thinking there is a lot of perfectly unnecessary isolation going

Hector's unit building a pontoon bridge during training near Brightlingsea, Essex – probably taken from Point Clear Bay, looking north towards the town. | *Family album*

---

[1] Dedham is ten miles north of Brightlingsea, Essex. The Ashwin family had befriended Hector.

[2] Nicolai Schou served as reeve of the Municipality of Burnaby from 1893 to 1903. He was a relative and neighbour of Charles Sprott, a major shareholder of the Fraser Valley Nurseries, Ltd.

on.[1] It will take a lot to get me back to anything quiet after the War, except as a change: if we don't get much money anyhow we see life. And it seems quite natural to start afresh at any old place they stick us down at.

I prefer the Canadian officers I have come across to any of the others, except a few exceptions. Of course they are only Territorials and Kitchener's Army that I have seen on the Course.[2]

We are getting pretty sick of the Mess and general arrangements here, and there will be trouble: it appears that the Mess in the past has had debt, and this S.M.E. Class is expected to pay it off, but it won't.[3]

I believe Davis and I are going to hire a yacht and live in it instead of a billet. I can make 4/6 a week by doing so, and be absolutely independent into the bargain.

I must finish now and give someone else a chance.

Your affectionate,

HECTOR

3. 7. 16 (cont). So the mystery has been satisfactorily explained, have the payments been coming in right along?[4] I have got off parade this morning as I am on another Board of Inquiry about some lost stores. I am decidedly glad, as there is to be a Battalion parade and inspection which means hours of waiting and fooling around. We have an Officers Ride this afternoon, with a certain amount of jumping. I am fearfully out of practice, and am sure to be stiff for a few days after.

We have just had another draft of Officers transferring from Infantry battalions into the tunneling company, but that never appealed to me.[5]

If my eyesight had been perfect I would have transferred into the R.F. Corps[6] as they are calling for volunteers, and I am beginning to understand motors now. I had my machine right down, and gave it a general cleaning up, and with another fellow, I worried out the timing of the magneto.

I can see I am going to have a hard job getting my £12 expense

---

[1] Gerald was being home schooled because of their financial situation, the lack of a nearby secondary school and Moses and Rosa's experience with teaching. As a result he seldom left the isolated farm.

[2] British volunteer army set up at the beginning of the war.

[3] School of Military Engineering.

[4] This appears to refer to the payments of Hector's "Assignment" pay.

[5] Tunneling companies were set up to dig tunnels under enemy trenches and then destroy them with huge amounts of explosives packed in the tunnels.

[6] Royal Flying Corps.

money from the Pay Office. Courses are an expensive luxury, and mine is no isolated case. Our band has just started which means the Companies are moving up; it is a full dress parade. Luckily for me my section is taking 6 days leave from today, and I am going to apply for some myself if I can raise the price. I have miles of letters to get off somehow.

　　　　Your affectionate,
　　　　HECTOR

　　　　　　　　　　　　　　　R.E. Mess,
　　　　　　　　　　　　　　　School of Military
　　　　　　　　　　　　　　　Engineering,
　　　　　　　　　　　　　　　Brightlingsea, Essex.
　　　　　　　　　　　　　　　12. 7. 16.

Dear Marg,

　　　　I am awfully sorry I have not written for so long but I have kept on putting it off as I have done with all my mail, as we are on a class here and have work all day and notes the rest of the time. Your letters and one from Ags have always found me. I heard from Oscar a few days ago, he has joined up in the D.C.O.R.[1] and has hopes of a Commission as he is getting influence to bear.

　　　　We are doing all kinds of Engineering down here: trench work, pontooning and trestle bridging, also demolition and all kinds of other stuff. Just now we are working with a field coy.[2] of Territorials putting up a trestle bridge across the Colne 320 ft. I have a few photos of the work and will get more when the sun gets out. I am going to see Dr. Rendall very soon, he lives at Dedham quite close to here.[3] The Crisps have a house, Wenham Court near also, but I don't know if they ever live there.[4]

　　　　I have not heard from Rupert since he left, but anyhow I have never written so it is not unusual. There are 6 Canadian and 10 British Officers down here and about 30 N.C.O.s; we are billeted in the town. Will write some other time but really am fearfully busy.

　　　　Your affectionate,
　　　　HECTOR

---

[1] Duke of Connaught's Own Rifles, the same unit that Hector had joined in Vancouver.
[2] The Engineers were divided into Field Companies of approximately 100 men.
[3] Dr. Gerald Henry Rendall, clergyman, born 1851, who had retired from the headmastership of Charterhouse in the same year that Hector left for Canada.
[4] The Crisps from Godalming.

THE BATTLE OF THE SOMME

R.E. Mess,
School of Military
Engineering,
Brightlingsea, Essex.
15. 7. 16.

Dear Mamma,

We have had 4 weeks of the course already and things are cheering up somewhat. The work is fine and quite like old times and after all it is merely a little theory with loads of common sense and actual experience, which is one thing B.C. can teach. I had charge of a Tidal Ramp for a bridge across the Colne, there is a 15' variation in tides and we have to have part of it on floating piers. The 6 Canadians had a trip today in a Submarine Chaser twin screw patrol boat about 300 H.P. We were doing over 15 knots and were out 4 hours. We passed a King Edward type battleship and got out to the boom across the channel with submarine nets.[1] Sub Lieut. Viner was in command and he gave us a fine tea.

We have a 3 day fair at this place and tonight is the last night. There ought to be great times as we are making an organised party from the Mess. Last night I had a hand full of confetti down my neck and scattered it all over my Billet.

Hector (left) enjoying a day out from the SME on a patrol boat. | *Family album*

---

[1] The King Edward class of battleships were launched by the Royal Navy between 1903 and 1905.

In the English Channel (Hector 2nd from left). | *Family album*

Dr. Rendall has asked me over for Sunday week and I have three other invitations from Dedham for tennis and boating which I will have to give up for various reasons. Davis is away on weekend leave and I am feeling rather lost at present. We always go out for a 2 or 3 mile run about 10.30 at night and I don't feel much like going alone.

There was a slight scare when about 12 big guns were fired off Clacton, it was only a Monitor at night practice.[1] I heard from Oscar and have replied, but not from Rupert.

Your affectionate,
HECTOR

The Cups,
Colchester.
4. 8. 16.

Dear Mamma,

I have completely given up writing for about 3 weeks now except absolutely necessary letters, thanks to a rush of work. The Class ends next week and I am applying for 6 days leave to get around. We have been doing

---

[1] A shallow draft vessel with heavy guns.

defense schemes just lately, and have to measure up the various houses to see what men they would hold; it is rather fun and the people don't mind in the least. Booker and I went all round the village of Alresford and took details of about 15 houses including a school.[1]

I came over to Colchester in the Ford to get my machine from the shop where it was being overhauled, and then I am going to say goodbye to Dedham. Davis and I had a fine time there last weekend on the river with a Mrs. Layers and party. Two Australian Officers were there on sick leave and we made a fine party of 15 in three boats. I have absorbed quite a considerable amount of Military Lore, but will not be sorry to get back to Shorncliffe even though it does mean tents instead of sheets and a decent bed.

The Canadian Govt. owes me £11 as we have so far had to pay our own billeting and Ration Allowances so I am fearfully hard up. Luckily there is nothing to spend it on here. I have an enormous collection of photos taken by myself and others, but no prints except those in my book.[2]
We have been having hot weather and Zepp raids for the last 10 days, the bombs were dropped quite close two nights running.

Hoping alls well,
Your affectionate,
HECTOR

After eight weeks at the School of Military Engineering at Brightlingsea, Essex, Hector completed the course on August 11 and transferred directly back to his tented billet in the camp at Shorncliffe, sufficiently trained in military engineering to be sent to the front in France.

The day before he returned to Shorncliffe, the bulk of the newly trained 4th Canadian Division crossed the channel for France. In spite of the losses during the ongoing Battle of the Somme, the Engineers had more officers than were required, and Hector was not needed immediately. He wrote in one of his letters that he did not believe that he would be called on to go before the end of the year. In the meantime he was determined to enjoy his social life while he could.

---

[1] Three miles north-northwest of Brightlingsea, Essex.
[2] It is not known what happened to Hector's loose photographs that were not in his album.

Officers Mess,
R.E. Barracks.
Shorncliffe
14. 8. 16.

Dear Mamma,

Back again on the old stamping ground, but have not got down to work yet; that does not start till tomorrow. It is funny to get back to Camp routine and everlasting bugles after 2 months of general slackness. I have made arrangements for plenty of tennis both up at the Mess, and outside, and mean to pile in as much as possible in the time.

I got to know two very decent families through a fellow called Fraser. I scarcely know him, but happened to meet him on the Leas and he suggested going to tea with friends, Colonel Tremaine. Later on we went to another house and finished up with the younger members of the family at a dance at the Grand. I am going to see if I can pick up dancing as it appears to be the only way to meet people here, and goodness only knows how long we may stay on here. There are 102 Officers in the Mess while 30 could do the work.

I did not stay in Town on my way down as no leave was given so will take one later in September. There is a general rumour that the C.E.T.D.[1] is shifting to Bramshott at the end of the month, it will suit me absolutely, and will add one more camp to the many. I don't know if I have mentioned the Collingwoods at Dedham, one of the boys who was at Ch'ouse has just been killed.[2]

I am going to make an attempt to write off some of my millions of replies that are waiting, but it will be a long job; this is a beginning.

Your affectionate,
HECTOR

The Grand Hotel in Folkestone in 190?... surviving today. | *Archival photo*

---

[1] Canadian Engineer Training Depot.
[2] Captain Carlton Collingwood was killed on August 8, 1916, aged 26.

Shorncliffe
14. 9. 16.

Dear Gerald,

I have been intending to write for ages, but have finally actually started. We have just started to get cold weather, it is a fine moonlight night outside, but beastly chilly and I have lit my little oil stove to keep things comfortable. I am settling down to solid continuous work again, as I have No. 1 Section of A3 Coy; all my last men have been divided up between A1 and 2 Companies and I had 40 new men in yesterday.

My old bus[1] is simply great and takes me all over the place, the only drawback is the petrol shortage but I can get various ways of getting around it. Will you tell Mamma I am stopping the $16 assignment but it won't take effect for Sept., as there is not time, so I should have had it from March to Sept. inclusive. I want a pair of Shoe-packs knee high, a real heavy laced pair any price around $10, but get good ones as I will need them.[2] I am afraid the Scarborough shell splinters are off as Davies (he is in the Imperials) gave almost all to Bradford school museum.[3] Still I ought to be able to collar something with luck, if I keep going long enough.

We keep on sending drafts off now, I can hear the cheering now.[4] I suppose it means some more starting off.

Best of luck to all,
Your affectionate,
HECTOR

———————————

Hotel Metropole,
Folkestone
24. 9. 16.

Dear Mamma,

No I am not in France and as things go, have not much chance this year. I know when I get across I will hate it and wish myself back again, but it feels rotten hanging on here indefinitely, and there is no chance of volunteering; when officers are needed they are told, and have no further say in the matter; men volunteer when a draft is called.

———————————

[1] Hector's motorcycle.
[2] A moccasin-like boot made of a single piece of leather to keep out water.
[3] Hector probably meant Lowestoft, not Scarborough although Scarborough had been shelled by the German battleships *Derfflinger* and *von der Tann* in 1914.
[4] Batches of the 4th Canadian Division were being dispatched to France.

I came down to the Leas to listen to the band with Clemes who was at Brightlingsea, Essex with me, but saw Colonel and Mrs. Tremaine who have been away for a month, and decided to have tea with them; that is why I came here to get cleaned up and write a few letters in the mean time. I don't know if you have heard that Ione Rideal has got her peoples consent (grudging I should imagine) to go on the stage. I must get up and see the first night if poss: she ought to make rather a success as she is awfully pretty and really quite clever.

I am living in a continual state of minor insolvency which is annoying; I generally keep going somehow, but there are all kinds of small extras. One of these days I will catch up but not in Folkestone as everything is filthily dear.

Marg and Tiger keep up a perpetual complaint that I have not visited them.

> Officers Mess,
> R.E.Barracks,
> Shorncliffe.
> 25. 9. 16.

I have just got back to Camp after some rather nice tennis and feel pretty weary. Am playing again tomorrow; the weather has been behaving splendidly. Unfortunately the motorcycle is undergoing repairs at the

The Leas, a sea-front promenade in Folkestone, during the First World War. |
Archival photo

A.S.C.; when I saw it they had the magneto off and could not find the trouble. I called on Mrs. Boldham-Wheatham, who lives here last night and am going down to dinner on Friday night. I have not heard from any of the Hill-Tout family for weeks now, people are gradually giving up the idea of writing to me; I know I don't deserve letters, as I have been fearfully slack. Lights out has gone all over the Camp because of a Zepp raid somewhere up the coast, so I have to finish this in a great hurry. One of these nights they will drop bombs here, but they have not done so yet, and people are careless.

We move into a new mess tomorrow and I am having a room instead of a tent. No one knows when move out takes place.

I have stopped the $16.[1]

Across the English Channel in the Somme, the fighting continued unabated. The Canadian Divisions had mounted a successful attack on the western end of the zone, using tanks for the first time. They captured the village of Courcelette but then, in spite of strenuous attempts, they made very little more headway against the well dug-in German defences in the so-called Regina Trench.

The French continued to beg the British to keep the pressure off Verdun, and the Allied Command decided to try to break the deadlock in the Somme with one last push before winter set in. They planned to focus their efforts on the eastern end of the active front. More troops were required, so the Allied High Command decided to again use the Canadian Divisions. However, the newly arrived 4th Division was still undermanned; additional reinforcements were needed from the rear to bring it up to strength.

Hector's view that he was unlikely to be sent to France that year was to be proved very wrong. In mid-October, just three weeks after making this prediction, he received word that he was to leave for France in a matter of days.

---

[1] Remainder of letter missing.

Hotel Metropole,
Folkestone.
20. 10. 16.

Dear Mamma,

We are on the move at last, 45 C.E. Officers are warned for tomorrow night for France. We have had leave since Tuesday and I spent it as usual with Mr. Ward in Town, and had the usual splendid time; just one last "Bust". I went to try "First Light" to see Ione start her stage career, and four of us had a Supper after the show. I hope the piece catches on and is a success as it means a lot to her.

You will be glad to hear that I have had a photo taken at last but have not seen the proofs yet. Since it was taken I have shaved off my mustache as the Order has been changed. I thought I had told you I had the "Daily Light".[1]

I could not recover £5 from the Govt. It was a beastly swindle. Davis is in the R.E. Territorials[2] so I don't expect I will see him again though we write occasionally. Only yesterday he met a C.E. man and asked to be remembered to me. I wonder if you have heard that Mrs. McClellan died last June. I went round to say good bye and found some relation keeping house for Edie Edwards. When I was up in May she looked awfully ill and was being treated for acute indigestion; it was cancer and they did not realise it.

I will have to be getting back to Camp.

Your affectionate,
HECTOR

I am selling the Bus with luck to a fellow in the Mess.

The formal portrait of Hector as a newly-commissioned Second Lieutenant, taken in England, before he left for France. | Family album

---

[1] A small book with a short bible quotation for each day of the year, which Hector carried in his pocket throughout the war.

[2] Royal Engineers.

Hotel Metropole,
Folkestone
20. 10. 16.

Dear Marg,

Thanks for your last letter; we may be moving any day and I am staying around for news. I was up in Town for 48 hours getting kit, and came down yesterday.

I don't believe there is anything I want, thanks all the same. I hope your plans work, they seem rather fine. Olive Berners appears to be engaged to a fellow in the R.F.C.,[1] I saw it in the papers. Have to scrawl a few more letters, and then back to Camp.

Your affectionate,
HECTOR

----

[1] Royal Flying Corps.

Chapter 4

France at Last

Hector shipped out across the English Channel to France on the night of October 21, 1916. His vessel sailed under cover of darkness to foil prowling German submarines and aircraft. He had been in England for some seven months.

The most recent Allied offensive on the Somme, the Battle of Le Transloy, had been launched three weeks earlier but soon bogged down when the weather turned and the battlefield became a quagmire. A report to Canadian Headquarters described how "with the bad weather the men's clothing became so coated with mud, great coat, trousers, puttees and boots sometimes weighed 120 pounds." The Battle of the Somme was reaching its final crescendo and the German forces were putting up a violent and desperate defence while the knee-deep mud was proving a terrible handicap to the attacking Allies whose casualties continued to be horrific. The attacking armies desperately needed reinforcements to bolster their forces.

After landing in France, it took Hector ten days to rejoin the rest of his 10th Field Company, Canadian Engineers, part of the 4th Canadian Division. The unit's commanding officer was Major (later Lt. Col.) Wilgar. He had set up base in the recently captured village of Courcelette, five miles northeast of the town of Albert, and less than a mile behind the front line. There had been rain on sixteen of the previous twenty-one days and the roads and trenches were in an appalling condition. Most of the trenches had collapsed with the combination of the saturated conditions and heavy shell fire. The 10th

Field Company was working frantically in bitterly cold conditions, to build defences in the newly captured area, and to ensure roads were passable to troops and equipment moving to and from the front. Hector arrived in Courcelette on November 1, 1916. That same night he was sent to the front line as part of a working party east of Courcelette, near the road from the town of Albert in Allied held territory, to the German held town of Baupaume.

On the following night the official war diary of the 10th Field Company records that Hector was assigned responsibility for a group of infantry consisting of an officer and fifty-six men from the 7th Division Pioneers,[1] to construct an observation post.[2] Four of the group were wounded during the night. Hector wrote home for the first time since arriving in France, after returning to his billet early the next morning, already sounding like an old hand. Censorship regulations forbade him from describing his exact location.

France,
3. 11. 16.

Dear Mamma,

I can quite sympathise with Rupert in the matter of letter writing; of course I can go on talking shop by the yard but when the novelty wears off there is nothing to say. I have been out with working parties 2 nights running and am out again tonight I am afraid to finish up a job. We leave at 4.15 and ride out for 3 miles, leave the horses there as the road is pretty tricky and the shells are pretty thick at times. From there it is a mile wade through mud and loose road metal, with intermittent swimming of shell craters; the road to the mill can hide its head in shame compared to this one. We get on the job about 7 p.m. and work for 5 hours getting back to camp at 2.30 or 3, and have a meal and then bed. I am writing this in bed while I am waiting for breakfast, then I am off to sleep again. I am wearing a pair of 16" boots, but the mud comes up to the top and is like glue. I suppose you got my letter asking for Shoe-packs, they have to be really high.

The first night I went out, we were working just behind the front line now; the shell fire got on my nerves after a bit, but that has all passed now, and it is only when one comes really close that I actually

---

[1] Combat Engineers responsible for constructing trenches and clearing mine fields.
[2] Observation posts were usually sited on high ground or in shell holes in no man's land to give early warning of impending enemy attacks.

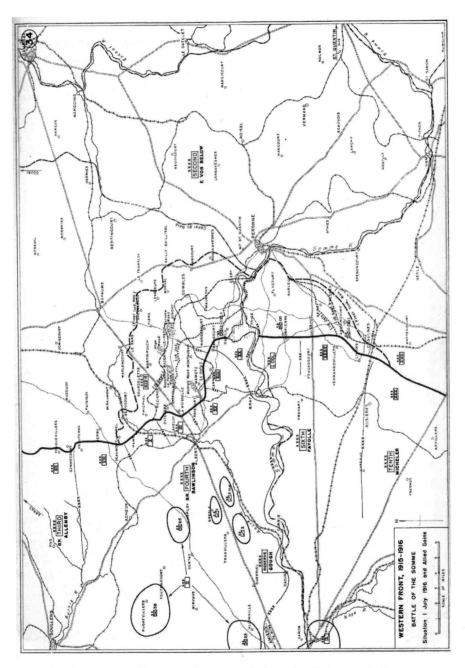

The front line moved only a few miles during the five-month-long Battle of the Somme.
| *Archival photo*

notice it, as the firing is continuous and the scream keeps up like a kind of Aeolian harp with a large explosion at the end. You can hear them coming and have plenty of time to think how close, just like dodging London traffic on a bicycle, it becomes second nature, and I go on explaining the work to be done. We have had so far few casualties, which seems wonderful considering. I must get another sleep now before lunch, so will stop.

Your affectionate,
HECTOR
10th Field Coy, 4th Div:
Army P.O.

———————

10th Field Coy,
4th Div.
Army P.O.
7. 11. 16.

Dear Mamma,

Just got your note about the Shoepacks. I have been out here 7 days now, and have been on night work with parties four times which is about an average, as we have plenty of Officers at present. The photo should reach you about the same time as this letter, I am enclosing a proof with the hat on, it is in itself an answer as to why I did not get any done that way.[1] I had to have the peak back, so he said, or it would shade my eyes too much.

We had a grand old firework display last night, at one time eight flares were shot up together, and various coloured Star Shells.[2]

The Officer in charge of my working party was a son of Pryce Jones,[3] the Mail Order people who pay carriage; he is quite young and decidedly English. All Engineer working parties are in charge of an infantry N.C.O., or Officer if there are over 50 men; we take along a few Sappers to help us explain what is needed. They look upon us as absolute experts, and do anything we want. Last night we were cleaning out a front line trench and as it was moonlight they saw us and gave us the benefit of

---

[1] The formal portrait taken before leaving England.
[2] The flares provided light if an enemy attack or advance into no man's land was suspected; star shells were used as signals.
[3] Lieutenant Rex Pryce-Jones (aged 20) was killed eleven days later on the last day of the Battle of the Somme, November 18, 1916.

their shrapnel and H.E.[1] mixed, the men were great and stayed with the job right along.[2] As soon as the fire was over for the time, they cleaned up the earth that had been knocked in and went on.

    I must go off to dinner now,

    Your affectionate,

    HECTOR

               10th Field Coy, 4th Div.

               Army P.O.

               8. 11. 16.

Dear Marg,

    Many thanks for your letter; just scribbling a reply to show that all is well so far.

    We are having plenty of work and pretty rotten weather to do it in, but our quarters are good enough, though quite temporary. The mail here

Two French soldiers, one carrying a German helmet, walk past a body dismembered by shellfire near Courcelette, the Somme. | *Archival photo*

---

[1] Shrapnel shells were generally used against infantry and high-explosive shells against buildings or vehicles.

[2] Casualties from this group were 1 killed and 3 wounded.

is quite an event and so far people have been fairly good in sending letters, we get it just as we are leaving for night work in the Lines. Rupert seems to have left here as I can get no word of him; am writing by this post to see if he can let me know where he is.

Must close now,
Your affectionate,
HECTOR

———————————

10th Field Coy,
Army P.O.
9. 11. 16.

Dear Gerald,

I am not out tonight so have time for a few letters before I get to bed.

As things are now we go out on alternate nights for work in the Lines. We usually get our Orders from 2 to 3 in the afternoon, stating the nature of work, number of Sappers and N.C.O.s in charge, and number of infantry for a working party. Also the Rendezvous and Time. We get a kind of High Tea at 4 and then ride out as far as it is tolerable safe, join up with the infantry and take them to the job; it is usually going up and coming out we get the Casualties. Just lately there has been a fine moon and a party of 150 in single file 5 ft apart takes up a lot of room when shrapnel gets at all busy. Last night I was working with seven pioneers and we ran into what they call a Barrage that is a continuous line of shrapnel and Whizz Bangs[1] on a given line of road to stop troops or supplies getting by. As luck would have it, it was taken off just before we got up and no one was touched, but it felt uncomfortable marching right up to it; as I was leading the party. If I had had any sense I would have taken cover, as I found out later the other parties did, but I was not going to stop with the others behind.

I heard from Rupert today, it seems he is only 3 miles away; the letter took 4 days to get to me as it had to go to the Field Post Office and then back. The trains here just crawl along. Coming down here I got out as it was moving; I was in the front and it must have been 200 yds. long, had a wash in the canal along side and got on at the back, then walked up to my carriage partly on the footboards and partly on the track.

_____

[1] A term describing any German artillery shell, although originally derived from the noise made by shells from German 77 mm. field guns.

The trouble is the enormous amount of freight which has to be shunted off at different sidings, they may as well go slow steadily as go fast and wait. The ground here was left in a hurry, and is covered with all kinds of rifles and ammunition, but I have seen no helmets yet with a spike. I picked up one of the plain kind but it is no better than our own as a curio; the bombardment here must have been simply fearful. In cleaning out trenches I have come across 3 remains of Germans deep down which must have been simply buried by shell fire.[1] Aeroplane photos which are used for making the official maps, look like photos of the craters of the moon through a high powered telescope, or like melted lead pocked with air holes.

We have got a fine little goat here as a kind of mascot, eats anything, and comes round for its rum ration; it just loves a cigarette to eat.

I suppose the Hill-Touts are still going strong. I hear from them at intervals, or rather from Lilian, as the others only answer letters of mine

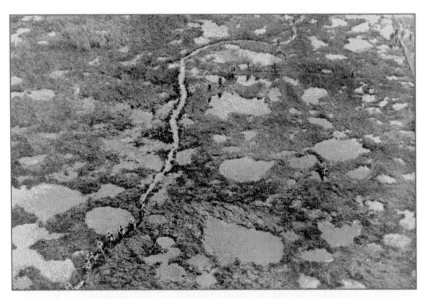

Hector described the ground at the Somme as looking like the surface of the moon through a high powered telescope. | *Archival photo*

---

[1] There are numerous reports of trenches with the rotting remains of legs or arms. protruding from the sidewalls which were simply ignored or partially covered by a sandbag.

when their conscience pricks them extra badly. What became of the bike, did Oscar take it to Vernon by any chance?[1] I had to leave the old Bus in Folkestone with Lady Lawson as I could not get a reasonable price, there is a small trouble in the magneto winding, but otherwise it kept in grand shape.

The men are getting their goat skin coats now, and it is getting about time; I believe I will get hold of a leather jacket myself to wear under my tunic. I have a Sapper's tunic to save my own as every night I come in just plastered with mud. I also have an issue of hip rubbers so keep dry around camp, they are useless for Trench work when there is much walking around, simply stick in the mud.

Must stop now,
Your affectionate,
HECTOR

Allied troops were initially issued goatskin coats to ward off the winter cold, but this was later discontinued due their impracticality in the clinging mud of the trenches. | *Archival photo*

---

[1] 200 miles east of Vancouver, British Columbia. A military training camp had been set up there in 1913 and this was presumably where Oscar had been sent, perhaps with the 26th Field Company Canadian Engineers.

The Battle of the Somme had swung back and forth for five long months. On November 11, 1916, the 4th Canadian Division made one last effort to break through the German lines. In a remarkable attack, the Canadians captured Regina Trench, an enemy position which had held out against many previous attacks. By the time the Canadians finally took possession, it was no more than a slight depression in the pulverised ground. They managed to push on a few more yards to capture the grotesquely misnamed Desire Trench but on November 18, 1916, heavy rain and the first snows of winter caused the armies of both sides to become bogged down in an exhausted stalemate.

In the five months of slaughter on the Somme, the combatants suffered about one million dead or wounded. The Allies had succeeded in pushing back the Germans a mere six miles. In truth, neither side could claim to have won the battle. However, the Canadians emerged from this carnage with a reputation of being able to succeed where others had failed. British Prime Minister Lloyd George later wrote:

> The Canadians played a part of such distinction that thenceforward they were marked out as storm troops; for the remainder of the war

British and Commonwealth dead being buried during the Battle of the Somme. | *Archival photo*

they were brought along to head the assault in one great battle after another. Whenever the Germans found the Canadian Corps coming into the line they prepared for the worst.

Hector saw considerable action on the Somme and touched upon his experiences in his next letter home, written the day after the battle officially ended, and four weeks after he had arrived in France. In spite of the cessation of the suicidal infantry advances, artillery duels and skirmishes continued.

10th Field Coy.
19. 11. 16.

Dear Mamma,

Alls well and the real fun has been going on all around us, as you can see by looking at the papers of this date. I am afraid the Vanc. papers will be full of names,[1] but they did fine work. I have not been out for two nights now, so am pretty certain to be up tonight and tomorrow night also. The last time I was out I had my first real experience of those devilish machine guns,[2] they put up flares till it was light as day and tried to wipe out my party of 40 men. We promptly rolled into shell holes and played an exciting variation of musical chairs, the difference being that shell holes were chairs and we were only allowed to move when the music stopped. We got safely back to the trench just in time to be clear of the artillery bombardment, it lasted an hour and was as warm as necessary, but our guns behind got busy, and we were able to get out and finish the job. The only casualty was one man got someone's iron heel in his face in the rush for a "Chair".

I saw Rupert in his quarters a few days ago and had lunch at their mess. He should be getting leave soon as the pressure lifts, and a Captaincy. They have a fine dry place about five miles from our place, but have since moved three miles further away. I must go and see him again if I can get a chance, especially if we think about moving ourselves.

You can have no idea what our trenches are like here; this is supposed to be one big forward movement so they are not made permanent, just a chain of shell holes joined up under fire and improved next

---

[1] Casualty lists.
[2] The German army was equipped with Maxim machine guns that had a firing rate of 600 rounds per minute.

night. No revetting and seldom any bath matting under foot.[1] The stories you read about massive earthworks don't apply to our part of the line.

I hear from several of my newly made friends and get things sent out. But the old standbys are not so good at writing except Lilian who is a splendid correspondent. I am glad to see that Dedham has not forgotten me and some of the girls I met at Lady Lawson's for tennis have promised various things. We are quite cut off from the outer world here; every village we get is a total ruin when we arrive and what remains is loaded in sand bags into wagons and lorries and used on the roads. So luxuries are not thought of, just the Army Ration for the men with a little fresh meat when we can get it, and tinned fruit.

How is the wood problem this year? Ours is nearly as acute as the Applegarth at its worst. We get ours from captured German Dugouts and have to haul it several miles, but it is good stuff, oak and birch with a little fir. We had three days of heavy frost and everything dried up and the mud froze like sharp rocks, but we have had two days of rain and are back "as you were". Leave is beginning for the Division very soon as they have been out three months. My turn should come just about as the last of our fellows gets it. So I can count on getting mine about Feb. unless I get my V.C. before that date. One of our fellows has been recommended for the M.C.[2] for good work the night I was last out. Right up in "no mans land" they were caught the same way as us, and had to duck but he got the party started again and was fired on again. Finally he left his shell hole and brought in the Infantry Captain i/c of the covering party who was wounded, with a machine gun playing on him all the time. These are great times, and quite worth going 7,000 miles to see.

Your affectionate,

HECTOR

A week after the fighting died down, and a month after he had arrived on the Somme at the height of the battle, Hector's unit was relieved from their front line position and marched fifteen miles northwest, via Puchvillers and Beauquesne, to the tiny town of Beauval. Beauval had become a major casualty-clearing station situated well behind the front

---

[1] Revetting: sandbags or planks to support the sides of trenches. Bathmats: wooden grids to raise the floor of the trench above mud and water.

[2] Military Cross, an award for "an act of exemplary gallantry during active operations against the enemy."

line. There, the unit was able to get some much-needed rest and recuperation before leaving to join the main body of the Canadian Corps which had moved to the Vimy Ridge area, twenty miles along the front line, to the north. Hector's next letter to his mother was sent from Beauval which appeared to live up to its name, Beautiful Valley.

10th Field Coy.
27. 10. 16.[1]

Dear Mamma,

Please imagine me now taking a well earned rest. We have great billets in a farm house with an open fire and all the comforts possible. Clarets, Champagne, Scotch and Benedictine on the table and nothing to do. No gun fire or Whiz Bangs within miles, in fact it is a fine War. The country here is fine, no shell holes and all the farmers are ploughing cultivating the fields; there is some winter oats making a fine showing. I wrote to you about meeting Pryce Jones. I have just heard he was killed in the last Show. He never seemed to have much hope of getting out and now he has got his. It was pitiful to see the battalions coming up to hold the line; one time a Company came up to hold 500 yds of trench, 1 Officer, 2 N.C.O.s and 35 men,[2] and they were pretty well played out before they got up.

I saw Jack Aitken (Hill-Touts), he got through though the man next him was killed.[3] He seems very decent. It is wonderful how local the shells are in their destructive power; one of our sappers was handing a pick to an infantry man when an H.E. burst right close killing 4 men and wounding 15. The infantry man was blown to bits and the sapper was untouched though they had hold of the same pick. Burrows who used to be my section officer in the old 7th field coy. at Bordon was killed two days ago. The trouble is we have been spoiling the infantry and doing all the tricky jobs which are really theirs, as well as our own technical ones.

We had great fun at the last village with the people at an "estaminet".[4] I felt so pleased to see a female instead of endless khaki and to hear a rooster crow that I scraped together all my available French, and with their attempts at English we got on beautifully even if we were noisy. But it was the fault of 5 weeks of trench warfare, a Rhom

---

[1] This letter is dated 27. 10. 16, but from the content and the reference to 5 weeks trench warfare in paragraph 3, it should have been dated 27. 11. 16.

[2] Out of an original 5 officers and 100 men.

[3] John Glendinning Aitken of the 47th Battalion, originally from Chilliwack.

[4] A small café, selling beer and wine, and sometimes offering accommodation.

omelette and Heidsieck Champagne. People send me all kinds of cigarettes but they can't tempt me, but I never did draw the line at a little "quelque chose a boire", as long as it is small.

I have a German rifle I picked up in the line, and several shell cases that I have had sawn off short, but so far not a helmet; the infantry get the first chance at that.[1] We have an organ in the billet and work it for all we know, but the pedal is not equal to the occasion and keeps on giving out, so we have given up the attempt till we can get some wire to fix it up.

You can't imagine just how much pure luck and providence counts in this war as I never feel safe once I start out for my work till I get back, and even then the aeroplanes do their best to bomb us, but no one even takes the trouble to look out of the door when a raid is on (which is usually twice a week) even though the bombs are bursting quite close, and their machine guns are busy up above; the danger is so insignificant compared to the line. I know this must seem an exaggeration, but it really is an actual fact.

Up in the line the shells come down in a way which seems till you get used to it, as absolutely without method and all over the place but gradually you can recognise the various whines and know just where to expect them to burst; the shell seems to be going about 15 miles an hour by the sound, and if there is a chance of moving I can usually pick out a safe spot. Every now and then an eccentric one comes over and upsets my theories, but as long as it does not hit me it is all right. It is a great thing to stand up and watch one of our "Barrages" at work on their lines. The earth just keeps up one continuous upheaval along a certain line, they can move that line as close as 200 ft. ahead of an infantry advance with out any fear of firing into our troops, and the guns themselves are two or three miles back and quite out of sight, just firing from a map and observation at the other end of the phone.

To turn to more cheerful subjects as I intend to forget the war for a little, I just can't make up my mind, what to do after the war, engineering is obviously the best thing, as if I can get a job I know I can hold it as I have got a bit of training and can handle men to a certain extent, but I would like to mix a little of farming with it. It just makes me itch to get hold of a plough, when I see the way the old fools of French peasants drive their horses along the roadside, turning long furrows. They had the horse power and the land, and of course they must spoil it all by hitching up their horses absolutely the worst way possible and using,

---

[1] Souvenir collecting was popular among the armies of the Western front, and a German *pickelhaube* (spiked helmet) was considered a special prize.

except in a few exceptional cases, the most absurd plough you can imagine. And even then they get the work done.

I had a parcel from Miss Brown from Grenfell Sask. I met her skiing at Ottawa, and we have kept up a desultory correspondence ever since. I still hear from Olga Bell.[1] I certainly must see her again when I pass through. Leave has started for the Division, and the Major has got his already; mine unfortunately is a thing of the distant future. I don't suppose barring a comfortable "Blighty"[2] I shall see England till the middle of Feb. Speaking of Blighty I had a great chance of a leg wound as I lay on my back in a small shell hole listening to the zip of machine gun bullets overhead; just lift up one leg and there you are. But I preferred the shell hole even though it was wet.

I must be getting to bed now as we are having an early breakfast. I feel as if I can go on soliloquizing all night but it is a foolish habit and I am sleepy. Anyhow the fire is going out.

Your affectionate,
HECTOR

---

28. 11. 16.

Dear Mamma,

I only wrote last night but as I have just got two letters from you I am answering various things right away, as we have nothing to do and all day to do it. You seem to have quite unnecessary fears for my solvency and general outlook from one of the letters; first of all the Engineers get no more pay than the Infantry in the Canadian forces, which is unfortunate, and then the price of anything is far away ahead of what it was in pre-war days, but I don't get into any sized debt in spite of it all. I have a theory that it is better to have a good old Bust for a few days, and then become a hermit till next pay day.

Thanks very much for getting the shoe packs, I hope they come out soon, as the mud is just as filthy as mud can be. I don't suppose they will need any extension flaps, but anyhow I will get them fixed by the Company Shoemaker. You can bet your life I have a sweet tooth still and can always do with any extra sweets. My days of expenses are done now till my next leave, but really I don't spend an awful lot; out of £23 monthly, £3 used

---

[1] Olga was the daughter of Dr. Bell who had provided hospitality to Hector when he was in Ottawa, en route to Europe. She was four years younger than Hector.
[2] A wound requiring evacuation back to England.

to be assigned, £6.10 mess fees, and about £5 unavoidable extras (Batman and wear and tear) which does not leave an awful lot for amusements.

I have heard from Vera a few times but she never speaks of Gerald her affianced. I heard from [indecipherable name] by today's mail, he is at Shoreham, but I am afraid I have missed him for some time. At Shorncliffe, I was at the training Depot and no fixed command; the men just pass through and we never keep the same for any time. Here I am a supernumerary but for the time I am section officer of No. 2 Section, 45 men as we have had two casualties.

Your affectionate,
HECTOR

Hector's stream of letters faltered during the first part of December as the 10th Field Company was on the move again. After a week's rest and recuperation in Beauval, the unit moved thirty miles northwest and then another forty miles northeast to the back area of the Vimy Ridge sector of the front line. There, Hector and his unit rejoined the rest of the 4th Canadian Division. The journey took a week, marching for about six hours a day in cold, wet winter weather. The unit billeted at the small settlements of Remaisnil, Blangermont and Bours on the way, staying mainly in local hostelries, but occasionally in grander houses. The men finished their route march at the small coal-dust blackened, war-weary town of Bruay-la-Buissière, forty miles northwest of Arras, and twenty miles west of the key German-held city of Lens.

Hector's unit then spent ten days at a military training school at Pernes, a few miles to the west of Bruay, where the engineers were occupied with the mundane task of building a new firing range.

9. 12. 16.

Dear Mamma,

To wish you all a Merry Xmas and Happy New Year. Have not heard a gun now for nearly two weeks and have been able to get in a fresh supply of necessities. All going along splendidly except the usual rain which has just started. Have had three steaming hot baths in five days, the first since I got out here.

Heard from Oscar again yesterday. Rupert seems to have got leave and his Captaincy at last. I don't suppose I will get any for months as they have crowds to get through before me, and then expect to hear that all leave has been cancelled owing to perennial Spring Push.[1]

It is almost like peace times again. Clean buttons and leggings and an apology of a town.[2]

Your affectionate,
HECTOR

———————

9. 12. 16.

Dear Marg,

Thanks ever so much for the socks and the letter. They both were awfully fine of you. I am glad Oscar managed a leave while Rupert was free, it makes things ever so much nicer, especially the first leave. You seem to have got through a fairly extensive programme in the limited time.[3] Just now we are in Rest Billets in a dirty part of a dirty town, but we will be starting earning our living again soon.

My mail comes in fits and starts, but it is as good as I can expect considering the way I let it drop at Shorncliffe. I have been revelling in the luxury of hot baths, the first since I got out here, some of the men were just "Walking".[4]

Must get off to bed now,
Your affectionate,
HECTOR

———————

15. 12. 16.

Dear Mamma,

I got two letters from you last night, in answer to my first one from France, and as they are full of questions some of which I think I have since answered, I will, as you used to say, comment on them. As you already know I was where Rupert used to be, and worked all around that

---

[1] Spring offensive.

[2] Bruay.

[3] Oscar had apparently completed his Canadian training and arrived in England in September or October, a short time before Hector left for France.

[4] He had been in France for almost six weeks by this time.

part, the town itself was in a pretty rotten condition, as they shelled it about 3 days a week, putting over 30 or 40 shells from what seemed like a naval gun.[1] I used to hear them whistling over my head at night, and then came the explosion.

I hear pretty regularly from Marg and Tiger. Marg has a good job, and Tiger seems cheerful for a change. I saw the same picture you saw at Folkestone and since then have seen the real thing in proper war weather, with the noise thrown in.[2] In the other Divisions the infantry do most of the front line work, and in the Imperials just about all of it. We have spoilt our infantry, who expect us to do everything, even clean out their trenches, while they sit around. Of course we only supervise, it is an infantry working party who do the actual work. "Snaps"[3] now are never heard of and curios are hard to get out of the country. When I get leave I will bring some with me and post from England. I got the cheque alright

Oscar Jackson, one of Hector's younger brothers, soon after arriving in England after enlisting. | *Family album*

but no sign of boots yet. My address only needs Rank and Name, Can. Eng, 10th Field Coy, France. Nothing more is necessary.

I get socks still from friends not from any Red Cross Societies. Mrs. Rendall sent me a pair, also Marg, several pairs.

The Zepp wire was from the one Robinson V.C. brought down, but it might just as well be from any piece of polished hay wire for all you could tell. I heard from Oscar yesterday. I never can help smiling when I read his letters, they are so serious and in such quaint English withal; I quite miss the long 'S' and other relics of the 19th century. But he seems

---

[1] The town of Albert was about two miles behind his billet at Tara Hill.
[2] The silent motion picture *The Battle of the Somme*, was released on August 21, 1916 and was viewed by close to twenty million Britons in the next two months.
[3] Photos.

fearfully keen and full of interest in his work, which is a great change after Applegarth.

I thought I told you I had lunch with Dr. and Mrs. Rendall one Sunday; he still does a lot of work and is on the school board for Colchester, as well as doing great work in Dedham. I also, as you have heard, got to know the Ashwin family there, Dr. Ashwin is the last "Reader" of Dedham Church, an old post dating back for hundreds of years, but when he dies it becomes extinct.[1]

Miss Ashwin, a very nice maiden lady, has become my adopted Aunt, and keeps me supplied with parcels.

I have all the kit I want now. Clothes cost nothing, as I draw what I need from stores. If we get really cold weather, I will get a sheepskin coat the same as the sappers. My trench coat is as good as can be expected considering the rate all kit is being turned out, even Burberry's things look cheap after a month, as the demand is so great. All the original men here are new to me as they were formed as a Division at Bramshott,[2] but the reinforcements come from Shorncliffe and Crowborough. I wish I could lose some of my stuff as it is a beastly nuisance to pack around.

I have not heard from Ione lately, she only had a small part in a farce at St. James's, and is to be in a panto at Xmas. I believe she has an idea that tragedy is her real forte; her voice is really, next to her face, her strong point.

I did not sell the Bus after all, just left it with Lady Lawson at Folkestone. It will come in handy for Oscar if he gets his Commission. In our last place we had canvas huts for the Officers and Mess, and captured dug outs for the men, but while we are in Rest we have billets in houses with real beds. We marched for 7 days, about 15 kilometres a day, billeting with the villages we passed through. Twice we managed to get Châteaux, but usually it was in Estaminets.

I think that answers all your questions. You must excuse the beastly scrawl, but I am writing in bed. I have just got over one of my fever attacks and get up tomorrow.[3] We have not shaved for 4 days so must look an awful sight. I have a splendid batman who makes a good nurse, and does absolutely everything. He has a son about 20 in the same section of the

---

[1] Dr. Hamilton Ashwin was a Church of England clergyman in his early eighties.

[2] Very close to Bordon Camp.

[3] "Trench fever" was a common affliction on the Western Front. It was later discovered to be due to lice bites; since Hector had had to go without a bath for six weeks it is not surprising that he had been bitten. Symptoms of "trench fever" included headaches, acute pain, rashes and eye inflammation. Recommended treatment usually involved twelve weeks off duty, although this was obviously seldom possible.

Company. Was foreman of C.P.R.[1] at Winnipeg drawing about $200 per month and expenses.

There is some delay about Xmas cards so they will be late in arriving. I wonder if you got the Mênu or whether the Censor would not let it pass because of the names[2].
Your affectionate,
HECTOR

_____

_____

[1] Canadian Pacific Railway.
[2] Individual dishes on the menu in the officers' mess had been named after places where the unit had been based.

Chapter 5

Stalemate

After completing the work at the training school at Pernes, the 10th Field Company Canadian Engineers returned to the front line, this time marching twenty miles east, to an area nearly sixty miles north of their previous front line position. The unit was based six miles northwest of the pulverised city of Arras, and immediately northwest of German-held Vimy Ridge. The area had been fought over by the two sides since 1915, with the front line ebbing and flowing over the area. Most of the villages and woods had been largely reduced to rubble and splintered matchwood.

The Allied high command planned a major spring offensive in the Aisne area, seventy-five miles to the southeast of Vimy Ridge. To ensure the success of the plan, the generals ordered a smaller diversionary attack in the six-mile portion of the front stretching from the town of Arras in the south, to Vimy Ridge in the north.

Vimy Ridge is an unimpressive feature that runs from northwest to southeast and rises a mere 120 feet above the surrounding plain. However, this was high enough to provide the German forces with a clear view of the Allied lines. The German artillery, sited just behind the ridge, could be brought to bear on the Allies with deadly accuracy. Vimy Ridge had become a key anchor point on the German lines. As a result, the Allied commanders deemed its capture to be critical to the larger war effort, and Vimy Ridge was shortly to become the object of one of the largest offensives launched on the Western Front. As at the Somme, Canadian forces again played the key role in the attack. The battle for the ridge has been described as an event that marked Canada's coming of age as a nation.

Hector's new area of operations was opposite the northern end of Vimy Ridge, near a small hill known as "the Pimple" that played an important part in the battle that ensued.

The unit arrived in the new area on December 18, and set about arranging billets for themselves and the infantry of the 4th Division. Because of the large buildup of troops, the engineers were billeted in the shattered remains of several small villages spread over an area three miles by three miles. These included the villages of Carency, Gouy Servins, Maisnil-Bouche and Souchez. For some time at least, Hector's billet was in Carency, located four miles behind the front line. There he passed a peaceful, albeit cold, wet and windy Christmas Day.

26. 12. 16.

Dear Mamma,

I have not written for some time, and also have not heard from you. Xmas passed off fairly satisfactorily though I spent most of my time in bed on the 26th. So you see the war is not all that it is painted in Canada. I have not been within 4 miles of the line now since Oct. 25th, we are the last to go up this time for a change. And also I have had orders to report for a 4 weeks course on Jan 1st, perhaps that will show you that we don't spend all our time in the trenches as I used to think.[1] Although the infantry certainly do get a pretty poor time of it right along, and deserve all the sympathy they get, as well as what I have been getting undeservedly. The funny part is that they would not change jobs with us. They only see us when we are having a bad time of it; when we are resting they seem to forget to put it to our account.

I have been chasing around various villages fixing up or rather estimating the work on existing billets and huts. It is good practice for my French and really lots of fun, but making up the report at night rather spoils the fun.

No sign yet of the boots, I have written to Mr. Ward about them. The cheque posted to my account in the Bank, as it was easier than getting it changed out here. I am getting my Xmas letters and parcels late this year, but they are coming along steadily.

---

[1] The course was at Corps School but it is not clear where this was situated. Hector left the front on January 1, 1917, and rejoined his unit on the evening of January 26.

The Mess at present is just surfeited as I was afraid. At other places some of the parcels would have been godsends as nothing could be got, now boxes of chocolates, preserved fruits, marron glacés,[1] pâte de foi gras and numberless cakes are lying around for anyone who wants to be ill, while issue cigarettes are fed to our goat. In a few weeks the famine will set in again. Rumours of Leave starting up again give me hopes of getting to England about Oscar's birthday.[2] I only wish it was June or July.

I had a nice Xmas Card from Ione from an original pen and ink sketch of hers. So you see there is some swank in her these days. She will be running around in her closed limousine by next Xmas.

I have not heard from Rupert since his leave though I suppose he is still around the same parts; I must make time to write to him tonight and let him know I am still above ground. I do quite a lot of riding these days, we have all kinds of horses just now so can have two a day if I have far to go. I know all around here pretty well but what I really want is to get hold of a motor cycle and take a day off to get to Paris and see if it is up to all the glowing accounts.

I suppose food prices are simply absurd. People on the prairies with something to sell ought to be making money. Eggs here are ruinously dear, 3d. and 4d. each and the estaminets make plenty of money out of omelettes which they certainly have reduced to a fine art. Any time I can't get back to lunch I get a 3 egg omelette, coffee and cheese, usually roquefort. Sometimes they have English beer, it costs anything from 2 to 3 francs which is quite reasonable. Our messing here is about 120 francs a month which is really the only necessary expense except for about 50 fr. incidental, such as toilet necessities (soap etc) and food. So I can start saving. It sounds rather funny to me, but if our new War Cabinet decide to make peace this year I may as well have some money to show for it.[3]

It is just dinner time now. Best wishes for the New Year,
Your affectionate,
HECTOR

---

[1] Chestnuts cooked in syrup.
[2] February 15 – Oscar was turning 22.
[3] Lloyd George became Prime Minister of the wartime coalition in December 1916. There was considerable disagreement in the Cabinet, especially between Lloyd George and his commander in chief, General Sir Douglas Haig, whom Lloyd George suspected of unnecessarily squandering the troops' lives.

26. 12. 16.

Dear Marg

Many thanks for your letter. I suppose Xmas hols are going on much the same as ever, in spite of newspaper threats.

We had a fine Xmas in good quarters, everything even to crackers and paper caps etc. Just now we are not in the line though our Rest is over. We are not the same as the infantry, we keep going for weeks on end and then come out for a rest. Sometimes we are attached to Brigade but just now we are Corps troops and are on Huts and other repair work behind the lines. Which is the first time since the Division came out that our work has not been front line. I have a job of billets and huts, horse lines, and water supply and all that kind of junk in various villages around.

Avez vous ici place pour des soldats? Ou est ce? Voilà tout en-face. Merci Madame. Bon Jour. And then I measure it up and figure on the number. And go on to the next. It is really all kinds of fun though it gets monotonous especially making out reports when I get back. So you see the danger is very minute at present, in fact I will have to be broken into shell fire all over again.

If Oscar gets a Commission in the Engineers (Signals) there is not much chance of him going out till Spring 1918 at the rate things were moving.[1] All the time I was at Shorncliffe there was not a single Signal Officer sent across.

I am awfully pleased that you are getting such a good time now, and hope it will last when I get leave. I might just as well come up and see you if the people don't mind, but the leave problem is pretty desperate just now. The socks are just fine. I have not worn outer ones yet, but the inners are beautifully warm and comfy. I think Rupert is right about the waterproof qualities of socks. I have had a few Xmas letters but so far none of the promised parcels have arrived; there is a general mix up in the mails I suppose. I heard from Ags today, and Mr. Ward, but nothing from B.C. The Canadian Xmas mail seems to be late. I must write to Rupert again, I never answered a letter of his from London. Tell him S.W. by S. 30, N.E. by E. 46. It was rather lucky finding myself right alongside of him when I first got out because the Ambulance has been moving around quite a lot.[2] Just now it is pouring like the dickens and the wind has dropped. We have been having tremendous wind storms for the last

---

[1] The signallers provided a vital service, linking the trenches with headquarters. Most signals were via telephone line, rather than radio. Signallers fell under the engineers' organization.

[2] Rupert was attached to the 91st Field Ambulance.

week, which played havoc with half built huts.
>   With best wishes for the New Year,
>   Your affectionate,
>   HECTOR

---

5. 1. 17.

Dear Mamma,

I just got two letters from you with an enclosure from Gerald, and am answering right away though I have only just written.

I am at the Corps School on a training course and am having great times. There are officers and N.C.O.s from all the Divisions and battalions. The School is divided into 10 Platoons, 3 officers and 7 N.C.O.s with an average of 15 in each and we certainly are kept busy. Reveillé 7 a.m. and work right ahead till 11.30. Jerks, platoon drill and bayonet fighting, with a lecture by some "Brass Hat" as they call Staff Officers. After lunch at 2 p.m. the engineer officers take up parties to the works and we work on a system of trenches. My special job is a communication trench which has to be dug out and revetted, and the various platoons come out as working parties. We have a good camp, with band and concert parties most evenings, and there are a very decent lot of fellows here, especially a pioneer (67th Western Scots) who used to teach at Columbian College, New Westminster.[1] We have struck it off pretty well and get on well enough together; his name is Thomas. Everyone has to be in Camp by 9, and Lights Out sounds at 10.30.

I heard from Mr. Ward today, he says the boots have arrived at last. I don't think I need any more just now as I can always draw a 16 inch pair from Q.M. stores, they are not especially fine but cost nothing. We wear any colour now.

To continue answering your letter, what I wrote was shrapnel and H.E. mixed, not simply shrapnel. H.E. meaning High Explosive.

I don't know much about Lady Lawson herself; her husband is dead and the daughters run the place. I used to play tennis there, anyhow twice a week, and met a lot of very nice people, especially Miss Horne who keeps me supplied with letters and food. I am leaving the bus[2] in England so that Oscar can take it over if he likes, anyhow it is just as well there as any other place.

---

[1] The Columbian Methodist College was established in New Westminster in 1897.
[2] Hector's motorcycle.

We have batmen out here who do all our work which is just as well.

This was started some time ago, and I lost it but will send it in case of any news.

———————————

27. 1. 17.

Dear Mamma,

I have numerous things to thank you for now, and have time to do it as the Corps School Course is over.[1] I received the boots and candy about four days ago, both were most welcome and unmixed, also the socks. Next day I got the lard pail of Xmas food which was fine, and today your letter (31. 12. 16).

The Langley parcel has not turned up so far, I expect it was lost somewhere, but I have got all kinds of others from Ottawa and English people, so don't worry. I see there are several questions to be answered before I give what little news there is.

When we go up the line here we move up to advanced billets with the batmen, who stay there. It is only the infantry officers who stay 2 or 3 days in the front line that take batmen with them; we have runners in case of accident or especial message.

I have a Wolseley Valise sleeping bag with a 3 ply bed, and 3 Army blankets (issue from Q.M.S. Stores) so can usually keep warm[2]. Just now we have a cold snap in full swing so I help things out with newspapers and great coats. The blank sheets of paper are really unnecessary now as we are within reach of civilisation, and I have laid in a good store.

I came back from the School last night and am on general work again; just now I have the heroic job of putting in three culverts.

We had two exams at the place and though I say so as should not, I came out top; 97 and 100 out of possible 100 each. Also to lay it on thicker still my report was the only one V.G. all through.

I know an officer out of each battalion in the Canadian Corps as one was sent from each, and we had 4 weeks to know each other which in itself does a lot to create good feelings between the battalions.

In this part of the line we send two sections and two officers up in the line for two weeks at a time, which is quite a change to the last place where everyone was liable any night; here we get a definite rest.

———————————

[1] Hector had completed the course the previous day and returned to the wintry front line.
[2] The Wolseley Valise was a commonly used bedding roll with built in padding and a waterproof cover.

I heard from Mr. Housman a few days ago and will answer tonight if possible.[1] All the time I was away my mail accumulated as I got no time to answer; I must have 30 letters to answer which is an appalling task, but I ought to get through it in 3 days with luck.

German 7.58 cm. Minenwerfer trench mortar or "Minnie". | Archival photo

I heard from Muriel Atwood a few days ago, she is going to work at the Admiralty and I have got to stay with them part of my leave. If I went to all the places I have been told to I would have to put in for 3 months so I won't attempt to. I can't find my pen anywhere and am reduced to this. I hope it is not lost for good as they are hard to replace just now around here. I have a letter of Gerald's to answer which must be attended to, but I don't see any chance of sending any souvenirs till I get leave, as it is against regulations.

Remember me to everyone,

Your affectionate,

HECTOR

———————

29. 1. 17

Dear Gerald,

I have a letter of yours to thank you for, and as the Corps School has finished I will do so right away.

I got back from my first trip up in this Area with the Major to see around in daylight.[2] We made quite an imposing cavalcade up as far as advanced billets (ours are in a cellar among the ruins of a village) as we had a Brigadier and two Staff Officers, with all their grooms along with us. The whole place is on hillsides and drainage will be a problem as soon as the thaw sets in; just now the sides of trenches are like iron and there is a

[1] Housman was still at Trinity College, Cambridge.
[2] The northern part of Vimy Ridge.

light covering of snow. Snipers are busy and got a corporal while we were up, also "Minnies"[1] and trench mortars keep up the general interest in life, luckily you can see them in the air and so have an average chance of getting behind cover as they make a crater the size of a 6" shell, so it is just as well to keep clear.

Aeroplanes are pretty busy as we have been having clear bright days and nights and photography and observations are splendid. The Boche certainly has some great machines and know how to use them in spite of all the bosh written in the press about air supremacy. They have a large type painted red.[2] It was attacked by five of our smaller planes and charged right among them firing away in fine style with the machine gun. One of ours was hit and dived straight nose first for 2,000 odd feet like a piece of lead, when the pilot got control again and spiraled down to within 200 ft. of the ground though the machine was obviously badly alight. Suddenly he fell out turning over as he fell and the machine came down in a crumpled . . . [remainder of the third sheet is missing].

. . . beginning at last, oldest inhabitants call it the coldest winter for 40 years, but anyhow it keeps dry which is the great point.

Who is Helen and how old is she? Is she the only pupil? My leave is a thing of the far distant future as it keeps on shutting off for indefinite periods. Anyhow I am saving a

German Albatros DLII biplane. | *Archival photo*

---

[1] *Minenwerfer*: a German 7.6 cm mortar which fired ninety-four kilogram high-explosive or gas bombs that tumbled as they flew.

[2] This may refer to the aircraft belonging to Baron Manfred von Richthofen, 'The Red Baron'. Others in his squadron painted parts of their aircraft red, but von Richthofen's plane was the only all-red aircraft. At that time, he flew an Albatros DLII biplane, not the famous Fokker Dr.1 triplane he later used. He scored his 18th air victory in Jan.1917 (when this letter was written) and received the "Blue Max." In all, he was credited with shooting down 80 Allied planes before being shot down behind Allied lines on April 21, 1918. The month of April 1917 became known by the British as "Bloody April" due to the Royal Flying Corps's aircraft losses.

certain amount of money.

I had quite a good time on the course and learned a certain amount, but chiefly French, it is not half bad now, another 6 months and good teachers should work wonders.

Your affectionate,
HECTOR

————————

30. 1. 17.

Dear Marg,

I have two letters to thank you for. I was fearfully busy for the last four weeks at the Corps School and scarcely wrote any letters. So I am making up for it now.

I went up in the line yesterday for the first time in our new Area and had a general look around with our Major. We are back in billets just now about 5 miles behind and sent up two officers and two sections into advanced billets. Ours are in the cellar of a ruin of what must once have been a good house, but only part of the front wall is standing now. I go up in a few days for a two weeks spell and intend to make myself as comfortable as possible while it lasts.

The Xmas parcel arrived safely a few days ago, as did also the boots. As far as I can see the leave chances are pretty slim, as it is going by division instead of brigade, and keeps shutting off completely at most unexpected times.

We have been having a cold snap for the last two weeks with a few inches of snow, and now it has started to snow again. But I prefer this to what we are going to have once the thaw starts.

Hospital is the best place for Oscar in this weather, he may just as well hang on there for another month for all the good he will get outside in this weather.[1] One of these days they will realise that training in winter is not worth the time spent the way they do it now. I hope you are going to be a permanency at G., it must be a decent billet.

I have simply crowds of letters to answer and must get through them in the next few days.

Your affectionate,
HECTOR

————————

---

[1] Oscar was still in England, and suffering from a severe respiratory tract infection.

3. 2. 17.

Dear Mamma,

I had a splendid mail tonight when I got I back from the line; 7 perfectly good letters. No duds. I have had two baths since my Xmas Bust, while I was down at the Corps School.

Thanks muchly for the Quinine, I will keep it handy in case of emergency, though I don't think I have any bad after effects from the chills.[1] As it happens, the last time[2] I was in bed 5 days with a temp for $3\frac{1}{2}$ of them, and got up at 10 a.m. At 12.30 I was taking two sections back to our old quarters as I was the only officer available.

I must have mentioned the Ashwins before. I met them under what may seem peculiar circumstances but actually was quite normal for me in those days of no work and a motorcycle. Davies and I at Brightlingsea, Essex had got tired of all the various people around, so chased around on our machines to unearth some new ones. He took me to a lady doctor at Colchester where he had been billeted, who was out at the time, but the governess gave us tea, and mentioned Rendall's name. So next Sunday I chased over to Dedham to find Rendall; he was in Cumberland. I had not gone 15 miles for nothing and wanted lunch, so struck the nicest house I could see and asked if Dr. Rendall was in. No! Dr. Ashwin. So I asked to see him. He was hospitable as I had expected when I said I was hoping to see my old Head Master, and made me stay to lunch and meet his daughters who were at church just then. They are very nice middle aged people and awfully kind. So there you are. All this sounds very cold matter of fact on paper, not to mention heartless, but actually it was lots of fun, and Davies and I got tennis and canoeing parties to waste, in fact we had to refuse most.

I have lost touch with Eric Buckley and Noel just lately and must write and find out what kind of a war they are having.[3]

My latest job is decidedly open to Sniping, so the least conspicuous I look the better I like it. So far they have had no luck, but it isn't for lack of trying. We had an unfortunate piece of luck yesterday, one of my working party got a beastly looking wound from one of our own guns. Of course I reported it and there it a certain amount of excitement, as of

---

[1] On the Western Front, quinine was taken as an anti viral treatment, as opposed to its more common use against malaria. It was not effective against trench fever.

[2] Six weeks earlier.

[3] Noel Robinson and Eric Buckley both survived the war. Robinson became a well-respected journalist in Vancouver. Buckley settled in St. Catherine's, Ontario where he married Edna Honberger in 1925.

course they will do their best to prove that it could not have been our own, but I know better. We have a little glimpse of real comedy-tragedy at times; one piece of line just by my trench is obviously in view of the Boche, and it is quite a thrilling sight to see an officer cross it and hear the bullets zip and knock up the snow, near him, all work stops and he pretends to be unconcerned. I know just how he actually feels because I had six shots fired at myself only this afternoon as I crossed. Most of them are low and mean a comfortable "Blighty" but there is always the chance of one being a little straighter than necessary.

Another "thinkable" sight is to see a party going up for a Raid, our pet form of warfare at present; it keeps the enemy on the jump and also is useful for identification purposes. At the last one pulled off,[1] the men came right by my party on their way through to the jumping off place, and they obviously understood just how serious war can be, I saw one man recognise a fellow from my party he had not seen since Canada, and as likely as not would not see again.

This letter is getting hopelessly serious. Lilian sent me a really good photo of herself, not in the least artificial looking and very cheerful.[2] I like reading her letters awfully as they are just exactly as she talks, discussing anything and always nicely. I have started yet another correspondence, it is from a girl in N. Vanc. whom I have never seen, but who is a friend of all the girls I met while I was at the Drill Hall. It started in a peculiar way; as I censored a letter from her Cousin in our Company to her, signing my name, she had a girl I know staying with her and the fun started, as she insisted on paying me back by censoring this girls letter to me, and adding a short note to the effect that it was fit for human consumption. So as I always have room for more letters I replied. She is an especial friend of Lilian McNair's also, who is one of the Hewlings many best girls.[3] So you see how small and compact this world is.

---

[1] This is probably referring to a major Allied raid into the German lines on Hill 145 (known as the Pimple) on Vimy Ridge, in which Hector's 10th Field Company participated. The raiding party attacked at 9:00 p.m. on the night of February 3. The party blew a hole in the barbed wire entanglements, rushed the enemy trenches, killing a number of Germans, capturing a machine gun and destroying a mine shaft that the Germans were digging under no man's land to be packed with explosives and detonated under British lines. Several Canadian troops were wounded in the raid. It was the first of a number of raids made that month.

[2] Possibly Lilian Hill-Tout, from B.C.

[3] Lillian McNair was the daughter of James McNair, who was one of North Vancouver's wealthiest residents. Lillian married William Townsey, a member of a prominent Vancouver family, in 1925.

I picked up two more shell nose caps yesterday, and we unearthed an old French tin hat, also a box of bombs in the trench, there were enough there to wreck a house if anyone had put a pick in by mistake.

Had two more parcels from Ottawa full of all kinds of eats, they are very nice to get, but really unnecessary for the winning of the War.

Having splendid weather though the ground is like iron, and am feeling in fine shape. Must get cleaned for dinner.

Your affectionate,
HECTOR

---

9. 2. 17.

Dear Mamma,

I have just about finished my job on the trenches and am having a day off for a change, and am writing this in an estaminet out of sound of the guns.

Oscar wrote yesterday and has fear that he may go with the rest of the Signals and be drafted as infantry reinforcements. I have seen enough of the work of the Infantry to keep him clear of them if poss, though of course someone has to do the work, but as things are now, they work till they drop. I wrote to him and O.C. Can Eng at Crowborough to get a transfer put through in the Signals Engineers and I think Osborne can get it for me.[1]

We are having great weather now except it is filthily cold at nights; there is still snow on the ground but a fine warm sun which is better than what it will be like in the thaw.

I had a letter from Nan Bostock a few days ago. Jean is in London now and I have to look her up on leave, which makes about 20; they are back in Ottawa and so is Olga Bell. She has been spending all summer and autumn at Rathwell driving the team and feeding small stock.[2] Goodness only knows why; three of the other girls I met are over in England as V.A.D. workers.[3]

I may get a leave sometime in March unless it is all shut down as I expect it will be just to spite me. Anyhow I am saving money as I must

---

[1] Crowborough camp was in Sussex.

[2] Possibly close to the farm belonging to Moses' brother, Robert Jackson, near Winnipeg.

[3] Voluntary Aid Detachment Hospitals, staffed mainly by volunteers, were set up all over southern England to receive sick and wounded from the Front who had travelled along the Army Medical Corps' evacuation chain.

have £30 somewhere, so perhaps it is just as well I don't get leave for a few months. Living costs about £8 a month though it cost a whole lot more while I was on the Course.

Oscar seems to have had rotten luck with his throat right along and I expect he will be going back again to hospital; they usually half cure people. I have almost got to the end of my ideas, biscuits and coffee and I have to get back to Head Quarters but this walk has been a change to the last week. The roads are full of motor transport and any time I feel tired of walking I stop a lorry and jump aboard; they make about 10 miles per hour so it does not take long to get away from the line.

I will write to Gerald a birthday letter in a few days.

Your affectionate,

HECTOR

---

11. 2. 17.

Dear Marg,

Thanks for your letter, there must have been one of mine lost as I wrote to you from the Corps School. I was there till Jan 25th and have been up in the Line since except for the last two days. I may be back again any time now.

We do not get rests like the infantry, as things are now we have Rear and Advanced Billets, and usually stay in an Area for 3 months at a

A typical transport truck as used by the Canadian Corps. | *Archival photo*

time. Two officers go to Advanced Billets at a time, and are liable to go out day or night for two weeks. I have been out so far on special work, my real time starts next week.

I heard from Tiger a few days ago, she seemed cheerful enough, but did not say she had imported her cat with her.

We have had a Cold Snap here for three weeks now, the thaw is just ... [letter unfinished] [1]

---

14. 2. 17.

Dear Gerald,

This is to wish you many happy returns of the day, it may get to you any time as mails appear rather irregular just now.

I am up in the line for my two weeks steady Tour, which means every day or night and if necessary both; we are billeted in a cellar and things are pretty cramped as is natural. Two partitions 8'x12' with a low roof 6' in the centre for 4 officers sleeping and 8 eating, luckily we don't often eat together. I was up last night and this morning so won't be out tonight, the trenches are just starting to thaw out and will be most beautifully sticky all next week even if it does not rain. We have been really awfully lucky with our weather since Xmas, no rain at all, just 3" of snow and 3" of hard frost. I suppose the creek has flooded pretty badly again this year and the Dog Salmon should be up.[2] Has any clearing been done at all on any large scale? I suppose it keeps you busy keeping up what we have going. I could phone up Brigade and turn a working party out on the job if it were anywhere around these parts, and they would consider it a pretty good job after some of this stuff, as we have chalk and flint mixed in places. One man last night had bad luck, he struck a Mills bomb[3] with a pick; of course it started sizzling (a 5 sec. fuse) and being new men they did not recognize the sound, looking all round to find out where it came from. I don't think it was very serious.

Your affectionate,
HECTOR

---

[1] This was a busy time and the 10th Field Company took part in a very large four-hour raid into German trenches starting at 4:00 a.m. on the morning of February 13. The raiding party killed a German officer and destroyed German trenches and mine shafts over a wide area. There were eight Canadian casualties. Hector was only indirectly involved.

[2] Bertrand Creek at Applegarth was well-stocked with chum salmon..

[3] Hand grenade.

P.S. I almost forgot; I believe there is some money to my credit in Canada; take out $10 for your birthday to get any small things you want.

On February 19 the unit made yet another raid into German lines, destroying further trenches and dugouts with explosives.

This pattern of raids and destruction of the German defences was part of a much wider effort. Throughout the winter of 1916-1917 the German army had been preparing to withdraw from an untenable part of their front line, to a position many miles back. There they were constructing what was to become the Hindenburg Line, a formidable complex of double or triple trenches, fronted by extensive barbed wire entanglements almost a mile deep in places, and supported by deep concrete bunkers and machine gun nests. The Germans cleared the ground for many miles in front of the line, leveling French villages, filling wells and removing all vestiges of vegetation to clear the field of fire and deny the Allied forces any shelter from either weather or shellfire. Incredibly, the Allies seemed unaware of this while it was taking place.

With the Hindenburg Line completed, the Germans began a twenty-five to fifty-mile tactical withdrawal on the night of February 22/23, from their vulnerable old front line, back to their new seemingly impregnable fortress. This withdrawal was completed over a six-week period. Vimy Ridge formed the anchoring point at the northwest end of the Hindenburg Line, and there was no withdrawal in that sector of the line. The ridge was a position the Germans were determined to hold. They wanted to be able to command the high ground and to accurately shell the Allied troops and the city of Arras, located seven miles to the south. The Germans had enjoyed their advantageous position for the previous two years, steadily reducing the city to rubble. The ridge also provided protection to the city of Lens with its critical coal mines and the many factories producing ammunition and other materiel to feed the German front line. The Allied commanders were equally keen to gain control of the ridge, both for its tactical value and also to allow them to recapture Lens. They therefore began planning to storm the ridge in the spring of 1917.

The city of Arras in May 1917; the city was pulverised by German artillery for several years. | *Archival photo*

26. 2. 17.

Dear Mamma,

Just a scrawl to say everything is fine but beastly busy, as is natural.

We have been flooded out of our cellar (6" water) and have built a sandbag house; the place is pretty comfortable.

Am working day and night just now and getting anything from 4 to 6 hours sleep, as I have to go up with both parties. We are a little short handed and very much rushed for work, only a few more days though, and I will get a relief.

Oscar seems having a fairly decent time, I heard last night from him.[1]

Will write later.

Your affectionate,

HECTOR

---

[1] Oscar was still in England waiting to transfer into the Canadian Engineers (Signals).

4. 3. 17.

Dear Mamma

    I am back again in Rear Billets after 4 weeks of front area work, and have kept pretty fit right along thanks to plenty of exercise.

    Our work here is quite different to the Somme where everything was disorganized as we were always moving forward and had no chance of getting a fixed Base of Supplies. Things were arranged for us by Brigades and the O.C. of our Company, and we just acted as policemen to see the work was carried out right. Here we have Advanced and Rear Billets that are 8 miles behind the Line and pretty comfortable. Advanced are well up and within easy range of guns, but seldom get touched. I will make an attempt to show you what we do; all Brigades don't do the same thing but I believe it is their misfortune, as it works out well. And the Army Commander complimented the Brigadier . . . [Unreadable section] . . . pretty well to the section officers to fix up for themselves.

    The day usually starts for me at 9:30 after breakfast in bed; at 11 I get hold of my bicycle and ride up to a few hundred yards of the line and walk in, look over the 5 or 6 jobs started and then see the Works Officer of the Battalion, and if necessary the Colonel, get back about 3 p.m. and detail the parties for the night and next day to the Section Sergeant. Then if necessary look out again at 7.30 p.m. or send out one of the infantry officers to look around (Sappers take charge of all parties up to 50 men). The reports are usually all in by 1.30 a.m. when I make out the daily report and get to bed. We make out weekly reports as well. We had to build ourselves a new Forward Billet with sandbags and corrugated iron roof as our cellar had 4" of water when the thaw began, and everything got damp. Leave seems pretty far away just now. Oscar has hopes of a transfer now, I hope there is no hitch and he gets into signals as the work would suit him absolutely.

    I have another batch of 30 letters to answer as I absolutely had not a moment to myself during the last weeks. I never knew I could get along with so little sleep but except that I am a bit thin in the face I feel great.

    Ione has left the stage temporarily and is living with her mother in Town, I wonder how long the fit will last. I owe her a letter.

    Your affectionate,
    HECTOR

---

6. 3. 17

Dear Marg
    Thanks very much for your last two letters. I have lost your last one and with it Mrs. S name so cannot write to thank her for the socks. Please tell her that they are a perfect fit and look altogether too swanky for the wide rib to be hidden by leggings, and thank her very much for them.
    I am out of the line in Rear Billets now as I have just finished 4 weeks of front line work and needed a rest and a little fattening up. The weather is not too bad just now, all the snow has gone and no rain just lately, so the trenches are almost passable. Fritz has been behaving himself just lately except for "Rum Jars"[1] and the casualties have been comparatively slight.
  No talk of leave yet.
      Your affectionate,
      HECTOR

---

23. 3. 17.

Dear Mamma
    I have not heard from Canada now for over 2 weeks thanks to submarines, they seem to have got a large Canadian mail in one of the liners sunk.[2]
    All the country is white again now, the last few days have been too absurd, bright sunshine, then a hail storm followed by sun again, and usually snow at night.
    There has not been much doing with me lately, of course the usual routine of Trench Maintenance, a little more perhaps as the Section I relieved let things go badly, and this weather is pretty trying. I put in a new piece of Front Line one day last week to straighten out a bad kink, which makes another trench to my credit.[3] I had never been in the area before and had no idea of where Fritz line came, so sent another officer to the far end where I was to strike the old line again. He was to send up a flare to show he was ready, followed by a second to give me direction, and if I was not across in 5 minutes to fire a third.

---

[1] A bomb fired from a large trench mortar.
[2] Germany had begun "unrestricted" submarine warfare from February 1, 1917. Two days later, the United States severed diplomatic ties with Germany and then declared war against Germany on April 6, 1917, after a number of American ships were sunk.
[3] The Company diary shows that Hector was back in the forward billets in the village of Ablaine St. Nazaire by March 17. As the Germans gradually retired to the Hindenburg Line, the Allies continued to inch forward in the area of Vimy Ridge, which required

I had a sapper with me, and we cut across making for the direction of the flare, just behind our front wire right across, joining up small shell holes, and missing the large crumps[1] which were full of water, laying the tape as we went. Then got hold of our party of 100 and placed them along the line and let them go to it. Fritz was pretty harmless and only fired about 100 shots with his machine guns all night. Which was just as well as we were right out in the open as plain as day when a flare went up. I am not really as hard worked this Tour as we can do very little night work, it is much too dark, so I just make a daylight tour to see the Battalion in the line and try to help them with their worries, and see the various working parties. We have quite a good sized Mess up here now, 3 Engineer Officers, 5 attached Infantry, and 2 Brigade Wiring Officers,[2] so we can have plenty of amusement any time we happen to be in. The Infantry Officers are here for a month at a time and the wirers more or less permanent. We had some "Heavies" in here a few days ago pretty close to us; the nearest was 40 yds. and plastered us with mud and bricks, blew the door open and tore the canvas windows; we were lucky as one billet got a direct hit, killed 3 and wounded 7. I had a fine view of the whole show from our place 200 yds. away. They must have put in 25 shells in about an acre of ground (village) and only had one direct hit, which is pretty remarkable.[3]

I have been having pretty poor mails lately. I heard from Davis who was at Brightlingsea, Essex with me, he has come out at last.

Your affectionate,
HECTOR

---

considerable repair work as well as construction of new trenches in ground that was previously either no man's land or held by the Germans.

[1] Old shell craters.

[2] Wiring units laid out the barbed wire entanglements in no man's land, in front of the trenches at night.

[3] This particular heavy artillery bombardement happened at 2:30 p.m. March 22. The billets were at the ruined village of Carency, about three miles southwest of Souchez, and within easy range of the German artillery.

Chapter 6

Vimy Ridge

On April 9, 1917, the Allies began their major offensive in the Arras area, aiming to break through the German lines at the western end of the well-defended Hindenburg Line. Such a breakthrough would allow them to outflank this formidable obstacle. Key to the attack was the capture of Vimy Ridge. The front slope of the low ridge was bare of cover and, on the crest and rear slope of the ridge, the Germans had built a warren of trenches and deep tunnels protected by concrete-reinforced machine gun emplacements. The French had attempted to take the ridge in 1915 but had been repulsed after suffering an appalling 150,000 casualties.

This time, the task of taking Vimy Ridge was assigned to the four Canadian Divisions on the back of their successful operations at the Somme. The commanders planned meticulously to minimize the casualties. Each battalion had an attached Engineer group, commanded by a lieutenant and consisting of a handful of sappers. Hector led one of these groups. The 11th Canadian Infantry Battalion was given the task of capturing the Pimple, the point of high ground at the north end of the ridge that had been the target of Hector's unit's raid three weeks earlier.

Over a period of months, the Engineers built up dumps of trench construction material for the coming attack and supervised the digging of twelve tunnels which allowed access for thousands of troops from the rear to the front-line trenches. The tunnels were dug through chalk at least thirty feet below the surface to protect the troops from shell, rifle and machine gun fire immediately before and during the attack. The underground system also had storage and assembly chambers.

The Engineers built a full-scale replica of the Allied trenches and German defences near the Allied headquarters at Château de la Haie,[1] marking the positions of key trenches and German defences on the ground with tape, so that the infantry assaulting Vimy Ridge would be fully familiar with the terrain.

The German defences were softened up by continuous shelling for a full week immediately before the ground attack. During this time, over a million shells were fired at the enemy on the ridge. Heavy rain fell during the week and the artillery fire turned construction sites, no man's land and the ridge into a quagmire. Hector's task the night before the attack was to repair the track crossing this churned quagmire to the ridge for the 4th Canadian Division troops to use during the assault. When it wasn't raining or snowing that night, an

Naval guns begin the bombardment of Vimy Ridge a week before the attack. | *National Archives of Canada*

---

[1] Château de la Haie was a French country estate that the British had taken over as their headquarters in the Vimy Ridge sector.

almost full moon made the work in view of the German lines particularly dangerous. An entry in the unit's war diary reads, "The moon was particularly bright and they were observed by the enemy at the beginning of the night and were subjected to continuous shelling throughout the night."

The next morning, April 9, Easter Monday, was miserably cold; the previously clear skies were obliterated by heavy snow-laden clouds just before dawn, and four inches of snow fell, giving way to sleet and rain as the time for the attack approached. Exactly at 5:30, in the first glimmers of the grey dawn, 20,000 Allied troops emerged from their tunnels and trenches. They attacked up the exposed ridge behind a creeping barrage of shells from their own guns, which advanced a few hundred yards ahead of them, providing cover from the German artillery. Earlier shell fire had largely destroyed the German's defensive minefields and barbed wire entanglements. The troops slipped and slid their way across the churned slough of melting snow and mud of no man's land. The surviving enemy machine gunners on the ridge had a clear field of fire and mowed down many of the advancing troops but despite heavy losses, the Canadians reached the crest of the ridge thirty

German prisoners help Canadian wounded from Vimy Ridge. | *Archival photo*

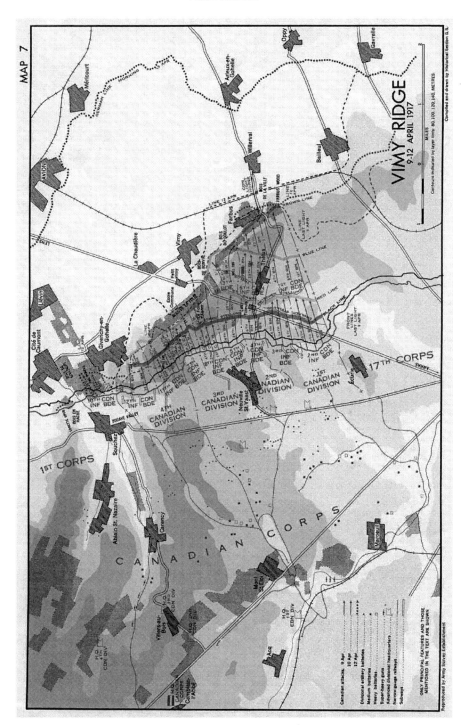

minutes after the start of the attack, overwhelming the German defenders in their front line trenches.

Hector followed the initial wave of infantry and arrived at the top of the ridge soon after the first attack had succeeded, where, during a momentary break in the sleet, he could finally look over the valley beyond, to the city of Lens.

By 3:00 p.m. that day, most of the ridge had been captured, but two hills remained in German hands: Hill 145 and the Pimple, which Hector's unit had raided a few weeks earlier. Hill 145 was captured the next morning (April 10th) but the 11th Canadian Infantry Battalion had failed to overcome the German defenders on the heavily fortified Pimple. The task to capture the hill was then assigned to the 10th Infantry Battalion, of which Hector's unit was then a part. Their preparations for the assault were completed only after midnight.

The next wave of the attack was launched at dawn on April 11 but again bogged down in the face of heavy machine gun fire and shelling. Defensive trenches were completed by 4 p.m. as the unit's diary records: "The tasks were completed by Lts. Jackson and Wood.

Canadian machine gunners setting up their weapons on the top of Vimy Ridge immediately after the successful attack. | *Archival photo*

Both these officers displayed great courage and zeal in the carrying out of the work."[1]

The final attack on the Pimple began at 5:30 a.m. on the fourth day of the battle, with the Canadian troops slogging through the mud as a howling wind blew heavy snow into the defenders' eyes. After day-long fighting, much of it hand to hand, the Pimple was finally captured late in the afternoon. The surviving defenders retreated to the German reserve line, some two miles to the northeast, and the last part of Vimy Ridge was finally in Allied hands. Fearing a counter attack, the Canadians worked through the night to prepare defences. According to an entry in the unit's diary at 6 a.m. on the 13th "Lts. Wood and Jackson, with their sapper parties, have worked continuously from 9 p.m. on the night of the 11th."

Hector had a close call during the consolidation of the captured hill when an artillery shell exploded next to him, killing another officer, Lt. Childe-Pemberton, and wounding three other men he was standing with. Remarkably, Hector emerged from the incident unscathed.

The Battle of Vimy Ridge was a turning point in the First World War. A total of 3,598 Canadians were killed during the attack, and more than 10,000 were wounded. Most casualties occurred in the first half hour of the first day, at a mind-numbing rate of over 400 casualties a minute. The German forces suffered 20,000 dead and wounded, and another 10,000 captured.

Hector finally had an opportunity to write a letter five days after the start of the battle.

14. 4. 17.

Dear Marg,

Just to let you know I got through our Show in good shape. I was lucky enough to be close up in the Show itself and had the most miserable time I have had for some time till the Ridge was finally taken, when I had a party up, and we put through a trench to connect up with our new line in the valley beyond, and helped the Infantry consolidate their line. We had snow 4" thick in the morning of the attack and small showers on and off during the day. I had a great time looking over the captured line and

---

[1] Hector's Commanding Officer indicated in a later letter that Hector was recommended for the Military Cross for his work here, but that the recommendation was turned down.

collecting some souvenirs which I want to get back to Blighty with. I am glad we had a chance of something big.

I suppose you had an idea of where I was from Rupert, as he seemed to know. We have been here all the year and our casualties have been pretty heavy, but our Division has made a name at last.[1]

Out of eight officers in the consolidation of our new line, we had one killed and four wounded; there was a group of four of us and two Runners hit by a shell, and I was the only one unhurt, my Runner got a slight touch of Shell Shock but he is quite recovered now, so I can consider myself lucky.[2]

The accounts in the papers are all a lot of rot, they reported the North end of the ridge taken 36 hours before we went over, and we could have taken the ridge any old time we wanted to if the people on our flanks had been ready to go ahead with us; our supporting artillery was fine.

Your affectionate,
HECTOR

Canadian soldiers celebrate after the capture of Vimy Ridge. | *National Archives of Canada*

---

[1] The 4th Canadian Division.

[2] The unit's diary indicates that this incident happened around midnight on April 13-14.

18. 4. 17.

Dear Gerald,

I have got two letters of yours to thank you for, and as the main excitement has passed I am getting off a few letters before we get too busy again.

We have taken the old Ridge at last after sitting in front of it since before Xmas and getting the benefit of every "Hate" that came along;[1] by the time you get this it will all be ancient history of course.

The day before the attack everything was just about normal, of course our guns were firing away in fine style, and had been for a week. I was lucky enough to be chosen from the Company to follow the attack on my old frontage and get a trench dug through to our new front line, and help the infantry consolidate. The night before the attack our party went up into advanced quarters, three officers of our company and five of a working party; it was snowing like the devil and everything was covered with several inches of snow. But our job was to mend the track across the valley,[2] which had been badly broken up by shell fire, to let the infantry get across.

We finished by 12.30 and got a kind of sleep from 1.30, though everyone was soaked and muddy up to the hips. Next morning we were awake at 5.30 and ready to move forward by 6, but stayed till 8.30 when word came down that the first attack had succeeded.

I got my party started on work that had been already arranged, and went ahead with two runners to get an idea of how things were before the party got up, and had my first sight of Lens and the Douai Valley beyond. As soon as the party was on the job I started exploring among the old Fritz trenches and dugouts, but it was a dirty job and did not find much as it was too far up in his lines. Most of the stuff was ahead in his Back Area.

I have thrown my rifle away as I hope to get a better one in this place besides plenty of other junk. I picked up a real typical Fritz pipe, armguards, bayonet and scabbard, a telephone set and a few odd things, but everything was too much destroyed to be any good.

We use this paper all the time for written messages and making sketches.[3] It is handy and I have not been near a place to buy note paper for months.

---

[1] Indiscriminate firing towards the enemy lines at dusk and dawn to prevent potential attacks were often known as "hates".

[2] Immediately in front of Vimy Ridge.

[3] Paper from official army signals pads.

I am sending you a German postcard I picked out of a haversack of a dead Fritz, it had a bullet right through it as you see. And I think I have a button off a tunic somewhere. Helmets are scarce and some of the men who get them are selling them for 60 francs. Out of the 8 officers in consolidation, one was killed and four wounded; all by shell fire. And except one, by the same shell that missed me. Five of us were together at the time, and I got away free, the only one.

The Canadians in London and the rest of England are having a great time on our reputation; if I get leave now there ought to be some fun.

Your affectionate,
HECTOR

---

6. 5. 17.

Dear Mamma,

I have not heard from you since I last wrote, but all Canadian mail appears to have gone groggy.

We have been working steadily ever since the Push but just now are having an unofficial rest, and luckily good weather for it.[1] I got hold of a Douglas motor cycle yesterday, and chased over to some towns I knew just to see how, everyone was, and found myself sitting next to Travers of all people at dinner in the Hotel. He was in Daviesites.[2] I think his photo is in my room. Just now he is on Corps Staff, but was Capt. and Adj. of the Queens (Surreys).

I had some unexpected news the same time; it appears that everyone was rather pleased with my work at the Corps School, and I have been applied for as instructor in Bayonet Fighting and physical culture. The application has gone into Corps, but nothing may come of it. I am just wondering whether I can satisfy myself that I have done my share before I get into a "Cushy" job like that.

We have had pretty heavy casualties as is natural these last few weeks. Oscar seems to be doing well with Signals. Must write and find out about Rupert.

Your affectionate,
HECTOR

---

[1] The work was mainly constructing new front line trenches immediately west of Lens, and repairing the road from Souchez to Givenchy to allow the artillery to catch up with the infantry.

[2] A "house" at Charterhouse School.

Hector on a motorbike. Date and location unknown. | *Family album*

11. 5. 17.

Dear Marg,

    Thanks for your last letter; this is just to say that I am alright still, and no hopes of Leave.

    We are not quite so far south as the place you mention, and have been out for some time.

    I had a letter from Rupert; he has got the "Croix de Guerre" for work with the French civilians in the last advance.[1]

    It is great weather just now except a little warm for work in the day. And there is lots of shell fire.

    If I ever get leave I must make London my headquarters, but I have so many people to see that I think I will be harder worked than out here, unless I can get an extension.

    Your affectionate,
    HECTOR

---

[1] Rupert was awarded the Croix de Guerre on April 7, 1917, on the citation of the Régiment No.174 of the French Army to which he was presumably attached at the time. Also in 1917, he was awarded the Military Cross for evacuating wounded from a field dressing station under gas attack.

16. 5. 17.

Dear Mamma,

We have not had a Canadian mail for some time now. I had a short note from you about a week ago answering one to Gerald.

I have had a great rest just lately. We left the Road work about the end of last month, and only started Trench work again on the 12th. I go up for a few days to relieve the officer up there at present.

There seems to be quite a lot of fuss about Pemberton, one of the officers who were killed in the attack on the Ridge.[1] He died of wounds after I carried him in. And it appears that his father is a great friend of General Byng's (Corps Commander).[2] I have had to send in two reports on his death, with a sketch map showing the place and direction of the shell. I suppose it is some comfort to his people to know something more than just "killed in action".

We have had three weeks of grand weather, only occasional thunder showers at night, just enough to lay the dust and bring on the grass. It is good news about Rupert's decoration, he must have got pretty close up to the Line and into a warm spot.

It is always just as well to take the hint when a shell comes too close. "Heinie"[3] has a nasty habit of lobbing over gas shells in our Area, Tear Gas with Phosgene[4] and some chlorine compound mixed in. It is not as bad as chlorine gas because it is pretty local, but quite effective if a shell happens to land close.

Rupert's Croix de Guerre. The medal is held by Rupert's son, Hugh Jackson. | A. Jackson

I met another O.C. a few days ago, also Daviesites, he is in command of 1st Corps Balloons. I happened to meet him in one of the Back Area towns, and paid a visit

---

[1] Edmund Childe-Pemberton , son of Lord and Lady William Childe-Pemberton. He was 22 years old when he was killed.

[2] Later, Sir Julian Byng, who served as Governor General of Canada from 1921 to 1926, and as commissioner of the London Metropolitan Police from 1928 to 1931.

[3] Heinie, Fritz and the Boche were British slang terms for the Germans.

[4] Carbonyl chloride, a colourless gas causes severe irritation and burns to eyes and skin and is fatal at high concentrations. Although the Germans were the first to use gas, the Allies soon followed suit.

Ref. No. 90-0

Mo.

The brilliant operations during the last month, culminating in the capture of Arleux and Fresnoy, seem to give me the opportunity of expressing to all ranks the pride I feel in commanding the Canadian Corps.

Since the 9th April, when the offensive against the VIMY RIDGE began, till the morning of May 3rd, when Fresnoy was captured and consolidated, it has been one series of successes only obtained by troops whose courage, discipline and initiative stand pre-eminent. Nine villages have passed into our hands. Eight German Divisions have been met and defeated. Over 5000 prisoners have been captured, and booty comprising some 64 guns and howitzers, 106 trench mortars, and 126 machine guns are now the trophies of the Canadians.

The training undergone during the winter has borne its fruit, and it is this training coupled with the zeal and gallantry which are so conspicuous in all ranks of the Corps, that will continue to gain results as potent and far-reaching as those which began with the capture of the VIMY RIDGE.

Byng.
Lieutenant General
Commanding Canadian Corps

May 3rd, 1917.

A message from General Julian Byng, Commander of the Canadian Corps, congratulating the troops on the capture of Vimy Ridge. | National Archives of Canada

to his mess and had tea. It seems very interesting work, and of course a Snap compared to our own. He was wounded last year and I suppose deserves a change.

I would not worry too much about how much money I am saving; I have always dropped on my feet, thanks to various things, and don't intend to come a cropper after the War.

Your affectionate.

HECTOR

---

26. 5. 17.

Dear Mamma,

We are expecting another Canadian Mail any time now, but as I have a day off I am writing without waiting for it.

The Company is back in the Line again with forward and rear billets as before.[1] And except for the weather, things are very much the same as before the Push. For the last two weeks we have been putting in a new Support Line which is just about finished, and then we go forward to the Front to relieve the other Company.[2] Leave has opened up very slightly and if it keeps on I may get mine the end of next month. But I will be too late to see Oscar as he should be across any time from what I last heard; he can't be very far from here when he does arrive, so I can get over and see how things are.

This time I will have to do a double tour thanks to a scarcity of officers, and won't be relieved when No.4 Section goes back in a few days. I stay on as C.O. Advanced Billets.

Two days ago when I was looking for a telephone I ran across Harold Galbraith, a 2nd Lieut. in the....... [indecipherable]. He has been along with us since Xmas attached to the Canadian Corps. He is more "Chops" than ever and I scarcely recognised him.

It appears I was recommended for the M.C. for the last month's work,[3] but it seems to have been turned down. Still there is plenty of time yet before the War ends.

---

[1] The forward billets were still at Ablain St. Nazaire, one mile north of the rear billets at Carency.

[2] Support line: a second line of trenches, used as a fall back position if the front line was overwhelmed. On May 28, Hector's unit moved east to the newly captured village of Givenchy, just northeast of Vimy Ridge, to work on the front line trenches.

[3] The capture of the Pimple at Vimy Ridge.

We are having grand weather just now especially in the evenings when most of our work starts.

Your affectionate,
HECTOR

———————————

Chapter 7

The Battle for Lens

WITH THE CAPTURE OF VIMY RIDGE and the withdrawal of the German forces to the Hindenburg Line, the Allied command planned to wear down the German Army with surprise attacks at various points then launch a final fatal attack in the Ypres area, well to the north of Vimy Ridge. One of these surprise attacks targeted the grubby, partially ruined coal mining city of Lens, attacking from the south and capturing German defensive positions in the outskirts of the city.

The 4th Canadian Division made a strong attack on the German lines on the night of June 2-3 after a preliminary gas shell bombardment of the German defenders. The unit's diary reported:

> At 12 midnight, night 2nd/3rd June, an operation was carried out by the 44th and 50th Battalions, the objective being the general line of enemy trenches from M.36.b.46.90 to T.1.a.95.50, including the CENTRAL ELECTRIC GENERATING STATION, BREWERY and LA COULOTTE.
>
> Considerable opposition was encountered and very severe fighting ensued. The Right Battalion parties reached their objective after suffering severe casualties but were driven out later by a heavy enemy attack and forced to retire on their original line. The Left Battalion, after heavy fighting, secured practically their final objectives, the line now held being M.36.b.42.06 to M.36.b.78.82.

At approximately 6:30 p.m. after having suffered all day a very heavy continuous bombardment of our newly captured positions on our Left Battalion front, the enemy attacked in force and our troops were forced to withdraw to their original line.

During a series of Canadian and German attacks and counter-attacks over the next week, the front line oscillated back and forth through the outskirts of Lens. Hector's sector experienced mobile urban warfare, in contrast to the months of static trench warfare leading up to the attack on Vimy Ridge. Much of the Engineers' work was focused on putting in new front line and support trenches (usually fifty to one hundred yards behind the front line trenches) among the ruins, setting out barbed wire entanglements to protect them and clearing rubble and debris from the ruined streets to provide a field of fire. The logistics involved in trench construction of this nature were considerable. Laffin (1991) reported that 2000 yards of front line put in near La Bassée required 5,036 bags of cement, 19,384 bags of shingle, and 9,692 bags of sand, quite apart from the material for revetting and the barbed wire entanglements. Hector spent part of his time in the back areas, only travelling up to the front line as needed.

9. 6. 17.

Dear Marg,

I think I had better make carbon copies of my letters and send them around to various relations. The pile I am supposed to answer is simply hopeless, as I had a double length Tour in the Line last time owing to lack of officers; the last week I was C.O. Advanced Billets, and was responsible for Liaison work with the Battalion commanders; finishing up the tour with the scrap you will have read about in the papers at the beginning of the month.[1] It was decidedly warm work and I must have had a charmed life. I am due for leave on the 10th but I give you fair warning that 10 days is not a tenth long enough to get around to see the people who have been keeping me supplied, and I will be relieved when I get back here again for a rest.

I heard from both Rupert and Oscar today. Oscar should be

---

[1] Referring to the attacks on La Coulotte, the Brewery, and the Central Electric Generating Station.

somewhere pretty close to me out here;[1] his Division is out on rest just now, and goes back into the Line in a week or so.

Our Division by the way has never been out for a rest since they came out. Of course we get occasional Brigade rests so we are not actually working all the time.

I am entering for the Horse Show tomorrow with my little mare in the jumps. I was riding the Major's horse but have decided to stick to my own after all.[2]

If this weather only lasts I ought to collect a pretty good time if everyone does a quarter of what they promise. Some duty calls have to be got through but otherwise they ought all to help to make things worthwhile.

Your affectionate,
HECTOR

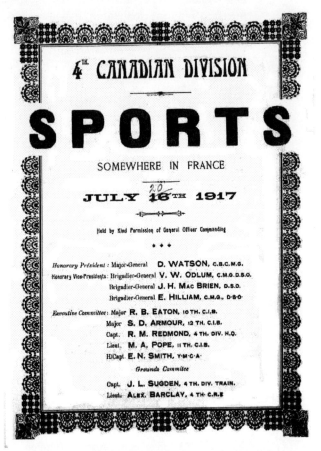

4TH CANADIAN DIVISION

SPORTS

SOMEWHERE IN FRANCE

JULY 16TH 1917

Held by Kind Permission of General Officer Commanding

♦ ♦ ♦

Honorary President : Major-General **D. WATSON,** C.B.C.M.G.
Honorary Vice-Presidents: Brigadier-General **V. W. ODLUM,** C.M.G.D.S.O.
Brigadier-General **J. H. MacBRIEN,** D.S.O.
Brigadier-General **E. HILLIAM,** C.M.G., D.S.O.

Executive Committee: Major **R. B. EATON,** 10 TH. C.I.B.
Major **S. D. ARMOUR,** 12 TH. C.I.B.
Capt. **R. M. REDMOND,** 4 TH. DIV. H.Q.
Lieut. **M. A. POPE,** 11 TH. C.I.B.
H/Capt. **E. N. SMITH,** Y.M.C.A.

Grounds Committee

Capt. **J. L. SUGDEN,** 4 TH. DIV. TRAIN.
Lieut. **ALEX. BARCLAY,** 4 TH. C.R.E.

Program for Battalion sports day held during a training break. Hector competed in the horse jumping competition.
| *National Archives of Canada*

Just think of leave.

---

[1] Oscar appears to have arrived in France in the first week of June and to have been assigned to the 1st or 2nd Canadian Division.

[2] Hector won the Officers' Jumping competition and returned to the front line on June 12.

Hector on his horse, somewhere in France. The horse's tail has been docked to prevent it from becoming caked in mud. | Family album

17. 6. 17.

Dear Marg,

    I am still at the War as my leave has been put off another week, that is half the fun in the Army: making plans for leave and changing them about six times.[1]

    We are not exactly being overworked this Tour but just get enough to keep healthy and take an interest in the War, the weather keeps glorious and makes things a whole lot better for everyone.

    I am going up in about an hour to finish off a trench we have been working on; it is pretty monotonous work, but it seems to be our job just at

---

[1] Hector eventually departed on leave on June 24.

present and I have known lots worse.

Oscar came over to our H.Q. to see me the day I left to go up so we missed each other, but he is not very far away and I can get over and see him next week when I get back.

I have just seen that Marion Bostock is an L.R.C.P., F.R.C.S.[1] etc, she and her sister are in London just now. They were at Priors Field girls school when I was at Ch'house with her brother.[2] I met the family again at Ottawa, so I suppose I must congratulate her even if I am a bit scared of all the letters.

There are some awfully nice roses in one of the broken up villages here, but I don't think that cuttings will grow at this time of year; there are rhubarb and cress also going to waste in very small patches between shell holes.

Our dugouts are not too bad only rather damp, and matches have to be put out to dry every day. I used to pretend I could not sleep in a strange bed, but that notion is completely finished with now. All you need is to come in at 4.30 after wandering around since 8.30 the night before, and the rest is easy.

You can expect me when you see me.

Your affectionate,

HECTOR

Chepstow Place, W.8.
26. 7. 17.[3]

Dear Marg,

I have arrived at last and am just scrawling a letter to explain things.

Can you get down here early Monday and get me by phone? I can't possibly make you and Tiger, so am writing her to get up as well. I leave Tuesday morning worse luck.

I have been out of Town for the weekend and am shopping all week and seeing people in Town. Mr. Ward wants to see something of you in Town when you arrive.

Mind you get away,

HECTOR

---

[1] Licentiate of the Royal College of Physicians, Fellow of the Royal College of Surgeons. Marion Bostock was one of Senator Bostock's daughters.

[2] Priors Field was a private girls' school in Godalming.

[3] Date should read 26. 6. 17, not 26. 7. 17.

51, Chepstow Place,
Pembridge Square, W.
27. 6. 17.

Dear Mamma,

My leave has come through at last and I am seeing all I can in the measly 10 days they allow us. Luckily the weather is good and I can get around in comfort. Marg and Tiger are coming up to Town to see me, and I am gradually working through the list of "Duty".

I am going on the River[1] today with Muriel Richardson after we have had lunch. Thursday is all shopping and seeing three people. Friday is lunch and tennis at Queens with the Maynard-Horne crowd, and dinner and a show with the daughter; after Sat. and Sunday at Dedham with my adopted Aunt and to see Rendall Monday, Tiger and Marg; Tuesday Lady Lawson at Folkestone, and I am off to France early Wednesday. So you can see how everything has to be worked in. When I get back I am glad to see we are on Division Rest for a month. I came straight out of the Line to go on leave; had been digging "Jumping off trenches" in front of our own line for three nights in succession. So I was not at all sorry to leave.

Oscar is at Bruay[2] but will soon change to Château-de-la-Haie[3] where we used to be. Keep an eye on Souchez River, Avion, Coulotte, Electric Station.

Your affectionate,
HECTOR

———————————

51 Chepstow Place,
Pembridge Square, W
4. 7. 17.

Dear Mamma,

It is all over and I have had a splendid time; am leaving for Folkestone this afternoon. Saw Dedham and the Rendalls etc, Marg and Tiger came up and went on the River and Theatre. But it is all going to be history in a few hours.

We are in Division Rest I think so should be out till the end of the month. Oscar is quite close. Lens, Avion, Souchez River (South) means work

---

[1] The Thames.

[2] Bruay-la-Buissière, twelve miles northwest of where Hector was based.

[3] Divisional Headquarters.

done by us, when you see it in the Papers.[1]

Everyone has been doing their best to keep things going during the leave. Mr. Ward the best of them.

Will write when I get across.

Your affectionate,

HECTOR

----

8. 7. 17.

Dear Mamma,

Just got back from Leave and have found a pile of letters to be answered but only one from yourself with one from Gerald, enclosed. Leave is a thing of the past and I have nothing to live for except the present. And the memory of a perfectly good ten days.[2]

I saw young Leathem in Town. He has the M.C. and a bar to it, and was just going out to rejoin his people again.

Then you speak of seeing Rupert on a motorcycle; it sounds as absurd as the Englishman in Montreal taking his weekend with friends in Vancouver. You have to get passes to get out of Corps Area and as for Army it is almost imposs: he is 3 armies away from me.

The Job at Corps School is by no means a Staff job, but it would draw extra pay. Anyway the Chief Engineer put the lid on it by saying no Engineers were to go on instruction. The Commandant of the School applied for me and told me so himself, and applied to Canadian Corps.

I have been having tennis and just now was out judging sports. I am making an effort to see Oscar this evening if he is where I think he is; we have been missing each other up to now.

I will answer Gerald's letter as soon as poss.

Your affectionate,

HECTOR

----

[1] Hector was able to mention these by name, as his letter from London was not subject to the military censorship.

[2] He returned to his unit on July 6. The unit had been relieved from the front line, and was training at the village of Maisnil-Bouché, two miles to the rear.

20. 7. 17.

Dear Mamma,

Still resting, but the weather has decidedly deteriorated and anyhow we will be back at our old tricks again, raising the righteous wrath of old Boche. Anytime we start holding a bit of line he gets rubbed up the wrong way, and never has a moment's peace.

The Corps School has started an honour roll and I see my name is down for Class V as first in the Class. They have had about 8 classes now, and the names and unit of the best people of each class are carved on it.

I gave Lady Pemberton[1] the operation Orders of the Pimple Attack (north end of the Ridge) and asked her to send them on to Golf Bungalow, Deal.[2] They will send them out to you; they are rather interesting.

We are getting plenty of tennis and I am getting fairly useful at it, except beastly carc . . . [indecipherable]; it always will be my fault slamming the ball anyhow into the net.

I am having more done to my teeth, they just keep up a steady decay and now my gums are getting Vincent or a mild Pyorrhea, but I think they have been taken in time. I have more money left after my leave than I expected to have, but I could not stand too many of those things. My next one will be spent in the country somewhere if I want to do it on a moderate sum.

At the Brigade sports this afternoon my mare let me down rather badly; it was really too wet for jumping as the take off was slushy and she did not get a place; just took it into her head that she could not jump, and we had a fine old argument about it.[3]

I have not seen Oscar yet, he is farther away than I thought, but I hope to get out before we go into the Line. I keep on intending to get over.

I don't know if I told you I was assigning $15 for current expenses, or anything that crops up; it is not very much I am afraid but I am going to make an effort to raise my Bank account for a change.

I will write to Gerald when I start next.

Your affectionate,
HECTOR

---

[1] Mother of Edmund Childe-Pemberton.

[2] Tiger's home.

[3] Held at Château de la Haie, the local Brigade Headquarters just one mile east of the training camp at Maisnil Bouché.

29. 7. 17.

Dear Mamma,

I had my first letter from you this month a few days ago (26.6.17). Before that I had May 11th, 22nd, 30th (with one from G.)[1]. All Canadian mail this month is scarce. Harold G.[2] is in artillery (Heavies), he came out first as a pte.[3] in the Motor Machines Gunners. His face is fatter than ever.

I have just finished having my teeth fixed for the umpteenth time, they are supposed to be O.K., but I have such hopeless Acid Mouth that they will need lots of work by Xmas. I must have had 8 stoppings, and it was lots of fun. Also my hair is getting bald on top, or rather decidedly thin, so I can see myself eligible for an old age pension by the end of the War.

I am enclosing a cutting which Olga sent from Rathwell. Dr. Bell was very nice to me in Ottawa, as were the whole family, and they must miss him. Also a photo of Ione, she was rather proud of her R.A.C. badge when I saw her and we had tea and a theatre, not to mention the River on the strength of it.

I saw Oscar, he seems cheerful and not overworked, among the guns and rather noisy, but comparatively safe.

Your affectionate,
HECTOR

---

29. 7. 17.

Dear Marg,

I have got a letter of yours to be answered, but I can't find it just now. We are in the middle of a sulphurous thunder storm;[4] it is only 10 a.m. but as dark as 10 p.m. and we have lamps everywhere.

I saw Oscar a few days ago, he was in Advanced Divisional work, up further than I expected to find him, but pretty secure except for the odd 5.9 that came over at intervals;[5] they are in dugouts in the grounds of a large house in the town. He has not changed, only grown more and has a

---

[1] His brother, Gerald.

[2] Harold Galbraith, an acquaintance from Abbotsford.

[3] Private, the lowest rank in the military.

[4] This was the start of an unusually rainy period which was to play a major part in the upcoming Passchendaele offensive.

[5] German 5.9″ howitzer, which fired high-explosive shells.

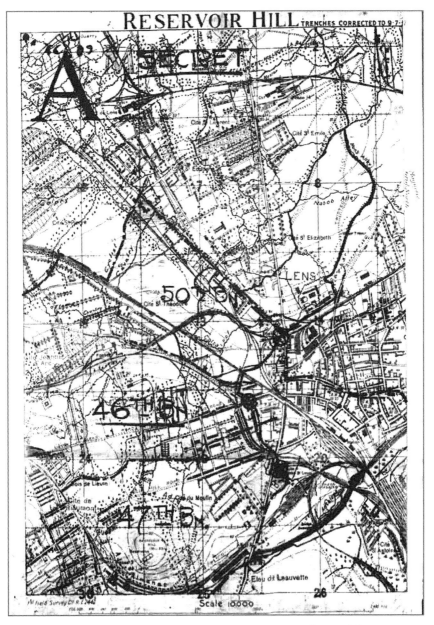

Allies' map of Lens during July 1917, showing the position of some of the battalions which were advancing eastward towards the centre of the city. Hector's unit was located just to the south of the 47th Battalion. | *National Archives of Canada*

very bass voice, and seems pretty satisfied with the war.[1] Anyhow he is doing work which will help him in civil life, and is pretty well on his own as far as officers are concerned.

You always ask for something I want. Can you see your way to make me a small House-wife?[2] My old one has disappeared and they are decidedly useful when we are up forward. Did you see the photo of Ione, it came out last week? She was wearing the R.A.C. Badge when I saw her and felt rather pleased with herself. It has a pretty stiff theoretical exam. I sent the Pembertons the Pimple Orders, and asked to have them sent to Golf Bungalow. We are all pretty fit now and up to strength.

Your affectionate,

HECTOR

P.S. I have got a pretty good chance of 2 weeks at Boulogne and a Rest Camp next month.[3]

This is a Menu we had at one of our halting places; we were lucky and stayed three nights.

Oh Pip = Observation Post ("P" is always Pip when signaling)

Tara Hill = Was our old Camp.[4]

Colt = a trench full of slush.

Ex Eleven Ack = a map location Brigade Headquarters

Regina = Our old front line.[5]

It is signed by everyone in the Mess.

Back in British Columbia, the need to supply the war machine in Europe spurred commercial activity in Vancouver. Munitions and explosives factories were running at full speed, and ship building was at an all time high. In the city, the recession was biting less severely than a year previously.

The economic recovery, however, did not extend to the countryside. With Hector and his brothers having been away from Aldergrove for almost two years, Moses and Rosa were struggling to keep the family farm going with the help of only seventeen-year-old

---

[1] This was the first time that Hector had seen Oscar in eighteen months.

[2] Sewing kit.

[3] This never happened, owing to the start of the Battle of Passchendaele, less than two days after he wrote this letter.

[4] On the Somme, immediately northeast of the town of Albert.

[5] The Regina Trench, near Courcelette, was captured by the Canadians in the last days of the Battle of the Somme.

Gerald. The soaring cost of potash fertilizer was crippling farmers and the overall cost of living in Canada had skyrocketed by more than thirty percent in those two years.

At the same time, the loss of a significant proportion of the men of British Columbia to the battlefields of Europe, and a resultant drop in the birth rate meant that demand for Applegarth's milk production plummeted. Income from the farm was insufficient for Moses to hire labour to help, even if it had been available. In spite of Moses and Gerald's best efforts, secondary forest growth was steadily re-invading the recently cleared fields, eating into the pasture needed for the dairy cows. Applegarth was trapped in a vicious downward cycle where everything seemed to conspire against it. The words of F.J. Hart's promotional brochure must have rung hollow in Moses' mind:

> The small farmer – the man who fills the mouths of the multitudes, whose vocation is affected by neither financial depression nor lack of employment, has not fears regarding the safety of his home.

The stress of the failing farm and the constant fear of the dreaded telegram announcing the death of one of their three sons at the front must have taken a psychological and physical toll on Hector's parents. Moses and Rosa tended to keep largely to themselves; their social life was apparently very restricted, with Moses preferring, according to an Aldergrove resident, to remain "where he couldn't see his neighbour's smoke."[1] Hector was aware of the family's problems from the letters he received in France, but perhaps not their full extent. In any case he could do nothing about the situation as he had enough on his own hands.

The Allies wanted to maintain the pressure on the German forces in the vicinity of Lens for two reasons. Firstly they needed to relieve the French troops in the southeast, and secondly they wanted to prevent the Germans from building up their forces in the northwest in Flanders, where the Allies were planning their imminent major spring offensive. To this end, the Canadians were tasked with capturing the city of Lens. The southern part of the city had already fallen to the Allies, and they planned to capture the remainder by gaining control of the high ground that overlooked the city from the north. This high

---

[1] *The Place Between*, p.153, Aldergrove Heritage Society (1997).

ground was known as Hill 70. The Canadian 1st and 2nd Divisions were assigned this task. The 3rd Canadian Division and Hector's 4th Division were to keep up the pressure by pushing east towards the centre of the city.

On July 25, after their retraining, Hector's Engineers unit moved, to Divisional Headquarters at Château de la Haie, just west of Vimy Ridge, to prepare for the attacks. A week later, on August 1, Hector returned to the front line on the western outskirts of Lens. He worked feverishly with his unit for the next couple of weeks as the Allies probed into the German-defended western portion of the city, preparing jumping-off trenches for the main attack.

Part of the 4th Division attacked on August 14 as a diversion for the main attack on Hill 70 which began early next morning. Preparation for and support of this activity kept Hector from his regular letter writing.

19. 8. 17.

Dear Marg,

Many thanks for the Housewife and chocolates. We are having concentrated essence of war. Houses all the time and you are not sure who has which in some cases.

No time to write,
HECTOR

The 10th Canadian Infantry Battalion carried out another attack on Lens on August 21, accompanied by Engineers. The Battalion succeeded in advancing the line about a mile to the edge of the ruined city centre, attacking and destroying German-held tunnels and underground shelters hidden in the rubble. Although Hector did not participate in this attack, some Engineers were from his section, and one of his non-commissioned officers, Lance Corporal Mitchell Crombie, was killed as reported in the Company diary.

5:30 a.m. 10th Canadian Infantry Battalion attacked and gained objectives. L/c Crombie wounded in right forearm, carried on and blew up tunnel. He was killed an hour later while directing work of consolidation. Sapper Randles then took over the work. L/c Brett and Sapper Sampson blew up tunnel entrances in Mill Hill Rd at N19d7.9. killing a number of Germans.

The city of Lens was virtually destroyed during the fighting and the ruins proved a nightmare for attacking troops. | *Archival photo*

The Canadians managed to hold onto their advances, and Hector spent the next day surveying the captured tunnels. Conditions during these attacks on Lens were unusually hazardous because the Germans began employing mustard gas and flame throwers against the Allies for the first time. Mustard gas was far worse than the chlorine or phosgene used by both sides until then. A relatively odourless, heavy gas, it flowed into trenches and penetrated clothing and available gas masks. Because it took six or more hours to take effect, the victims would breathe it unaware of its insidious damage. The gas attacked exposed skin to form mustard-coloured blisters. Victims suffered burning, gritty eyes and were racked by vomiting as they bled internally and externally, and mucous membrane was stripped from their bronchial tubes and lungs. Because of the intense pain, most victims had to be strapped to their beds for the four or five weeks it sometimes took them to die. Hector was later to have first-hand experience of poisoning by mustard gas.

The Canadians suffered over 9,000 casualties during the attacks on Lens, but they pushed the German defenders back, street by ruined street, to capture or dominate most of the western half of the city. More important than seizing their objective, this action prevented a build up of German forces in Flanders where the Allies were just beginning their main offensive. The Canadians' success at Hill 70 and Lens, on the heels of the capture of Vimy Ridge, sealed their destiny as the shock troops of choice at Passchendaele, just a few weeks later.

Some of the horrific effects of mustard gas can be seen on this soldier's back. It also attacked the eyes, throat and lungs of its victims. | Archival photo

22. 8. 17

Dear Mamma,

A Runner has just brought up our mail. Mine just consisted of one from you with an enclosure from Ags. Glad to hear that she is thinner if only a wee bit.

By now you will have the official Report on my leave from Marg and Tiger;[1] we went down to Richmond.

Muriel is working in the Admiralty now and seems to be getting fed

---

[1] Leave taken six weeks earlier.

25. 8. 17

Report on Sewer in Millue PS.

I examined crater at N 19. d.6.95.
the only tunnel entrance is in North lip.
It is in poor repair for the first 10' and
comes to a blind end after a right angle
turn.
The sewer running down centre of road
is broken in in a few places
but is still practicable for movement
of troops. It is of brick with
2½' head cover.
As far as I could see there were no connections with cellars.
All the houses alongside have cellars with
fair head cover. But most have the
entrances blown in. I was in a house at
N. 19. d. 3.8. The cellars are arched.
15' x 10' x 8' high the centre passing being
reinforced with 7"x 8" planting supported by
6" pil props. Five of these cellars
are joined up. The East house has also

Part of a report written by Hector after a survey of captured tunnels. | National Archives of Canada

up.[1] Anyone would be in this kind of weather in London. Mrs. Attwood lives with her and is always very cheerful. I met the Maynard-Hornes at tennis with the Lawsons. Dr. Hornes is at present in France with a Base Hospital. The boy is just leaving Harrow; the girl has been at Lady Lytton's Hospital till just lately, when she got typhoid and swollen glands and is convalescing.

It is very hard to take anything in the way of metal souvenirs out of France as practically all are forbidden.

I thought I told you I had seen the Pembertons. I went around about tea time and as the mother was out they asked me if I could come again some time, and I went a few days later. The photo you saw was quite a good one. I saw the original in the house. He was badly hit in the back and awfully hard to get out as the mud was up to our knees, and he had just rolled into it and was a mass of slime. The mother must have been very pretty once and is quite nice still with a rather fascinating lisp, but too hopelessly wrapped up in him and with the absurdest impracticable ideas.

Just now we are in cellars and are kept quite lively, but as usual nothing like the infantry have to put up with. The only thing that makes their job possible is that they don't last long.

The weather has been grand for some time now and that means quite a lot even though it is rather thirsty work.

Rupert is miles away from us as far as I can make out; they are having a rather quiet time. We are not. I lost my corporal yesterday morning. He and three others volunteered for an attack to destroy some tunnels and suspected machine guns and he was hit twice, the second time in the throat.[2]

I bet Ramsgate is scared stiff and I wish they could come out here and see a real mess;[3] the papers will have given accounts long before this letter reaches you.

I will send Gerald a letter some time,
Your affectionate,
HECTOR

---

[1] Muriel Attwood's brother, Langley, was a year younger than Hector, and had died ten days earlier from wounds received during an Allied attack at Messines on June 17, forty miles northwest of Hector's position. The Allies constructed nineteen tunnels under the German lines and laid huge amounts of explosives, which were detonated immediately before the attack. The explosion was heard 120 miles away in London.

[2] This fighting occurred about one mile southwest of the centre of Lens where Hector was surveying captured tunnels and sewers that had been used by the Germans to access their front line.

[3] There had been a major daylight air raid on Ramsgate on August 13, which caused a number of deaths.

The battle for Lens reached a stalemate on August 25 with the German troops still entrenched in the gutted city centre but virtually powerless because they were dominated by the Allies on the newly captured high ground.

Hector's unit was finally relieved from the front line in Lens the next day, and retired five miles to their rear base at Ablaine Saint Nazaire for a few days rest before returning to the same part of the front line to strengthen their defences.

1. 9. 17.

Dear Marg,

I wouldn't worry about what is happening out here just now; we are getting on pretty well as things go. I have been out the best part of a week just watching things. We had rather a warm time last week, at least the infantry did. Our job was nothing compared though I lost my best Corporal in the first attack, he was hit through the neck. I went out with a party to find his body a few nights later; it had been got in and is buried in the front line.

I must get up and see Oscar soon and find out how he liked his first attack; he should have been kept pretty busy. The House Wife is fine, thanks very much for sending it out. I believe I wrote and thanked you for it, but am not quite sure as it arrived at rather a strenuous time and we had quarters in cellars in the town.[1]

Give my best to Tiger,
Your affectionate,
HECTOR

———————

7. 9. 17.

Dear Mamma,

We have had a Canadian mail in now and I had a letter from you (Aug. 7th.) with an enclosure from Miss Lovejoy. She certainly gives a splendid lot of news. Next leave I must get down to Godalming and a take a few days so I can see some of the people, and of course, Ch'house.

---

[1] In Lens.

I am an awful sight just now as my head is as bald as an egg; I have had it shaved right close;[1] you have no idea how comfortable it feels except for flies, but it ought to be thick again by the end of next month when the winter comes on.

I was in Kendell's form all the time I was on the Army side,[2] he was a lieut in our Rifle Corps and got the M.C. early in the war.

It seems an awful pity that all the old clearings should grow up again after all the work that was put into them, even though it was spasmodic and all out of season; still it did show some results.[3]

Rupert must be having a grand old time if he is back with the V.A.D.s and all those kind of people.[4] They are back in the unattainable officers' heaven, a place I think about but never get a chance of even glancing at. Still he has been out some time and anyhow someone has to be there. Oscar is doing Advanced Division Signals when I saw him, he has moved a few miles now and is not so far from us, so I must get a look at him before I go up in the Line again.

Have they started paying in my Assigned pay yet? I suppose the first payment may take a little time.

There has been quite a lot of real slaughter round us, more like the early parts of the War as far as I can see, as the old Boche is determined to make a stand and well, he has the Canadians against him and they have a bad habit of getting what they go after, and don't want prisoners.

Langley Attwood was killed in the Messines show, he was in the "Heavies" as a lieut; Muriel feels it worse than I thought she was capable of.

I will try and make a collection of small curios and send them to Gerald.

Your affectionate,
HECTOR

P.S. If you can get a damp proof screwed in face (for the watch) so much the better.[5]

---

[1] Probably to remove lice which infested the clothing, bedding and hair of virtually every soldier in the trenches.

[2] In his last two years at Charterhouse.

[3] Referring toApplegarth farm in Aldergrove.

[4] Presumably Rupert was having some temporary relief from his posting at the front in France.

[5] The Allies issued their officers with pocket watches with screw-on back and front covers for dust and damp-proofing but, by 1917, wrist watches of a similar design were available.

---

10. 9. 17.

Dear Marg,

Just got your letter by runner and am writing by return; yours seems to have taken a long time to arrive. I expect you got my last letter just after writing; anyhow it was only a short note, the same as this one is going to be.

Yes we are still at it; of course it does not mean everyone is out all the time as some fool papers would like you to believe. We have Divisional, Brigade and Battalion reliefs going on all the time, so that everyone has a shot at it. But it is always the Canadian Corps for all the papers know; and I suppose it is just as well or it might muddle the poor old War Correspondents' weak heads.[1] I am up this time all alone in an old "Heinie" Dugout, and we are luckily having splendid weather with very useful early morning mists, they make moving about a whole lot easier.

Applegarth seems finally going to pot. I wish there was a large volcano started under the whole thing, and nothing short of that will make them[2] leave the rotten old place.

We get plenty of gas shot over here; our cat was gassed a few nights ago, but we had no casualties among the men.

When you go up to Town I wish you would get a wrist watch from Harrods or some such place. It must be good and luminous dial. Anything up to £4. You can see the adverts in the Tatler, Sketch etc.[3] I can send you a cheque or get Montreal to send it to your account.[4]

Your affectionate,
HECTOR

---

30. 9. 17.

Dear Marg,

Many thanks for watch, it seems fine.
HECTOR

---

[1] War correspondents often complied with officialdom's needs for glowing reports on the war's progress, earning them little respect among front line troops.

[2] Hector's parents.

[3] *Tatler* magazine covered the activities of the wealthy and aristocratic, and the *Sketch* was a British national tabloid newspaper.

[4] Hector held an account at The Bank of Montreal.

_____

9. 10. 17.

Dear Gerald,

I believe I wrote to Mamma a few days ago, but anyway I may as well write now as I have a little time to spare which I won't have for the next week or more.

I am just taking over the Line again but have not gone over the Area yet as Rogers, whom I am relieving, has not come in yet.[1]

The Old Boche certainly is a worker. I know that sounds pretty stale news, but I realise it more every day. Just now I am in an old gun position of his: dugouts under a ruined house with sleeping accommodation for 2 officers with lots of room to spare, mess room, kitchen and orderly room. And the men are just across the road in a dugout holding about twenty with kitchen as well. All of this is 15 feet underground in a perfectly flat piece of country.[2] The old gun pits are just near with his ammunition just as he left it. He was as safe as a house here all last winter and we were having a hopeless time with very little cover. And he has simply hundreds of these on this little frontage, this is quite a comparatively small one. There is always a certain amount of fun taking over a new piece of Area; every time we go in the other people have moved a little ahead and we find things quite changed. Trench junctions which used to be dangerous and passed at a quick shuffle are now in the safety zone, and new dugouts and cellars are unearthed and explored. Then we get busy and connect up posts and keep old trenches in some shape. The scouts Officer of one of the battalions got into a cellar and found a camera, a pair of field glasses, a revolver and a bundle of maps, but it is not often that you come across finds like this except in a large Advance.

I did not see Oscar this time out but he is not far away from us. This is a very warlike letter for some reason; I never am sure what my letters are going to turn out.

I have an idea that I am going to put in for leave for Nice and Lourdes as it won't interfere with my English leave about Xmas, but I am

_____

[1] Lieutenant R.A. Rogers, C.E.

[2] The German forces built very elaborate underground bunkers out of concrete with proper drainage, lighting, plumbing, heating and beds. The Allies, ostensibly in the interests of mobility, put up with far more crude accommodation that frequently flooded in wet weather.

not sure yet.[1]
> Write sometime,
> Your affectionate,
> HECTOR

I wonder if you got the photo of me. I forget how many were to be sent, but any over can go to Aunts.[2]

---

[1] The war put paid to this idea.
[2] Moses' sisters, Agnes and Irene Jackson in Mission, B.C.

Chapter 8

Passchendaele

On July 31, 1917, while Hector was involved with the urban warfare in the ruins of western Lens, the Allies launched their planned main spring offensive, some forty-five miles northwest of Vimy Ridge, in the Flanders area of southern Belgium. This was officially called the Third Battle of Ypres, after the ruined city that lay in the centre of the Flanders area. However, the battle became more commonly known as Passchendaele, named after a small village on an almost imperceptible ridge whose capture became the final objective. The Allies aimed to capture the high ground so that they could dominate the area and push the Germans back at least thirty miles to deny them the use of submarine bases at Ostende on the Belgian coast. The importance of this objective, which was promoted by the Royal Navy, was later shown to have been overstated.

For almost two weeks prior to the offensive, the Allies carried out their usual "softening-up" artillery barrage of the German lines. However, they had not learned from previous attacks because the artillery had the opposite effect to that intended. The approach to Passchendaele Ridge was across a low-lying area reclaimed from marshes, and the intricate drainage system was completely destroyed by the shellfire. The heaviest rains in thirty years began falling just before the attack and continued throughout the initial assault and for several days afterwards. Flooding from the destroyed drainage network rapidly turned the whole battlefield into a grim mire of

The iconic ruins of the Cloth Hall in Ypres. | *Archival photo*

sucking mud and flooded craters. In addition, the shelling removed any element of surprise that the Allies could have exploited, and the Germans were well prepared for the attack and remarkably unaffected by the artillery pounding.

The first ground assault, mostly by Australian troops, opened over a twelve-mile front on October 12. The attack was initially successful, but the Germans soon repelled it, and the Australians gained little ground.

The British and Commonwealth forces tried to renew the offensive over the next few days using newly introduced tanks, but they proved useless, subject to breakdown or churning helplessly in the quagmire of muck and splintered trees. Exhausted men and horses slipped into flooded shell craters where, too weak to pull themselves free, they sank beneath the mud and drowned. It was only after two weeks, when the rains subsided, that another attack could be launched. But this advance was equally ineffective and, in spite of intense fighting with huge casualties, a five-week stalemate ensued.

The Allied High Command were still desperate to take the Passchendaele ridge so that their troops could at least spend the winter on higher dry ground, rather than in the marshy morass below.

To support the offensive, the Allied command decided to reinforce their troops at Passchendaele with 20,000 battle-proven Canadian troops from the Lens/Vimy Ridge area, including Hector's 4th Canadian Division. Hector was withdrawn from the front line on the outskirts of Lens on the morning of October 10 after six weeks of continuous work, much of it under heavy shelling and conditions of urban warfare.

Without an opportunity to recover, Hector's unit moved to Passchendaele over a nine day period, travelling by foot and bus. The unit's route took them via their rear base at Ablain St. Nazaire, to Ruitz, Isbergues, and the village of Le Nieppe (fifteen miles west-northwest of Hazebrouck). There the engineers had five days to dry their equipment, rest their horses and prepare for their new role.

By the time the Canadian reinforcements arrived, the Australian troops who had borne the brunt of the recent fighting in the Passchendaele area, were exhausted. Conditions at the earlier Battle of the Somme had been appalling, but those at Passchendaele were far worse. Barely a tree or blade of grass survived in the pulverized wasteland of churned mud and twisted military hardware. No attempts could be made to recover and bury the dead from the shrapnel-swept battlefield, and the stench of putrefying corpses and fermenting latrines hung over everything, permeating hair, clothing and even their food. Vast numbers of rats thrived in this miserable sodden environment, eating the flesh off the dead and any food left carelessly unguarded, and occasionally even attacking sleeping men.

Hector's unit moved by bus on October 17 from La Nieppe to the shattered city of Ypres where his 10th Field Company initially took up billets in a disused nunnery in the remains of the city. Although there was no attack in progress when the unit first arrived, German shelling continued unabated, with extensive use of mustard gas. A number of Hector's unit were killed or wounded within hours of arriving in the new area. The unit's war diary entry on October 21, four days after their arrival, reported:

> 10 A.M. Billets heavily shelled. 18 men of 123rd Battalion (3rd Pioneers) killed by 1 shell in front of Nunnery. 4th Div. car burned. Driver seriously wounded.
> 4:30 P.M. Shells hit Sgts. kitchen and Sgts. Quarters of 10th Field Co. in Nunnery. Sgt Machon M.M., Sgt Spink killed. Sgt Morron wounded. Corporals Rosam M.M. and Burrows buried but unhurt.

Immediately after this incident, the 10th Field Company wisely moved their billets from the exposed nunnery to the more shell-resistant local jail.

When the Canadians arrived in the Ypres sector they found that much of its infrastructure had been neglected or destroyed. There was a dire need for roads, mule tracks and railways to move troops and supporting artillery and ammunition closer to the front. Immediately after his arrival in Ypres, Hector was deployed with a large number of troops to upgrade the badly damaged road running northeast from Ypres towards the German-held town of Zonnebeke. In the first three weeks following their arrival, the Canadian Engineers laid nearly two and a half miles of planked roads and a similar amount of rail line but suffered more than 1,500 casualties from the German artillery's continuous shelling.

Troops build a plank road for heavy wagons under supervision of the Canadian Engineers. | *National Archives of Canada*

The Passchendaele campaign was to be the hardest fought battle of the First World War, and it pushed the British and Commonwealth troops to the limits of their endurance. The overwhelming number of casualties sacrificed for so small a gain drained troop morale to its lowest point in the war. Passchendaele became a byword for the crushing futility of trench warfare. In spite of this, Hector appears to have remained unfazed. He wrote a brief letter home three days after arriving in the area.

20. 10. 17.

Dear Mamma,

We are out in Back Area for a few days, and I saw yet another town. One of the real kind you read about in Under the Red Robe,[1] and those books. Military of course, what is not these days, but awfully picturesque and old world.

I must be quite close to Rupert now but have not got in touch with him, he should be back from leave any time now and I will try and find him out through Signals.

There have been several plane fights around us, as the weather has been pretty fine and there is lots of activity. I saw two Boche planes brought down in five minutes, one had a wing burned clean off and came down spinning like a dry leaf, and the other came down like a dart and then crumpled right up. But I have quite decided that individually the R.F.C. is the fourth safest job in the Army, as the fighting has developed now. Infantry, Artillery and Engineer come in that order for danger; during normal times we drop back again to a safer place.

Some people talk about an extra $1 a day for "Subs"[2] in the Canadian Forces to be postdated from March or April. I don't believe it exactly but an extra £40 in a lump sum would help matters quite a bit if it ever came through.

Your parcel has not arrived as yet, but there has been very little Canadian Mail at all just lately, it seems held up somewhere.

We are on roads again now,

Your affectionate,

HECTOR

---

[1] A novel set in France, by English author Stanley J. Weyman (1855-1928).
[2] Subalterns, i.e. lieutenants.

Canadian stetcher bearers negotiating the tortured landscape of the Passchendaele battlefield. | *Archival photo*

25. 10. 17.

Dear Gerald,

Thank for your last letter and the Maple Leaves. Also please thank Mamma for the parcel which came today; the cake and sweets were fine, also the socks.

Just now we are in a warm part of the Line as you will see by the papers around this date, still there is always luck to be taken into account. Oscar must be up here as well but I have not seen him. Any how I don't expect his language will be fit for publication as it is his first sight of a real war. The Somme was pretty rotten but nothing like as much.

That pistol sounds pretty good if it lasts and you can always keep stocked with ammunition; [1] just keep enough of the money I sent over to pay my Insurance, and use the rest anytime you see a chance of having a decent time.

I am enclosing a menu for a dinner we had a few weeks ago; except that Benedictine is much stronger than it should be, and I had to ride a bicycle back.

My head is pretty well proof against headaches, but my ears hurt like the dickens when I get near a 60 pounder or some of those big Devils. [2]

---

[1] This probably refers to a 0.22" revolver that Gerald obtained for target shooting.
[2] The Canadians were pounding the German defences with heavy artillery in preparation for the attack the following morning.

The King was round our billets when he came over[1], not that he knew that they were ours; all the troops turned out on the roads to see him go by in the near Areas.

Our billets are known as Oxford Circus and Leicester Square and they look like a tube station. We had to get out of our last ones in a hurry as he got 3 of our men and twenty infantry in about 2 hours. Still it might have been worse as we had awfully good luck, though it may not sound that way.

Cheerio,
HECTOR

Australian troops navigate the duckboards across a flooded shell crater in the remains of Château Wood, Passchendaele. | *Archival photo*

---

[1] King George V visited the Vimy Ridge area (Maisnil Bouche) on June 10.

The Allies launched their next attack on Passchendaele on October 26, after painstaking preparation. The Canadians spearheaded the assault, advancing through mist and drizzle under a leaden sky, clawing their way from shell hole to flooded shell hole under heavy fire. After the first full day of fighting, they had gained a mere one hundred yards.

The weather improved marginally for the next four days while they prepared for the next push. But just before the launch of the assault on the ridge on October 30, the rain returned with a vengeance. Over the next six days, the Canadians resumed their advance, inching forward across the tortured landscape in thick mud and under constant artillery and machine gun fire, repelling numerous German counter attacks. Hector spent much of this time in the front line or no man's land laying out trenches and tracks.

The battlefield of Passchendaele, littered with dismembered bodies and the debris of war, half buried in mud. | *Archival photo*

A FINE VIEW OF THE SHOW

28. 10. 17.

Dear Marg,

I haven't written much just lately for obvious reasons; there was nothing much I could say as it was only War. I am up just below Rupert's which is no great secret, from the papers anyhow.

Rumour has it that Leave may come around sooner then expected. If it does for me I am going to spend very little time in London unless it is more attractive than I imagine it can be. Godalming will see me, and I might be able to get up your way. Bairnsfather has pictured Flanders mud but even he can't do it real justice because he has not been out during this show.[1]

The view is pretty depressing, "Pill Boxes"[2] and ammunition dumps and Tanks in all states of repair are all that you can pick up in the general waste. Except guns, and there are unlimited supplies of them; all sizes and shapes, more than axle to axle. I saw the Somme last year and our own pet show in the Spring[3] but this has them all beaten. But we have him going now if the weather gives us a chance. There are no trenches in the accepted sense of the word; men just dig little holes alongside shell craters (to collect the water) and sleep as best they can. We have a front line of course, but I was along there a few days ago and went overland most of the way. This ground does not allow for underground work, there is too much water.

Oscar must be having a pretty thin time just now. I must write and find out how things are going. This seems to be a sketchy kind of letter and does not say much after all, but it all amounts to this in the words of the Passing Show 1915 "I'm here and you're here so what do we care".[4]

The watch seems pretty useful but it needs to be, as it has been badly bunged up with mud once or twice already. How are Tiger and her job? I must write.

Your affectionate,
HECTOR

----

[1] Bruce Bairnsfather, who rose to the rank of captain in the British Army, regularly submitted articles and drawings from the Front to the British magazine The *Bystander*.
[2] The German concrete pill-boxes housed light Bergmann machine guns, whereas the heavy Maxim machine guns were usually fired from outside the concrete bunkers that protected their crews during artillery barrages.
[3] The Battle for Vimy Ridge.
[4] *The Passing Show* was a well-known revue show in London and New York, with music, dance and comedians.

30. 10. 17.

Dear Mamma,

I don't think it was very long ago that I last wrote, but anyway I may as well write now while I feel in the "Mood" as Oscar used to say. I have just finished breakfast and the others are eating their's at the present moment; there has been a great moon these last few nights and bombs of course have been dropped by the hundreds every night, still so far everyone is O.K. and we are doing the same to him, and better.

When we get out of the Line I will see about the photo. There seems to have been quite a General Post around Aldergrove in the way of changing farms and I don't blame any of the people.[1] Thanks very much for the "Queen" cutting. So far I have not had a chance to start it up, but this high pressure can't last for ever.

The lamp seems pretty nice for dark nights around the place and would be a great help out here. But the old Boche does not allow them, so we go about our work like a cat. It is no joke taking 150 men out to a job

Canadian troops bringing more duckboards to the front at Passchendaele, watch as German prisoners under guard carry out Allied wounded on stretchers. | *Archival photo*

---

[1] The hard times in the farming community were forcing the sale of a number of properties.

over ground you have scarcely seen before and start them working, with trenches and trails everywhere, and everything as black as pitch.

The enclosure from Ags never arrived so I suppose it was not to be found; if I was not so beastly lazy I would write to Irene and her myself;[1] but I am, so if they want any news you might enclose mine when you write.

Italy has had rather a bump in the last few days.[2] Leave is now 14 days and I want to get over for Founders Day.[3]

Your affectionate,
HECTOR

An Allied soldier with a fallen comrade at Château Wood, Passchendaele. | *Archival photo*

---

3. 11. 17.

Dear Mamma,

Everything going on pretty cheerfully here and Canada is doing the impossible once more, and paying for it.

I saw Oscar yesterday for little; he had just come up and is not very far from us. There is no news of course other than what is in the papers, but things are happening to the Boche that need some explaining away in his home papers. Of course Italy has given him all kinds of Morale and he hates to leave his Pill Boxes on the ridges and go down into the low plains behind.

Oscar is very anxious to get up and see some more of the war before his commission comes through; he does not appear to suffer from "nerves", very far from it, but is not exactly despondent over the chance

---

[1] Agnes and Irene Jackson , Hector's aunts.
[2] On October 24, Austrian and German forces broke through the Italian lines at Caporetto. Italy was a member of the Allies.
[3] Founders of Charterhouse School.

of spending Xmas in England.

I have another little job at 3.30 tomorrow morning fixing up a road for the guns; it is all guns here, everything depends on them, and if the roads are not fixed, the attack just hangs fire until they are.

We have just got in about 30 new Records for the gramophone, some of them are not at all bad.

Your affectionate,
HECTOR

The Germans finally yielded the pulverised morasse that had once been the village of Passchendaele on November 6 and retreated from the ridge.

Hector once again emerged from the battle unscathed, with nothing more serious than a rip in his trench coat, sliced by shrapnel from an exploding shell. He was later awarded the Military Cross for his actions during the battle for Passchendaele. Characteristically, he made little mention of it in his letters, referring to it in passing as "the Booby prize" in a letter to his brother Gerald. Hector offered no explanation in his letters of what the award was for, but the official citation read:

<u>MILITARY CROSS</u>
<u>DEED OF ACTION</u>
Lieutenant Hector John Roderick <u>JACKSON</u>
<u>Canadian Engineers</u>

For conspicuous gallantry and devotion to duty in marking out and digging a trench under heavy fire. Having completed the work, he made a reconnaissance, with two sappers, to look for wounded, and finding two brought them five miles to the dressing station.

(Authority: *London Gazette* number 30507, dated 4 February, 1918.)

It was only when the village of Passchendaele was finally captured that General Haig's pride allowed him to call a halt to the carnage. During the battle, the Allies suffered some 310,000 casualties (more than 10,000 casualties for each square mile captured); the Germans suffered a further 260,000 casualties of their own. Over three quarters of the 20,000 Canadian troops involved in the Battle of

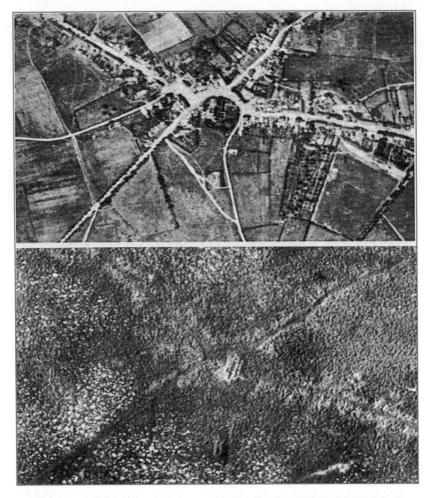

Before and after air photos of Passchendaele show the complete destruction of the village, and the density of shell craters. | *Archival photo*

Passchendaele were killed or wounded. The cemeteries of "Flanders Fields" were filling fast.

The winter of 1917-1918 set in around the middle of November, and both sides began digging in yet again for the long wait until the regular spring offensive.

On November 16, Hector's unit was finally withdrawn from the front at Ypres/Passchendaele. For two days, the engineers travelled by foot, truck and train twenty miles southwest, to a camp near the small village of La Brearde, three miles northeast of Hazebrouck. After a short rest they travelled on, apparently mainly on foot, a further twenty miles south, back to the Bruay-la-Buissière area, twelve miles northwest of Vimy Ridge. There Hector's unit spent from November 26 to late December retraining and recovering from the exhaustion of Passchendaele.

There is a six-week break in Hector's letters from the climax of the Battle of Passchendaele, through the move back to Bruay. Only after he was unexpectedly given two weeks leave in the middle of December did the regular flow of letters resume. It is not clear whether this gap was due to the pace of the war and an inability to write while on the move, or because letters went astray. The lack of any mention of the gap in his ensuing letters, suggests the latter. German submarines sank well over 100 Allied vessels during November and the first half of December. No doubt many of these lost ships were carrying letters from the front.

Hector left his unit for England on leave on December 11, 1917, and wrote to his mother the following day.

> 51, Chepstow Place,
> Pembridge Square, W.
> 14. 12. 17.

Dear Mamma,

I have managed to pull down another leave, which came rather unexpectedly. I had not counted on one much before the end of Jan.

The 12th was Founders Day, so naturally I went down there and had a look around. After the service having seen Tod and Miss Turner I had a meal at Revills, as Tod was going up to Old Charterhouse,[1] and went to tea at Sylvesters. Finishing with a supper at the Lovejoys where I ran across Mrs. and Maud Goddard, and so to bed and Town next day.

This evening I am off to Tunbridge Wells to see the family of Cole and then am free to look up London people; unless I make one more stab at travelling and see Mr. Housman.

It looks remarkably like rain today worse luck, which is cheerful for my leave.

---

[1] Alexander Tod had been Hector's housemaster; he was a close friend of Lord Baden-Powell, the founder of the scouting movement, and taught at Charterhouse for forty years. Old Charterhouse was the original school site in London which was used for the youngest pupils.

This is an awful nib. We will be back in the Line when I get back to Lens again, unless they decide on Cambrai for a change. Passchendaele was our worst trip yet and the two weeks rest was very much needed.

I will send my old Trench Coat back as a souvenir, and put some more in the pockets if I can.

Your affectionate,
HECTOR

Savoy Hotel,
London W.C.2.
20. 12. 17.

Dear Mamma,

I have nothing much to do for the time, so decided to come in here and write letters.

I've had a splendid time so far with a few days left still. At 1.30 am having lunch with Mr. Ward and on Friday am going down to Cambridge to see Mr. Housman.

Everyone was very well at Tunbridge Wells and they gave me a fine time. We had an air raid here last night; an awfully feeble attempt after Ypres, but it stopped the theatre party.

There is a dickens of a fog now which may get worse. I saw Marg and Tiger again,

Your affectionate,
HECTOR

Ici,
Now.[1]

Dear Marg,

Just got back from Cambridge and came into see what you were doing. I have tickets for Pamela tomorrow night (Monday). With any luck I can come in again but don't know for sure. I suppose Tiger can't get away. Sorry to have missed you.

HECTOR

---

[1] Probably Marg's accommodation in Leinster Square, London, Sunday December 23, 1917.

Hotel Folkestone,
Boulogne-sur-Mer.[1]
26. 12. 17.

Dear Mamma,

Well "Thats That" and I am on the first stage of the return journey after a fine leave and a long one.

I saw Mr. Housman and stayed a night at Trinity,[2] and then spent the last four days in Town. Saw Florence Horne before she went back to Esernck [?] to nurse Pembertons once more. And Marion Bostock, the eldest sister who is a House Surgeon. And Marg and Tiger at intervals. On Xmas day I went to St. Paul's with them for the service.

There should be lots of mail for me when I get back including some from Aldergrove. And parcels. So far I have had three Xmas presents, not so bad for war time, including an awfully nice leather case from Auntie Zoub, Vera and Dulcie.[3] And another for photos from the Pembertons with a photo of the boy who was killed.

I wonder if you knew a Murray Hamwick, Secretary to the Governor of Madras. I met the daughter who was at tea at one of the many places of call, and knew the brother in Gownboys.[4] Also Gowie[5] in charge of Indian Police in the same part of the world.

It is snowing outside and I have to stay overnight for a connection. Your affectionate,
HECTOR

While Hector reveled in his leave in England, the rest of his unit completed re-training and returned to Ablain St. Nazaire, near its base in the Vimy Ridge area. Hector rejoined them on December 27 and was advised by his commanding officer, Colonel Wilgar, that he had been awarded the Military Cross for his work at Passchendaele.

---

[1] A port on the French coast, across the Straits of Dover from Folkestone.

[2] Trinity College, Cambridge. In a letter to Moses dated August 24, 1918, Housman wrote "Hector stayed here a day or two in the winter, and has grown up rather a distinguished-looking fellow."

[3] Members of the Cole family. Auntie Zoub was Elizabeth Muirhead Cole, Moses' elder sister.

[4] One of the Houses at Charterhouse.

[5] Spelling uncertain.

Hector returned to the snow-covered front line next day to continue strengthening the defences and preparing machine gun emplacements in western Lens, very close to where he had been immediately before his unit's transfer to Passchendaele. Conditions were generally much quieter than when the unit had left in October, although the shelling by both sides continued and aircraft bombing had reportedly increased slightly.

30. 12. 17.

Dear Gerald,

I got back from leave a few days ago and went right up the line in the Lens / Vimy Ridge area the next morning which was rather a jar. But we are having it pretty easy, just like peace after Ypres, so it is not so bad.

Oscar is out on Rest and I won't see him for some time, but he can't be very far away.

I had a splendid leave and lots of it, saw most people I intended to see and some I had not expected, including Marion Bostock the eldest girl who is house Surgeon at St. Georges Hospital, and quite a knut [sic].

I posted a letter to Mamma that I forgot to send, written before I went on leave.

You may be interested to hear I have got the Booby Prize at last after four attempts, and am enclosing a piece of M.C. Ribbon.[1]

We have snow everywhere; but it is milder today and rather slushy for a change. I bought a fine pair of Musquash[2] gloves for the cold as I intend to keep warm; in fact I spent more on clothes than I did on leave, which was very cheap.

The Pembertons have sent the Vimy papers to Tiger who is copying them and sending them on, I believe.

Mrs. Rendall sent me 60 woolen knitted caps for wearing under the Tin Hats for the men in my section. And I had lots of parcels including a fine one from Mamma. We are having the pudding for New Year.

Your affectionate,
HECTOR

---

[1] The Military Cross. Hector had been put up for the M.C. on three previous occasions, one at Vimy Ridge, the others unknown.

[2] A beaver-like animal with dark glossy brown fur.

4 th. Canadian Division.

A. 42-226.

C. R. E.,

4th. Canadian Division.

Under auth ority granted by His Majesty
the King, the Field Marshall Commanding-in-Chief has
awarded the undermentioned De corations.

Please con vey to the receipient the
congratulations of the Army, Corps and Divisional Commanders

The awards will be published in the
London Gazette in due course.

The Militar y Cross.

Lieut. H. J. R. Jackson   10th. Field Company, C. E.

Authority M.S./R/7675 dated 1 6-12-17, Canadian Corps
M.S.21-4-103 dated 23-12-17.

(Signed) D.H.Barnett, Captain
For D. A. A. G. (a)

*The official message announcing the award of the Military Cross to Hector. |
Source: Library and Archives Canada*

8. 1. 18.

Dear Mamma,

Many thanks indeed for the parcel which arrived in fine condition
just as I was going forward, it was awfully nice of you to send it, and the
pudding was fine, we had it for New Years Day in forward billets. Also the
cake and fudge.

Conscription is going to stir some of the country people and make a change. Glad I got away before it started, and Oscar too. Gerald of course will be exempted as the last.[1]

I won't be a Captain if the war lasts five years, the way promotion goes. We do the work of Majors of infantry, and never argue with anyone below that rank; mere lieutenants in the infantry don't count while we are on the job; but a lieut I am and will remain.

I hear that the Vimy papers have been sent off at last. Thanks for the enclosure. I suppose I better send something along to our mutual enemy, he was quite jovial when I went down there.[2]

I see Marg puts M.C. after my name on letters. I don't want it; it's quite unnecessary and looks rotten, I think.

Must see Oscar some time and find out the news. Xmas parcels still coming in from unexpected people. Ottawa still fruitful.

Your affectionate,
HECTOR

---

8. 1. 18.

Dear Marg,

Just got your letter and the correct address. I was half afraid my coat would have gone astray. I don't remember what I have in the way of souvenirs, the thing you speak of is a fuse, more commonly called "Minnie". Something like a "Rum jar". I got it from a Boche dug out on Vimy Ridge, but the explosive has been taken out. The tray I beat out myself down at the Somme from an 18 pdr. shell case from Courcelette.[3] Thanks very much for sending them; let me know the damage. Also I would like a pair Chamoix leather short drawers for cold weather. Army and Navy Stores keep them.

The Xmas show went off alright, Dinner with Mrs. Cowie. Marion Bostock was there also. Not too bad rather "heavy draught"; the party had more juveniles than I was prepared for but went hilariously enough.

I am back again from the Line now; we had a very quiet tour for a

---

[1] The Canadian Government exempted persons under the age of nineteen, and "farmers and farm help" from conscription, to allow farming to continue. Gerald was then seventeen years old. The agricultural exemption was rescinded three months later on April 20, 1918, after particularly heavy Canadian casualties on the Western Front.
[2] This may refer to Housman, whom both Rosa and Hector may have regarded as being a potential rival for Moses affection.
[3] Where Hector was based in November 1916, soon after arriving in France.

change. Oscar is away back at Rest just now, but I gather the billets are none too comfortable.

So sorry to hear you are seedy, hope things are brighter again now. Best luck,

Your affectionate,

HECTOR

P.S. It is correct I suppose, but I don't want M.C. after my letters.

[Part of a letter; date not known, probably to his mother at Applegarth]

I wonder if the Trench coat and souvenirs arrived. Note the tear on left shoulder blade, it was my nearest squeak, a shell splinter at Passchendaele. The blood on the right is not my own; young Pemberton's I think.

By the way, Lady Constance[1] sent me a nice little leather case with photos of him taken out here in Bouvigny Woods[2] the day before he went up with me to the Ridge (someone smuggled a camera). The large mushroom thing is a "Minenwerfer" fuse commonly called "Minnie". I picked it up from a dug out on Vimy Ridge and got out the explosive. The "Minnie" is 11" dia. and 40" long, a perfectly devilish thing for breaking in dug outs. I was 35 ft. from one when it exploded. The tray I beat out myself from an 18 pdr. shell case from Courcelette at the Somme and have been packing it around ever since. The others are Boche 77 fuses.[3]

HECTOR

---

19. 1. 18.

Dear Gerald,

Just got back from the Line again, and having most hopeless weather. Am enclosing a snap taken out here from last Spring at Ablain St. Nazaire, famous for the French attack from there in 1915 around Notre

---

[1] Lady Constance Pemberton.

[2] In the back area, northwest of Vimy Ridge, southwest of Lens.

[3] From German 77mm. field gun shells.

Dame de Lorette.[1] My billet, a very temporary affair in the background, I don't think it gives away any military secrets.

Hope to see Oscar in a few days now.

> Best luck,
> HECTOR

---

25. 1. 18.

Dear Mamma,

Just got a Canadian mail so I will answer any of your questions. No time for more just now though things are quite easy with us.

Thanks for the statement of the Insurance people and Zoub's letters. I did not expect to have as much on hand. Still it does no harm, and one of these days may come in handy to tide over. "Betty" had to be shot a short time ago which is rather rotten luck as she was in great shape and had wintered well.[2] Tetanus set in somehow and it was no use trying to monkey around with her.

We have had things easy except perhaps for Oscar's people who may have got drawn in.

> Must stop now for the time,
> Your affectionate,
> HECTOR

---

26. 1. 18.

Dear Mamma,

We are rather busy just now, and have at last had decent weather to work in. It gets rather monotonous wading around in water which comes up to your knees in a few places and above your ankles most of the way. But don't believe the photos or rather pictures you see of men standing waist deep in water, its all rot. Any man can find a shell hole which would drown him if he wants to after heavy rains, but 10" of water and mud is the limit of anything I have experienced, taken right along as an average; and that's pretty fierce.

---

[1] This was Hector's Back Area billet just before the Battle of Vimy Ridge. Notre Dame de Lorette is a local church where some 44,000 French soldiers who died defending against a German attack in March 1915 were buried.

[2] Betty was one of Hector's two horses.

Oscar and Rupert wrote a few ago, both were in Rest at the time, but should be up by now.

I suppose the Vimy papers have arrived by now, like most much advertised things they will fall rather flat actually. Am sending along the programme of our 4th Divisional Pantomime, all local talent, and the dresses and scenery are great. The Maple Leaf is our sign as you may have guessed. Also plan of our old dug-out to give an idea of the room we have. Last summer I was up there alone for 3 weeks, but we have had 3 officers, and plenty of room. It is great weather just now and the frost has all gone for the time.

Marg wrote today and seems to have left out the Minnie fuse I spoke of; it can go some other time.

I wrote a short note to Mrs. Berry[1] in acknowledgement of the Langley Parcel, but if it comes from Aldergrove after all you might thank them from me, though the men appreciate them even more than we do, as they have not the same chance of buying, or the money for extras above Army Rations. Still it shows people think of us. Do you know that I am eligible for three months leave to Canada in March[2], having left there two years on the 11th. Unfortunately it needs "Pull" from the Canadian end. I can put in, as I most likely will, but there are thousands of applications in all the time, and only a few hundred have gone. It needs persuasion and lots of luck.

Canada mail has been held up a bit just lately.

Your affectionate,
HECTOR

---

11. 2. 18.

Dear Mamma,

Have only time for a short note as we are pretty busy. Oscar phoned a few days ago that he was getting leave, so I expect he is in England by now. He has been pretty lucky, only seven months for the first leave.

We have had splendid weather for the last two weeks, but a change is coming on and I can see rotten weather ahead till March anyway.

I had letters from both the Bostock girls which rather surprised me as I had not written for over a year except for Xmas cards. Jean is a

---

[1] Lydia Berry, wife of a prominent dairy farmer John W. Berry. Mrs Berry was president of the Langley Prairie "circle" of the Canadian Red Cross, which sent parcels to local soldiers overseas.
[2] The leave never materialized.

V.A.D. of sorts at Waverley Abbey Hospital,[1] and the other is with her people in Vancouver.

Willie is engaged to one of Mrs. Hill Tout's cousins and is out here now somewhere quite close I believe.

I don't understand what you mean by a loan of $20. I did not borrow anything that I remember. Is there any money to my credit from assigned pay?

My old kit has just about had its day so I got myself a new outfit when I was on leave, from boots up to trench coat, and feel all the better for it.[2] We have been forward for about two weeks now. Very quiet as quietness goes, but have been living on 5 hours sleep a day for the last week, and thriving on it.

Have an awful pile of unanswered mail.

Your affectionate,

HECTOR

---

13. 2. 18.

Dear Mamma,

I find I had not sent a short note I wrote a few days ago, and have just got another from you full of questions about Leave. I think I have answered most since. This will be just answers as nothing has happened since 11. 2. 18. It is the same coat in the photos I sent off last December. The gas mask is <u>inside</u> the canvas haversack on the chest protected from wet. The choice of background was very limited, as no civilian photographer is allowed with a camera outside his studio area. The camera was in the doorway of the shop and I was on the road.

I must have written Dolly by mistake for Betty in the photos.[3]

Mrs. Rendall did not recognise me, of course, though a younger woman Miss . . . [indecipherable] perhaps thought she had seen me somewhere, before I said who I was. Branksome has quite a few boys, but all infants. Charterhouse is absolutely overflowing, 645 I think.

The interrupted theatre party during the Raid was with the Maynard Hornes. Swan and Edgars is going as strong as ever, cleaned up in a night almost.

---

[1] Waverly Abbey House, near Farnum, SW of London, was converted to a hospital for the duration of the First World War.

[2] Unlike enlisted men, officers in the British and Commonwealth armies generally had to purchase their own uniforms.

[3] Referring to his horses.

I don't know Tiger's latest job, she is with Miss Young near Holland Park. I met them usually at Marg's place, Leinster Square, and saw a show and a lunch and St. Paul's for Xmas.[1]

Must close,
HECTOR

---

19. 2. 18.

Dear Gerald,

I have an unanswered letter of yours, and anyhow I have not written to B.C. for some time owing to a war.

I think you will find several of the officers appear in the Mênu or perhaps it is only their nicknames.

Many happy returns for the 13th. I hope this arrives in time; as for a present it does not exist except of course take what money you want at any time from the monthly assigned pay, whenever you get a chance of a visit: mind you do this. I know the $15 doesn't go very far, but it is something, and is meant to be spent on 1st, my insurance, and then on necessities and any holidays.

Branksome was just as usual; a few more boys, but all very young, from 8 to 12. Mr. Newton is still there.[2] Miss Cunningham has left and is staying with a rich Godmother. Mr. Furnival is in Canada I believe.

Hector had his photo taken by a French village photographer. | *Family album*

---

[1] Holland Park and Leinster Square are both near Hyde Park.

[2] Joseph Newton was a schoolmaster at Branksome School.

We are resting again, but doing Rear Area work of course. So only get a few days off a week, and then have the usual parades. I was billeting officer again and had lots of fun. I could write a book on it.

> Must stop,
> Yr. Affectionate,
> HECTOR

---

26. 2. 18.

Dear Marg,

Just got your letter. It is rather a long time since I wrote last, and also thanks for the chamoix drawers. I don't know how much the postage on the coat was, but am sending £2 to cover them both.

Please congratulate Helen from me on her Exams, and take what is left over for yourself.

We have been having a fine moon for bombing just lately but have had nothing at all near round our parts, and anyhow the wind is rather high for flying.

How did the War seem to strike Oscar? I suppose he spoke very little about it, it's almost impossible to do so to anyone who has not come out; but get a fellow spirit and the job is to change the subject.

I am back just now, but working and have a clean billet in a farm house.[1] Have a silent feud with the people, the first time I have had that sort of thing, and I hope the last. I was billeting officer too, which makes it more absurd, but I think I have fixed them for a while now.

Why does Tiger insist on giving the wrong address?

> Your affectionate,
> HECTOR

---

18. 3. 18.

Dear Gerald,

I have not written for quite a time now for various reasons, chiefly laziness I suppose, but as we have been having Canadian mail lately with three from Aldergrove I intend to start up the War Correspondent Game

---

[1] On February 19, Hector's unit had moved to the village of Hersin Coupigny, six miles behind the lines. He worked in that sector for about three weeks, before returning to the Ablain St. Nazaire area.

once more. And will begin by commenting on the letters received, both yours and Mamma's, as I suppose mine will be read by both of you.

To begin with there is not much to write about my Leave outside of what I have already said, without going into diary details which have to be written up each day, or else are forgotten. Florence Horne I met at the Lawsons at tennis; her father is a doctor near Harley Street. She herself is one of the "Mayfair Beauties" as they are nicknamed, working at the Countess of Lyttons Hospital, with such people as the Ladies Eileen Wellesley,[1] Gordon-Cumming, Irene Denison,[2] Bettine Stuart-Worsley and that crowd, but is herself not in the least affected. I usually see a show and have dinner each leave. She had nothing to do with the Pembertons at all.

The Bostocks, Mrs. Nan and Ruth are in Vanc. or were all winter, but they may have left for Ottawa by now. Marg came over to Chepstow Place one evening for an hour before we went to a show. Mr. Ward was not in; he never dines at home now but gets home at ten, and I only see him at breakfast.

Now that the new Rations are in I will put up somewhere else after calling on him, as it will be awfully inconvenient to draw any extra.[3]

The cream cheese arrived in fine shape with only a trace of green under the paper, and was greatly appreciated in the Mess by everyone; it was certainly a fine specimen.[4]

As for the M.C., I have not actually seen the wording of the award itself, but it was for a trench by Passchendaele Church I believe. So far it has not been presented except by a fair demoiselle in one of the towns from whom I bought the ribbon and made her present it to me with "military honours". I suppose the Divisional Commander will give them out to all the batch. The Buckingham Palace affair is the time the actual cross is given.[5]

Our O.C.'s name is Major Wilgar, D.S.O. Trench names are chosen at random. The Staff before an offensive get hold of maps of "Heinies" Back Area and trench systems, then choose a letter which covers a certain Area, and every trench begins with that letter taken straight out of a dictionary. When we get the trenches from him they are ready named

---

[1] Daughter of the 4th Duke of Wellington, b.1887.

[2] Lady Irene Francis Adza Denison, b.1890.

[3] The food ration, controlled through "ration books", was progressively reduced in England as the war progressed.

[4] Probably home made from Applegarth milk.

[5] The medal is held by Hector's nephew.

except for signs; the new ones we dig of course are named after different people or any characteristic such as "mud", "slimy", "lovers lane" , "Phyllis Dare"[1] or anything that comes into your head. We had a trench junction of three with signs Chu Chin Chow.[2]

I certainly remember that Chalk Pit Episode;[3] I had my Leave Ticket on me at the time and did not see much chance of using it as the Boche put over everything he had. Luckily we had only about 10 casualties; half wounded. I am, on the contrary getting less used to shells dropping around me, the same as everyone else. The best chances of doing anything wonderful were the first day I landed, as I did not know enough to realise what a mess a shell can make of a party.

Mamma did not enclose Tod's letter; anyhow I don't suppose I could have read it. I see Verites and Gownboys had a fire, but have not heard what damage was done.[4]

Olga Bell is flourishing; V.A.D.ing for all she is worth, when she is not having or giving tea fights and skiing parties at Ottawa. She says the Cavendish girls are very pretty, which I don't doubt, but I suppose they must be exceptional by the way she speaks. Childe-Pemberton himself has no rank as he is not in the Army; I think he used to amuse himself writing and sketching in Europe before the war, from his talk. They live on Portman Street;[5] he is a Mr. by the way. He was in the 11th Hussars attached to us for work as a Cavalry pioneer unit but of course in the Imperials.

Mamma must have had an awful trip back from Burnaby Lake.[6] I suppose the Yale Road has not improved much during the War.

As for the socks, it is not worth while. I turn in my old socks to the Q.M. as it is an Army Order about wasting clothing, so they are not wasted, and I have enough socks sent out to keep me in hand knitted. I

---

[1] An attractive English actress.

[2] A very long-running London musical.

[3] Possibly referring to an incident during the fighting on the outskirts of Lens in early June the previous year.

[4] Houses at Charterhouse School.

[5] Immediately east of Marble Arch in London.

[6] Burnaby Lake is half way between Vancouver and New Westminster; the Yale Road was the main road into New Westminster from the Fraser Valley and ran through the village of Aldergrove. Rosa may have traveled to Burnaby to visit the Sprotts, who were family friends and lived at Burnaby Lake.

have to tell people not to send a bunch at a time, so now I have the supply regulated. Anyhow spare pairs make a good pillow in the head of my bed till wanted.

Thanks very much for the good wishes for the 27[1], in plenty of time this year.

The M.C. is correct I suppose but only used in official letters I get from Brigade and such. I am a Temp Lieut, no Mercenary so it seems superfluous to put it on their letters of course.

We have nothing to do with the defence of the Line except in an emergency. The only time I wander around No Mans Land is for jumping off trenches or reconnaissance of our wire. It is surprising how ten minutes change your views when we hear about a jumping off trench to be dug, or a piece of line to be straightened out. The first thing when parties have been arranged, tools and rendezvous and time fixed, is to go up and pick out the place by daylight, with the help of the battalion Scouts Officer, or Company Commander and a periscope. Then just at dusk I get out with a few sappers, about two, or three if it's very much to be done, and run

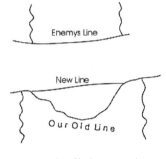

out the tape and get back in time to start the party, and tell them to dig like Hell and get done. You ought to see the dirt fly. The first time I get out it is crawling around when a flare goes up, and all kinds of caution; by the end we patrol up and down the line in a casual way, unless of course the Boche really gets nasty, when we make ourselves scarce till it blows over, as low to the ground as possible.

Oscar came over yesterday afternoon for a few hours; he is not very far away just now. He seems to have had a fairly good leave, but not having a commission jars a bit.

The weather is great now and looks as though it may last for a few days to come; planes are everywhere about and it feels like Spring. I suppose you will be getting a rotten end of the winter to make up for it. South Aldergrove is a poor bunch of Conchies[2] from all accounts, but I suppose you can't expect much else. If they are really needed they will go alright. But the West is away ahead of the East in recruits still, so the few who stay behind benefit by those gone, and will till the East balances things up again.

---

[1] Hector was turning 26 on March 27, 1918.
[2] Conscientious objectors and draft dodgers.

This is an awful long scrawl for some unearthly reason, but I had three of your letters and four of Mamma's to answer, and - a secret - I have six of Muriel Sprott's!
Must close now and write a few letters if I can expect any back.
Best luck,
HECTOR

———————

Chapter 9

The Last Spring Offensive

On March 21, 1918, the Germans launched a huge spring offensive, code named Operation Michael. Four months earlier, during Russia's Bolshevik Revolution, Lenin's Communist government had wrested power from Aleksandr Kerensky which had in turn overthrown the autocratic regime of Czar Nicholas II. The huge loss of Russian life on the Eastern Front under the Czar's inept leadership had been one of the root causes of the revolution, and it was obvious that the new Russian government planned to extricate itself from the war. It opened negotiations with Germany just before Christmas 1917, and these negotiations resulted in a peace treaty signed on March 3, 1918.

The Russian withdrawal from the Eastern Front freed a million German troops to shore up the Western Front in France and allow the launch of Operation Michael. By this time, American troops were starting to arrive in France, and the German high command realized that any delay would allow the Allied troops to be reinforced to such a degree that no offensive could succeed.

The German attack was launched on the morning of March 21 from the well-defended Hindenburg Line, over a sixty-mile front. The offensive targeted the Allied defences immediately southeast of Hector's sector of the line at Lens. The attack began with the usual earth shaking barrage from 6,000 pieces of heavy artillery, firing lethal gas and high-explosive shells deep into the Allied lines. The German infantry then rapidly advanced through the cover of a thick blanket of morning mist.

Although the German forces outnumbered the Allies by more than two to one in the Vimy Ridge area, they advanced little in that sector; to the south, however, on the Somme, they swept the Allies before them. In five days, they had captured the town of Albert, where Hector had been stationed when he first arrived in France and threatened to split the British and French armies completely.

The 1st Canadian Division was withdrawn from Hill 70 on the northern edge of Lens, to reinforce the line near Albert, and Hector's 4th Division was spread out thinly to cover the resulting gap. As part of this re-deployment, Hector's unit was moved to the village of Le Brebis, just north of Lens on March 24. There the engineers stood-to, i.e. at their action stations, for several nights in a row, in anticipation of an imminent German attack; the attack only occurred a few weeks later.

Buoyed by the influx of new reinforcements from the Russian Front, the Germans continued to advance rapidly southwest from the Hindenburg Line, overrunning the British and French lines and pushing many miles further into France, towards Paris. The British papers were full of gloom and doom at the Germans' rapid advance. Hector's constant movement prevented him from writing letters for a couple of weeks.

At the end of March, with the Germans still making headway, Hector's 10th Field Company was deployed ten miles south to help shore up the new defence line in the sector south of Vimy Ridge. The unit established its headquarters in the village of Auzin St. Aubin, immediately northwest of the ruined city of Arras, to whose shattered doorstep the Germans had quickly advanced.

31. 3. 18.

Dear Mamma,

We are having a little more movement than usual and I have slept in ten different places in the last fortnight, all kinds and shapes, from sheets to cellars. I believe the Kaiser was to be in Paris tomorrow, but as one of our generals pointed out he did not think it advisable to come our way.

Mail both ways has been held up a bit I believe, and I have not written a letter for weeks. This is only a scrawl. We only got here a few hours ago and I was out all yesterday on work, and this morning. Oscar must be near us but [I am] not quite sure of his location. I have heard from Marg and Tiger of Rupert's leave; he does not seem to get any too many.

Considering that there is a war on, it is quiet by us. We are just spectators for the time; rather a change for us. Thanks for the letters for my birthday. I spent the day wandering around a perfectly new Area trying to get acquainted and seeing historic places.

Must stop,
Your affectionate,
HECTOR

The German attack was more successful than its planners had expected. The defending Allies suffered 350,000 casualties in the first six weeks of the offensive and had to rush in additional reinforcements from reserves in England. The very success of the initial attack, however, proved its undoing. The German front troops soon outran their supply lines and the advance finally ground to an exhausted halt on April 7, just fifty miles short of Paris.

This first major German offensive was immediately followed by two more attacks to the north of Hector's area, south of Ypres. The attacks, collectively named Operation Georgette, began on April 9. The Allies (including the Portuguese Expeditionary Force this time) collapsed in the face of the determined German attack. Operation Georgette resulted in the recapture of the Passchendaele ridge that had been won by the Allies at such enormous cost just five months earlier, and pushed southwest for a further ten miles. Arras became a vulnerable bulge in the line, partially surrounded by the advancing German Army.

The British and Canadians finally managed to stem the advance, but they suffered an additional 100,000 casualties in the process. While Hector was in the Arras area, he and his troops stood-to periodically in anticipation of German attacks. These did not materialize, so he had a relatively quiet time reinforcing the defences that protected the remains of the city, while battles raged to the north and south. Hector seemed characteristically unconcerned by his precarious position when he wrote a short note to Gerald, two days after Operation Georgette was launched.

11. 4. 18.

Dear Gerald,

Have not very much time these days to write, but we are having nothing very exciting just yet. Noisy of course and the odd scare.[1]

Oscar wrote a few days ago and seemed alright. Rupert is held up or was at the Base like some of our officers on leave.

The weather has changed now for a month's wet weather I think, before summer sets in for good. Saw a fine show last night at the Divisional Theatre, but had to walk back an awful long way which spoiled things.[2]

Best luck,
Your affectionate,
HECTOR

———————

21. 4. 18.

Dear Marg,

All going strong only busy. I have been having an awful bunch of tearful letters just lately, but I can't see why; the old Boche has bitten off lots but has not digested it yet by a long sight.

Hope you are having as good weather as ourselves, it's great out at night. Only the moon seems rather superfluous and tantalising. Especially with all leave cancelled.

No time for more,
Your affectionate,
HECTOR

25. 4. 18.

Dear Marg,

O.K. Just got out of the Line for a few days. We had a quiet tour with lots of work and a certain amount of quiet fun. Heard from Oscar yesterday who must be south of us quite a bit. This war has rather put the lid on his affair. Can't possibly get over till the end of June at the earliest, unless the odd splinter comes my way.

Anyway England will improve further the next five months.

No news or time,
Your affectionate,
HECTOR

---

[1] The unit's official diary reported that enemy attacks were expected on April 18 and 19, but they didn't materialize.
[2] Presumably the show was at Divisional Headquartes at Maroeuil, two miles away.

2. 5. 18.

Dear Marg,

I am writing this in rustic simplicity sprawled out on the grass with a great sun and nothing to do. Everything fine as usual and chesty as ever; really am quite looking forward to something a little more like war. We won our first game of football a few days ago, against three companies combined, with half our people up the line; not so bad. I want Leave, this Spring weather is making me dream dreams, and look around for something to do.

Very little mail just lately but some should be on the way,
Your affectionate,
HECTOR

On May 7, 1918, Hector's unit moved by vehicle northwards back towards Bruay-la-Buissière for intensive training, initially in the hamlet of Hermin. The war had broken free of the old trench line and become more mobile; to meet the changing situation, the training concentrated on bridge construction and demolition.

There were also organizational changes made. Until the spring of 1918, the engineers had provided the technical expertise and leadership on engineering projects, while the infantry worked under the engineers' direction. The Canadian commanders decided to augment the engineer units with additional troops so that they could provide their own labour force for engineering projects, without the need to draw on front line troops.

As part of this reorganization, and with the growing need to adapt to the more mobile form of warfare, each division assembled its own specialist bridging unit, nominally consisting of a captain, two lieutenants and fifty to seventy non-commissioned officers and men. On May 23, Hector was advised that he was to be promoted from lieutenant to the rank of captain, although this did not take effect immediately. He was given command of the planned 4th Canadian Pontoon Bridging Transport Unit.

After two days in Hermin, the 10th Field Company marched fifteen miles northwest, to Burbure. The unit was officially disbanded the next day, and its members immediately became the nucleus of the new 4th Divisional Pontoon Bridging Unit. The new unit's war diary listed the planned complement as three officers, nine non-commissioned officers and fifty-four four other ranks. They were equipped with eleven wagons and sixty-six horses and mules to carry sufficient material to build three seventy-five-foot bridges. The unit was also provided with a motorcycle which Hector soon commandeered. He spent the next five weeks at Burbure, gradually building up and training his new unit.

On May 27, in spite of the exhausted condition of their troops, the Germans began their third offensive, attacking again just southeast of the Hindenburg Line, ninety miles southeast of Hector's area. Their ultimate aim was to capture Paris and so break the Allies resistance.

The Germans pushed the Allies back a further thirty miles before again being halted by the French 6th Army. For the first time American troops participated in the battle. This action did not affect Hector, although there were contingency plans to defend the line northwest of Vimy Ridge if a new German attack was launched there. The orders, recorded in the unit's diary, read in part: "Resistance is to be offered the enemy at every step and no ground is to be yielded. Units must fight their areas to the last." Nothing came of the threat however, and Hector found time to catch up on letter writing after a gap of almost four weeks.

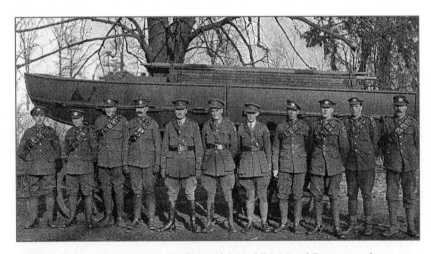

Officers and non-commissioned officers of the 3rd Divisional Pontoon and Bridging Transport Unit, a unit identical to Hector's. | *Archival photo*

28. 5. 18.

Dear Marg,

All serene and nothing special doing. I hope this applies to yourself. You can see I have had a dose of mail to censor. "Hoping this finds you as it leaves me."

I heard from Oscar today, which reminded me that I had not written for ages to anyone, so am going to make up for it now in a few cases anyway.

We are having priceless weather; not too hot and yet no rain, quite spoiled in fact for the kind we can expect soon. I have changed my job, or rather have had it changed for me, and will let you know when things are really more definite.

Its getting dark, and we get up early, so am off.

Your affectionate,

HECTOR

———————

18. 6. 18.

Dear Mamma,

I hope the tumble was not as bad as it sounds, and that you can get about alright now. I got your letter only a few days ago with a few other Canadian letters. I have not had any leave since Xmas and don't expect any for months the way things are at present, still we are not having anything very strenuous and, except for the monotony and sameness, it is a pretty Bon war.

I suppose you heard rumours of a change in my job; just why I am here needs a long explanation which can wait; and anyhow is not very important, but the fact remains that I am.

It is a mounted job in charge of pontoon and trestle wagons of the Field Coys. in our Division. So I am O.C. Bridges if things waken up and we have to bridge canals and rivers.

In theory I am O.C. (Captain) with 2 Lieuts and about 50 odd men and as many horses. Two horses for myself and a motor cycle and no more trench work. In practice I am a Lieut. doing all the work and very much tied down; the horses, motorcycle and extras are all in the future. Still it is a beginning.

But don't be surprised to see me back again at the old job, or one very much like it, just as soon as the novelty has worn off, as I know I

191

can't stick hanging around Headquarters for more than a few months.[1] My Captaincy comes through anyway, they are two a penny just now, or rather will be.

Somehow the weather keeps fine except for an occasional half hour shower; not enough to really lay the dust, and still the Boche seems to be waiting for an opportunity to start something.

I must stop now and see about things in general. This new job is giving me a much better idea of interior economy and orderly room work. The old job was merely trenches and shells with spells of Rest.

Your affectionate,
HECTOR

---

9. 7. 18.

Dear Marg,

As usual there is really nothing to write about; anyhow it is almost lunch time even though there is a war on.

As for the job, I think we will have to re-christen ourselves the Horse Marines. We have so far been known as the Navy; I think I carry the honorary rank of Commodore.

A few nights ago the Navy played the Army and got beaten 2-0 which was unfortunate.

I am quite near Rupert unless he has moved, and will see him one of these days. With any luck when I get up to strength in officers I will get my O.C.'s leave (every three months) its going to become rather expensive but I have only had two leaves since I came out, and the beastly money mounts up so fast; it takes three Banks now to hold it all.

You may as well write direct to my new address:

Lieutenant - - - -
4th Can: Pontoon B.T. Unit,
France.

I get a few pounds extra per month for doing less.

Your affectionate,
HECTOR

---

[1] The headquarters of the 10th Canadian Engineers Battalion in Maroeuil, a small village northwest of Arras.

After Hector's new bridging unit completed its training in open warfare techniques, it moved back twenty-five miles southeast again, to the front in the Arras area with its base at Divisional Headquarters in Maroeuil.

20. 7. 18.

Dear Marg,

I am sorry I have not written for so long but really there is lots to do for me these days as I am running a one man show.

When things get really started it ought to be a fairly good job as I have two Lieuts. to help out, and only about sixty men all told. But so far I am very much under strength and have no other officers at all. The pontoon equipment of the old Field Companies has been pooled now and I have the job of looking after it, and when necessary, taking it up for work where required. So far everyone has been busy cleaning and painting, and we have had no time to make ourselves comfortable. But I am still a Lieut.

I hope you get a decent lot of people if you try again not too far from Town.

Oscar can't be far away, and as I have a motorcycle now it will be easy to get over wherever he may be. Also Rupert.

Beastly hot these days, and lots of bombing, but a hut is a pretty small thing.

Best luck,
Your affectionate,
HECTOR

———

Chapter 10

The Final Push

On July 15, 1918, the German forces began their last attempt to breach the Allies' lines and capture Paris. The Second Battle of the Marne, as it became known, took place well to the southeast of Hector's location near Arras, and lasted three weeks.

By the end of July, the Allied Command realized that the Germans were overstretched, exhausted and demoralized. The great influenza epidemic sweeping the world had reached the Western Front and took a particularly high toll on the exhausted German armies.[1] In contrast, the ranks of the Allies swelled as American troops began to arrive in France. The Allies decided the time was ripe to launch a massive counter attack to drive the Germans back to the Hindenburg Line or beyond. General Haig ordered this attack to begin on August 8 from the area of Amiens, an important rail junction, forty miles south of where Hector was located at Arras. Once again, the Canadian divisions provided the shock troops at the centre of the line of advance.

The location and timing of the planned attack had to be kept secret for as long as possible. Orders were given to move reinforcements to the Amiens area covertly, and false radio traffic was generated by a Canadian Wireless Section to fool the Germans into thinking that the attack was to take place well to the northwest in Flanders.

---

[1] Popularly but inaccurately known as Spanish Flu, the devastating virus is thought to have originated in Fort Riley, Kansas. It was carried from North America to Europe by American troops in 1918. The virus killed over twenty million people worldwide in 1919-1920.

Hector received orders on August 1 to move his new bridging unit to the Amiens area in support of the attack. Along with many of the rested Canadian units, the engineers took an indirect route, keeping well back from the front for secrecy, marching by night with horse-drawn wagons carrying the bridging equipment. For a week they travelled thirty miles southwest on dark roads, to within fifteen miles of the coast. At the small town of Oisemont they turned back towards the front line again and traveled for another forty miles to just east of Amiens. The journey must have been trying, as the men raced to get to their destination on schedule, following over-crowded narrow and poorly signposted roads in heavy rain and darkness. Hector and his men joined the 4th Canadian Division camp in Boves Wood, immediately behind the front line but hidden from the enemy's sight, at 3:00 a.m. on the morning of August 7, just twenty-four hours before the Allies launched their attack.

This time there was no softening-up barrage of the German lines. When the attack began at 4:20 on the morning of August 8, with troops and tanks advancing eastward under cover of a creeping artillery barrage and thick mist, it came as a complete surprise to the enemy. The German defence collapsed, and the Allies advanced eight miles in the first twenty-four hours, capturing 15,000 prisoners.

Hector's bridging unit used horse-drawn wagons to transport material and equipment. | *Archival photo*

The Canadians had feared that the Germans would destroy all the bridges across the Luce River, but the attack had been so sudden and unexpected that they remained intact, and there was no need for Hector's pontoon bridges. Consequently, for the next few days, Hector's unit supported the attack, closely following the front troops, bringing up barbed wire, timber, sandbags and other defensive material. The unit did much of its work under the cover of night, but this precaution didn't prevent them from being heavily shelled and bombed. Fortunately the weather had improved and was mainly fine and warm. As usual, Hector relished the renewed activity and adventure.

The German troops' resources had been severely depleted during their earlier advances. The Allied attack soon extended along thirty miles of the front and swept the weakened German forces back towards the Hindenburg Line, resulting in the rapid recapture of much of the territory that had so recently been lost. For the first time, significant numbers of demoralized German troops surrendered in the face of the tank-led attack. German General von Ludendorff described August 8 as a "black day for the German Army" and advised the Kaiser to begin negotiations for peace. The Battle of Amiens, as this action became known, marked the beginning of the end of the war.

15. 8. 18.

Dear Marg,

This is the life. If I only had someone to help. As it is I am on my own, and it's no joke moving every day without any other officers, and the Sergeant Major on leave.

I am sending you a crossed blank cheque, I wish you would get me a small Primus Stove in a box and have it sent out. I unfortunately lost my watch on the move here and had to get a French one to replace it as I was in a hurry; have not had time yet to test it, but the man swore by it and gave a guarantee. It looks rather a pretty toy.

Things have settled down and the only trouble is bombing, which can be got over by digging a hole in the ground and trusting to luck.

Would you also send me ½ doz Summit collars, soft and fairly light in colour. 15½.

Must stop now,
Your affectionate,
HECTOR

23. 8. 18.

My dear Gerald,

We have been having quite a different kind of war just lately. More fun and movement than usual and of course more work. But our hardest time was getting here as we could only move by night, and then in a hurry. Quite a number of animals were beginning to show signs of chafing from the sudden change to real hard work.

During the show of course our part was insignificant though we had a few mules knocked out one night by shell fire.

I hope to get the Military Medal for two of the men for the work in getting the transport through. There are very few signs of war except in the villages which are badly chewed up.[1] Nothing to be compared of course with those of the old trench area which are pounded to dust, pretty near, but plenty of walls collapsed and roofs dented in. Tank tracks all over the ground and in places disabled tanks themselves.[2] In one place you could piece together the story of a duel between a tank and a couple of German 4.1 howitzers; both were knocked out. The Boche had evidently heard the tank coming around the corner of a bluff and they got the two guns out of the shallow emplacements by hand; lowered the sights and fired at point blank range, about 70 yds. No tank can stand that but either it or another accounted for the two guns and their crews.

Some of the country has obviously been won without much scrapping but any place near woods or where he had a trench system, had its own story pretty obvious for anyone to re-create.

One town with woods and chateau grounds had a cavalry attack.[3] It must have taken half a day to carry it; there were four lines of improvised one man holes about 200 yards interval, the last about $\frac{1}{4}$ mile off and from there on bodies of horses. They had been waiting in a wood close by till the infantry had worked their way close enough to cover them in the last charge; quite like the old days of war.

It has been fearfully hot and the dust is inches thick on some of the dirt roads. This part of France has the worst roads I have seen. It must

---

[1] Once the German began to withdraw, the battle line moved rapidly with fighting only where the retreating forces tried to hold a town or village to slow down the Allies.

[2] The Allies amassed 400 tanks for this attack.

[3] This probably refers to a battle between the 3rd Canadian Cavalry Brigade and German infantry just southwest of the village of Damery on August 10. The Canadians were repulsed initially before overwhelming the defenders. Because of the static nature of trench warfare, the cavalry was not used extensively before early 1918.

The Canadian Light Horse cavalry units were used on the offensive only during the last year of the war. | National Archives of Canada

be pretty hopeless here in Winter, and I can see where the Boche has either had to put on a grand attack or get out, the same as last year, to the region of Cambrai and St.Quentin where he belongs, that's if we don't kick him farther still.

Rupert's people were just around us and then got out and in again a little farther off, so I missed him. It is still keeping fine so things are pretty good in that way.

There are rumours of the Captaincy coming through. I am going over to Headquarters to find out; if so I will put in for leave right away and the pontoons can go hang. I may just be able to catch the end of the good weather & get some bathing. London, Tunbridge Wells and Felixstowe will be my addresses, and I am looking for a good time. Its ages since I have been anywhere in civilization as this job keeps me pretty well tied down.

Must stop now,
Your affectionate,
HECTOR

Five days after the start of the Battle of Amiens, the Allies had advanced thirteen miles. German resistance was stiffening, however, and the battle was stagnating back into trench warfare. General Haig decided to halt the attack and press the German forces farther to the north, back in Hector's old stamping grounds near Arras. On August 19, the Australians took over the Canadian positions, and the Canadians began to be re-deployed northwards. They had suffered over 11,000 casualties during the battle. Hector's bridging unit returned to its base at Boves Wood two weeks after the attack began. As anticipated, Hector's Captaincy finally came through.

On August 25, Hector received orders to return north with the last of the 4th Canadian Division to the Arras area, to support the Allies' new attack that was to be launched the next day immediately south of Arras. The unit moved to its new position two days later by train and truck, passing through Divisional Headquarters at Maroeuil. The unit set up camp five miles southeast of Arras, at Guémappe, a village that had been captured from the Germans the previous day following the breaching of the Hindenburg Line. Although the Allies were not to know it, they were about to launch the last great battle of the war.

The planned line of advance was crossed by small rivers and the Canal du Nord, then a wide partially-flooded trench. The Canadian bridging units were expected to be key players in the offensive. The 4th Division moved up to the centre of the front line during the night of August 31 in preparation for the next big attack, which was launched on the morning of September 2.

On that day, the Allies advanced rapidly and pushed the Germans back between one and two miles. During the night, the German forces withdrew a further three miles to the next defendable line, the Canal du Nord. There was little immediate need for the temporary lightweight floating bridges made of wood and cork[1] that Hector's unit had prepared to cross small rivers and swampy areas that the retreating Germans had flooded.

During the three weeks that followed the advance, Hector's unit

---

[1] Known as corked French mats.

spent much of its time repairing damaged bridges, filling craters blown in crossroads by the Germans, and transporting defensive material to the front as they consolidated the newly captured territory. In spite of the German withdrawal, shelling and night time bombing was intense and five men in Hector's unit were wounded and a number of horses were killed. The unit's base remained at Gémappe, six miles behind the new front line, but there was little time for letter writing and Hector's short note to Marg reflects this.

11. 9. 18.

Dear Marg,

Many thanks for your letters and attempts to get the Primus; don't worry about it any more. I will be getting my leave pretty soon and will see about it myself.

I have made the pontoons into a fighting unit in spite of 3 wounded and a Military Medal. Not bad for a start . . . [Missing section]
. . . at Boulogne or some such place. Very busy and still putting the wind up the Boche.

Your affectionate,
HECTOR

---

19. 9. 18.

Dear Marg,

With ordinary luck I am getting away on leave on the 23rd and will stay in Town till the end of the week, I expect, then spend a week visiting outside, and the last few days in town to pick up my traps.[1] That is the proposed plan but I'm hanged if I'll stick to it if I can see my way to make a better one.

The Captaincy has come through as far as the Corps is concerned, but still not officially gazetted, which means no pay. But that will come in a lump one of these days.

The Salmonds, Château Antigneul were very decent but I only had a very little time to see them in as we suddenly started a war and had to leave in a hurry.[2] The girl is inclined to be fat and has not the makings of a complexion; outside of that she is alright, I suppose.

---

[1] Hector's previous leave had been in December 1917, nine months earlier.
[2] The château is seven miles southwest of Bruay-la-Bussière. Presumably Hector visited it while stationed at Hermin in May that year.

Leave will be doubly welcome when it comes as things have not been any too comfortable just lately, and it will be a case of straight from a hole in the ground to comparative luxury. Though I have got a Better Ole than some I've seen.[1] The roads of course are badly chewed up with heavy traffic. No good for the motor cycle. Its almost a penance bumping along on shattered pavé, or ploughing through the messy side roads full of ruts.

Things were lovely for a while with us; being the bridging unit in open warfare is quite another matter to the "Park" during trench warfare,

"Well, if you knows of a better 'ole, go to it."

One of Bairnsfather's cartoons of life on the Western Front. | *Personal collection*

as we quite expected, and we followed right behind the Eighteen pounders.[2] Luckily the Hun spent most of his time getting his guns back and there were so many targets, we got off lightly. Only a few wounded, though the horses and mules suffered a lot. But it's a great feeling now the Mail[3] and the rest of the Panicky Press have stopped their dismal prophesies of the strength of the Hun. I'm quite sure they did more to cause the rot during March and April than anything else. The Hun is back where we want him, and in a more chastened mood.

---

[1] "A Better 'Ole" was a phrase immortalized by Captain Bruce Bairnsfather in his cartoons of characters in the trenches trying to make themselves comfortable in the shell hole pocked front line.

[2] Medium-sized artillery gun.

[3] The *Daily Mail*, the British tabloid.

Hoping to see something of you and Tiger if you are in Town. Or might be able to run up and see you if you can't get away.
Your affectionate,
HECTOR

P.S. Write c/o Ward and let me know how things are.

Hector left on two weeks' leave to England on September 19, a few days earlier than expected. Using his unit's motorcycle, he rode westward from the front to the coast where he caught a boat across the English Channel.

At the end of September, just as Hector's two weeks leave in England was ending, the Allies crossed the Canal du Nord and advanced on the city of Cambrai.

When he returned to France, Hector requested a transfer from the bridging unit to the 10th Battalion Canadian Engineers which his original 10th Field Company Canadian Engineers had been expanded to form. Although he had enjoyed the relative independence of the bridging unit, he seemed very happy to get back to his old group. He was apparently appointed second in command of D Company, which consisted of approximately 160 men.

While he had been on leave, the front had been pushed east and north and, on joining D Company, Hector found himself posted immediately west of Cambrai, maintaining canal crossings, roads and tramways and removing landmines and booby traps left by the retreating German forces. A few days after he returned, the 10th Battalion was relieved at the front and retired back to Maroeuil, near Arras, for a few days to rest and retrain.

On October 9, Hector's unit returned to the front, tavelling by train, truck and foot from Maroeuil, back to Gémappe. The Allies attacked that morning after having been stalled for the previous week while they consolidated captured ground. This attack was a complete success and it swept through the defenders, captured the remaining parts of Cambrai and then swung northeast, towards the next major city, Valenciennes.

By the evening of October 11, the Allied forces captured over fifty towns and villages and held most of the southern bank of the Canal de la Sensée. There they paused again to consolidate their gains and bring up bridge building material for the assault across the canal.

12. 10. 18.

Dear Mamma,

It's an awful long time since I wrote last and lots of things have happened.

I went on Leave on the 19th of last month and had a splendid time of course. A few days in Town to get things and saw two shows; one with Marg and Tiger and then a weekend at Tunbridge Wells. Dulcie was looking much better than last Xmas and as cheerful as ever. They all seemed very well.

I wish I could have stayed longer, but 14 days is only two weeks. Then I came back to Town again and left right away almost for Felixstowe to see the Ashwins who used to be at Dedham; two days only and even in that time I got some tennis and found myself quite hopeless. Town again and then two days at Folkestone before the boat sailed.

I saw Jean Bostock[1] who is driving a Ford for the R.A.F. at Hythe, and also the Lawsons who still stay at Folkestone. Had dinner one night with the Homes and tea with the Childe-Pembertons. So you can see how hopelessly full up a leave can be; and I always promise myself a rest to do just what I happen to feel like.

I have got back to the Battalion at last and the new address is: D.Coy. 10th Canadian Bn. France. It is quite a change after the old Pontoons where I did what I liked; but very much preferable.

Rotten weather just now and I hope the Boche is getting the full benefit of it. He retreats each night and has to fight next day so let's hope he feels sleepy, but he seems to have wonderful staying power. The motor cycle is still going strong and was awfully convenient getting down to the leave boat and back again as I saw some of France I had never seen before, and chose my own time.

Must stop now as I've plenty to do, we are near a C.C.S. and so I hope to get over and see if I know any of the nurses.[2]

Tell Gerald he should go to R.M.C. When he says he doesn't want to,

---

[1] Previously nursing with a Voluntary Aid Detachment Hospital.
[2] Casualty Clearing Stations were usually situated close to the front to provide the third or fourth step in treating the wounded, after the Aid Post and Advanced Dressing Stations.

it simply shows his ignorance of what things are like. I thought so too at one time, but now I know.[1]

> Your affectionate,
> HECTOR

On October 17, the Germans began withdrawing again and the Allies crossed the Canal de la Sensée with little resistance. The German Army's measured withdrawal became a full-fledged retreat to the northeast. Over the next four days the 4th Canadian Division advanced a total of fifteen miles until it reached the Canal de l'Escaut, which marked the western outskirts of the city of Valenciennes.

During this period, Hector's unit followed a mile or two behind the advancing front, repairing roads and building new bridges to allow reinforcements and the supporting artillery to move forward. As they retreated, the Germans left mines, some timed to explode days later, and booby traps that needed to be disarmed. They continually shelled the Allies with high explosive and gas shells to slow their advance and being behind the front line was certainly no guarantee of safety.

In the last few days of October, Hector's unit bridged the Canal de l'Escaut to the southwest of Valenciennes in preparation for a flanking approach around the south of the city to capture the high ground on its east. A frontal attack was precluded owing to the large number of French civilians trapped in the city.

The flanking attack was to be launched early on the morning of November 1. Orders from the brigade commander for Hector's Company were in part:

> "D" Company will be attached to the 10th Canadian Infantry Brigade for work under the G.O.C. this brigade. This Company will detail special parties to reconnoitre (within 10th Can. Inf. Bgde area) for Booby-traps, Land Mines, Delay Action Mines etc. Particular care will be taken to examine all approaches to canal crossings and adjacent ground suitable for deviations. The cellars of any houses near by should be examined for galleries leading to Bridge sites adjoining . . . They will arrange to place

---

[1] Gerald turned 18 earlier in the year and was preparing to volunteer for the military. R.M.C. is the Royal Medical Corps, the British Army's medical service. Gerald eventually went into medicine at the age of 32, after some years as a geologist.

Infantry bridges as required by G.O.C., 10th Can. Inf. Bgde., across the Rhonelle River,[1] as early as possible on the day the ground has been captured.

Hector was to act as Liaison Officer between these special Engineer reconnaissance groups, the commander of the various infantry battalions within the 10th Infantry Brigade, and the commander of his Canadian Engineers Brigade.

He left his billet at 3 o'clock on the morning of the attack to meet with two Battalion commanders. His next letter, three days later, described the events of that day.

4. 11. 18.

Dear Mamma,

I am writing this in the train on my way down to the Base as I was slightly gassed two days ago. Nothing much but there was a big casualty list at the time everything was cleared out, and I went down in the stream. I am not sure yet how far I will go before I stop, not much chance of "Blighty" I am afraid.

I have had a fine time since I got back to the Engineers, and in the last show was doing forward liaison with the infantry; it was great fun. Zero was 5.15 and I left my billets at 3A.M. with 4 sappers who were to act as runners. On the way up I picked up two more from forward sections and then pushed on in the dark to the Assembly point where I was supposed to find 3 Battalions' headquarters in a cellar.[2] It was my first real show since Passchendaele and I felt quite out of practice and the men were very green. Quite unlike the Field Company Sappers. I was going absolutely by the map as it was quite new ground and we ran into harassing fire. Of course he[3] knew something was going to happen. Luckily sunken roads are plentiful in these parts and my luck held till we were quite close up. Just as we got out of a railway cutting, or rather I had, a shell landed right on top of the party and got three out of my six.[4] One had an arm broken, and the others quite slight splinters, but we all got in ten minutes before the Barrage was due to start, and I found that my two battalions had changed

---

[1] On the southern edge of the city of Valenciennes.

[2] Probably in the village of La Fontenelle or Le Poirier.

[3] The enemy.

[4] There was only one railway on the southern approaches to Valenciennes; it ran north-south, parallel to the Canal, immediately west of the German-held high ground of Mont Houy, two miles south of the centre of Valenciennes.

their headquarters to about 2 kilometres away in the next village.

It was too late to get across so we stayed there for about 1½ hours while he bumped over the worst, and filled the whole place with gas, and then I started over with four men; the two worst had left for a dressing station.

By eight o'clock things were in full swing and his artillery was not so active, but I lost two more men who dropped out with gas. I had not been affected myself; it takes a lot somehow as I've found out before, when other people with me have got it.

About noon I ran across two cellars that the infantry had missed and got 16 Boche out of one. They came walking out in the true "Kamarad" style before I realised there was anyone inside, so we started them down in the right direction. I got two rather nice revolvers off them which I am sending over to Gerald when I get a chance. All the afternoon I walked around looking for souvenirs and hidden mines.

The villages are crammed full of civilians; anything from 10 to 40 in a cellar, who seemed crazy with joy, shaking hands and smiling all over. I was spared the kissing game here, and then my last two runners went down with gas.

About five in the evening the Hun put over a counter attack and gave us a dose of shells; gas and otherwise. Just as luck would have it I was out with a trench mortar officer for an automatic rifle we had heard of, and we had an exciting 2 minutes getting back. I think the last gas must have put the finishing touch on it all, as about 8 O'clock my eyes got bunged up, and next morning felt full of iron filings. So I gave myself up and passed through the various places, Aid Post, Advanced Dressing Station, Main Dressing Station, Casualty Clearing Station, and now, Base Hospital. Perhaps England.

The Sisters are splendid and do everything. But I feel ashamed of myself when it is so slight compared to a lot of cases on the train.

Must stop this endless diary.

Your affectionate,

HECTOR

The Canadians succeeded in capturing the city of Valenciennes that night (November 1-2), with the infantry crossing the small Rhonelle River and sweeping through the ruined shell of the city centre from the south, the west and the north. Owing to careful planning and precisely

Canadian troops entering Valenciennes on 1 November, 1918 during the final advance that broke the German will to continue fighting. | *Archival photo*

targeted artillery, civilian casualties were kept to a minimum.

The official war diary of the 10th Battalion Canadian Engineers reported on November 2, 1918: "Capt. HRJ Jackson evacuated wounded (gassed)."

Hector's military records indicate that he was initially evacuated down the chain of medical facilities at the front, and from there by train to the No. 8 General Hospital in Rouen, where he was treated for the effects of mild mustard gas poisoning.[1]

The Canadian Record Office sent an official telegram advising of Hector's gassing to A.E.N. Ward, who had previously been nominated as contact person in the event of death or injury. Ward sent a very brief telegram to Moses and mailed the original, with his own handwritten note at the bottom of the page, to Marg.

---

[1] Several military hospitals in Rouen attended to the wounded.

7. 11. 18.

Dr. M.J. Jackson,
C/o A.E. Ward.
65, London Wall.
0.2028 Regret inform you Captain Hector John Roderick Jackson,
M.C., 4th Canadian Transport Bn, wounded gas, 4th November.
Canadian Record Office.

This fortunately does not read very serious but we shall not have particulars for some time. I have cabled Mo[1] "Hector wounded gas" A.E.N.W.

One can only imagine the stab of icy terror that Moses and Rosa must have felt when the telegram was hand delivered in a sealed envelope to the farm in Aldergrove. They surely believed that their worst nightmare of one of their sons being killed in action was now reality. The sense of relief, after reading the telegram's brief wording, that their son was only wounded would have been dampened by the reasonable likelihood that he might still die from the effects of the gas or be horribly burned and disfigured for life.

This terrible suspense was endured for another week before Ward sent a second telegram, once Hector's location and condition had been established. He wrote another note to Marg:

65 London Wall
14. 11. 18.

Hector at No. 8 General Hospital, Rouen; gas poisoning slight. Informing Zoub, Ida[2] and Mo.
    A.E.N. Ward.

At 5:12 in the morning of November 11, 1918, just nine days after Hector was evacuated from the front, and after three days of negotiation, Germany surrendered unconditionally to the Allies. The declaration of surrender was signed in a railway carriage[3] on a siding

---

[1] Moses.
[2] Ida Caroline Jackson ("Tiger").
[3] The mobile Headquarters of the Allied Supreme Commander, General Foch.

in a boggy wood at Compiegne, northeast of Paris. The ceasefire came into effect at 11:00 that morning and at that hour, for the first time in more than four years, the guns fell silent.

In fact the ceasefire represented only an armistice; there was officially a state of war with Germany for another seven months until the Treaty of Versailles was signed on June 28, 1919. However, for the troops, the war had finally ended but there was no sense of euphoria evident on the front. A surreal sense of anti-climax pervaded the exhausted troops of both

Allied and German commanders pose after the signing of the cease fire in Compiègne. |
Archival photo

sides. It is interesting that none of Hector's surviving letters makes any mention of this momentous end to the first truly global war.

Hector's 10th Battalion Canadian Engineers' diary entry for November 11, 1918, recorded unemotionally: "Cloudy and cool. Armistice went into effect at 11:00 hours this date. Hostilities suspended."

While Hector was recovering in hospital in Rouen during the week before the Armistice, his unit continued to move eastwards for twenty miles, crossing into Belgium and eventually halting in the small town of Frameries, near Mons. It was in Mons that the last shots of the war were fired – between the occupying Germans and the Canadians.

Once they were established in Frameries, the troops of the Engineers Battalion underwent extended training to keep them occupied and to prepare them for demobilization and civilian life.

Hector (centre, clowning wearing the photographer's assistant's beret) with fellow officers whilst recovering from gassing; the photograph was taken a few days after the end of hostilities. | *Family album*

The day after the Armistice came into effect, Hector was transferred from the hospital in Rouen to No. 74 General Hospital in the Trouville area, on the coast of the English Channel and, eight days later, to a large house converted to a convalescent home for wounded Canadian officers at nearby Deauville-Sur-Mer. There he completed his full recovery from the effects of being gassed. Shortly afterwards he wrote to his aunt, Marg.

> Canadian Convalescent Home
> For Officers,
> Deauville-Sur-Mer, Calvados.
> Army Post Office S.83, B.E.F.
> France.
> 24. 11. 18.

Dear Marg,

    Many thanks for your letter. I have arrived down here and am having a splendid time. The eye trouble has quite gone, I think, and they are feeding me up in great style.

    Everyone is awfully fine and I have just finished my third tea. The house belongs to Rothschild and is very comfortable and quite near Deauville and Trouville, and I can get good golf and lots of places to visit.[1]

Had not the ghost of a suspicion that Rupert was engaged or thinking of it. That accounts for the French leave.[2]

Don't worry about the gas, it's all over now, and I am merely swinging the lead.
Must write to Rupert,
    Your affectionate,
    HECTOR

Rupert's fiancée Marguerite Marie du Pré de St. Maur, a French Red Cross nurse. | *Family album*

---

[1] The Deauville area had been developed as a major holiday resort for the rich and famous just two years before the war. Robert de Rothschild, a member of the Anglo-French bankers was one of those who built sumptuous houses in the area.

[2] Rupert became engaged to a French nurse, Marguerite Marie du Pré de St. Maur, whom he had originally met in Lannion on the Côte d'Amour in 1915 where she had been working with the Red Cross. They were married in Paris a year after the war's end, in December 1919.

Chapter 11

Long Journey Home

Nine million soldiers died during the First World War along with a similar number of civilians. At the outbreak of war, Canada's population was slightly under eight million. A total of 600,000 of these served in the Canadian forces during the war. 320,000 were sent to France and Belgium, and of these, two thirds were killed or wounded. For a new country just beginning to grow, this represented a fearful loss.

On the positive side, Canada came out of the killing fields with a reputation as a country that stood by its friends and allies in the face of terrible sacrifices. She had also earned respect for her fighting ability, proven under the harshest battlefield conditions. The names of Vimy Ridge and Passchendaele have gone down in history, and Canada's name is embellished on that history in gold. The war helped forge the Canadian nation.

Hector Jackson played only a small part in these events, no more than tens of thousands of others who fought alongside him. But without the contributions of Hector and these tens of thousands, the Allies could never have won the war.

Yet the Armistice was not a time for the victors to bask in glory. In truth there were no victors. With the war over, the priority turned to returning soldiers to their home countries to pick up lives where they left off and to rebuild economies worn down by more than four years of all-out war.

Hector's medical records recorded that he was discharged from the convalescent home in Deauville-Sur-Mer fit for duty, on December 10. Once discharged, Hector left immediately to rejoin his unit at its new base in Belgium.

E.F.C. Officers Rest House
and Mess,
Rouen.
11. 12. 18.

Dear Mamma,

I am on my way back to Base now, and hope to get up to my Unit again by Xmas, if not before.

Had an awfully good time at Deauville and met a number of Canadian Sisters and V.A.D.s.

I have been here a few times before and it always seems to be raining, so have never really had a chance to see much of the place.

There are lots of rumours going around demobilisation and war bounties, but nothing very definite has come out yet, except we get 3 months pay on leaving the service.

I was very sorry to hear of Mary Howes' death, the Howes family seem unlucky.[1]

The Childe-Pembertons heard of my gassing in the papers and wrote a very nice letter. They are leaving Town for good.[2]

Neither Rupert nor Oscar have written for a long time.[3]

Your affectionate,

HECTOR

HECTOR'S RETURN TO HIS UNIT in Belgium was aborted when he had traveled only half way to its location. On reaching the vast Allied military camp at Etaples on the estuary of the Canche River in northern France, he was assigned to assisting with the enormous logistical task of repatriating members of the Canadian Engineers, initially out of

---

[1] The Howes were neighbours of the Jacksons in Aldergrove. Mary Catherine (Howes) Hicks died in September 1918, a year and a day after her marriage in Aldergrove to Arthur Hicks. Her brother, Dempster Howes, was killed in action the day after her death.
[2] William Childe-Pemberton died in 1924.
[3] Oscar's signals unit was part of the 1st and 2nd Canadian Divisions that were selected to continue to Germany, to ensure complete disarmament and withdrawal of the German forces to the pre-war border.

France to England, from where they were shipped back home to Canada. Characteristically, Hector soon began to chafe at the mundane administrative tasks and lack of action.

E.F.C. Officers Rest
House & Mess
Etaples.
Dec. 15th 1918.

Dear Marg,

I'm at Can Inf Base Depot, on my way I hope to rejoin the Unit, but will stay here anyway for the end of the year I think, so address letters here. Have had no Canadian mail, only a few other letters for six weeks; they must be on the way somewhere I suppose. Hope we get out of this by May anyway if not sooner as it's not the same war it used to be. I'm right alongside Paris Plage and Le Touquet and the hospitals, a good combination during the war.[1]

I'm going to take dancing seriously for a change.

Your affectionate,
HECTOR

E.F.C. Officers Rest
House & Mess
Etaples.
30. 12. 18.

Dear Marg,

Thanks very much for the letter which I have not got with me. I'm still here. O.C. Engineers for demobilisation or some such rot, and we have lots of work and no thanks.

Please don't send any Xmas present, I've given none this year, as nothing can be got here, and anyhow this has been no sort of an Xmas.

Must get away and see the craft off,

Your affectionate,
HECTOR

---

[1] A very nice part of the city, on the sea shore.

E.F.C. Officers Rest
House & Mess
Etaples.
13. 1. 19.

Dear Mamma,

We are having wild rumours dished up to us at regular intervals about how and when we leave France. It seems certain we rejoin our Units, pass through England and get anyway seven days leave, so will be able to see people before I leave. Still nothing to do here so we get up dances & manage to keep things going. But mail is very irregular and I am getting no parcels somehow.

I heard from Oscar a few days ago from near Bonn, he was luckier than I at the end, but there is still a chance to take a short Cook's Tour as far as the Rhine.

These Expeditionary Force Canteen Clubs are one of the bright spots at the Base and Back area towns, as we see all the papers & periodicals, and there are officers passing through all the time. I am glad the Captaincy came through as living here is decidedly more expensive than up the line, but proportionally more comfortable.

I was sorry to hear of old 'Chummy',[1] but he was getting pretty old.
Your affectionate,
HECTOR

---

1. 2. 19.[2]

Dear Marg,

Sorry I did not ring you up before I left yesterday morning, but things went with a rush at the end.[3]

Had a nice dance here last night and met some quite decent people. As usual my luck and nerve started something. I introduced myself to an awfully pretty girl who looked lonely, who passed me on to a friend, who passed me on to her sister, who is going over to Brussels (her home) next week. Voilá.

---

[1] Gerald's pet Chow which he had brought over to Canada when the family moved from England, had apparently died.
[2] Hector was in Rouen for two weeks, sitting on a Court Martial.
[3] Left Etaples for his unit.

Hope you are having a good time and as good weather as we have had all day.

Your affectionate,
HECTOR

Lille.[1]
10. 2. 19.

Dear Mamma,

We started at last for the Unit.[2] Word came while we were at an afternoon dance, and we started next morning at 5.45 A.M.

It was a cattle truck and freezing like anything. We stuck it out as far as Bethune,[3] about 120 kilometres, and finally struck. It was then 10.30 P.M., and two of us got out and put up for the night in a very battered Estaminet.

We heard a train was to pass by at 12.30 next morning, but it finally arrived at 5.30, and turned out to be a civilian passenger train which we are not supposed to travel in without special permit, but we tumbled in kit and all and finally reached this place.[4] It is not badly hit at all except in a few places and life is fairly normal. I'm staying at the E.F.C.[5] which is an hotel and very comfortable, waiting for a car to take me up to Div. H.Q. at Brussels; if that is not poss, I suppose it means train again and I'm not very fond of them.

I met Randalls last night, he was in Verites with me & is now a Lieut in the R.A.F.

We are the last Division of the Corps to be demobilised and the Engineers are the last unit almost of the Division, so that I don't expect to get over for some time. I'm not worrying however as I think life here ought to be pretty "bon" especially if I find my salvage motor cycle is running as I left it.[6]

I heard from Rupert who has reverted to Capt. again and Oscar

----

[1] In France, very close to the Belgian border.

[2] Hector's unit was still in Belgium, but had moved from near Mons to the small town of Chastre, just southwest of Brussels.

[3] In the area of France recaptured by the Allies in the last days of the war.

[4] In the post-Armistice period, the Canadian troops' strong discipline partially collapsed and regulations were frequently ignored.

[5] Expeditionary Force Canteen.

[6] The motorcycle he left in Folkestone.

appears to be on leave.[1] I ought to be getting one pretty soon. I'm getting so many invitations in Montreal, Toronto and Ottawa that I could book myself for a year, but I rather hope we all go to Ottawa as a Unit and then I could see most people in a month.

> Must stop,
> Your affectionate,
> HECTOR

Chastre
17. 2. 19.

Dear Marg,

I've got up to the Unit again and this is the place ~50 Km. S.E. of Brussels about half way to Namur. It is a small very scattered village and the people are nothing wonderful, but there are better towns fairly close, I believe and lots of dances to be had.

I left Etaples on the 20th of last month for Rouen[2] to sit on a Court Martial, it took until the 4th of Feb. and I finally got back to Etaples on the 8th, going and coming by Paris but I only stayed half a day each way, just enough to make connections, and saw next to nothing of the place. I left the Base next day and stayed off at Bethune and Lille on the way up and spent one night in Brussels.

We aren't doing much here except education and games, and I've got to find something to pass the time.[3] Luckily the horse problem is simple and we have dances, but something else has to be found.

I hope you are feeling fine; we may pass through any time in May.

> Your affectionate,
> HECTOR

There is a long gap in Hector's letters here. Presumably he wrote letters, but they were not preserved. The following letter was written in early May, the day after the last of the 4th Canadian Division finally left France. Hector had arrived in England from the Continent a few days earlier to represent his brigade at the victory parade for Dominion

---

[1] Rupert ended the war with the rank of Captain (Acting Major) as second in charge of the 91st Field Ambulance Company, RAMC.

[2] Sixty-five miles west of Paris.

[3] The unit's diary shows a monotonous daily routine of "educational classes for all Ranks" that continued for several months in Belgium, after the Armistice.

The Victory Parade winds its way past Buckingham Palace. Hector on foot (front right of column) leading his company. The southeast corner of Buckingham Palace is on the left and the Victoria Memorial is in the background. | *Family album*

troops through London.

He had left Wavre, just southeast of Brussels, on April 29, 1919, and travelled to Le Havre by train and from there by ferry and train, arriving at Bramshott, forty miles southwest of London, on May 2.

The victory parade for Dominion troops took place through London the next day, passing west along the Mall to the Victoria Memorial and Buckingham Palace where it was reviewed by King George V and members of the Royal Family.

> (?) 6. 5. 19.
> The Grand,
> Folkestone.

[1] . . . part. All the day was spent by the men in cleaning up after the dirty journey. The morning of the 3rd we had reveille at 2.30 a.m. Marched down to the station and entrained at 6.30 a.m. Marched from Waterloo station to Hyde Park and had breakfast, then lunch at 12.00 noon and the final

---

[1] One or more pages of the letter, presumably to Hector's mother, are missing.

218

march at 1.40 (about 5½ miles).[1] There was quite a lot of enthusiasm and luckily the day was almost perfect; not too hot and occasional sun. At 5.30 we turned the men loose to rendezvous at the station at 8.30, and then reversed the process and reached Camp at 12.30 a.m. So you can see it was a pretty strenuous week.

I saw Tiger who happened to be in town, and. was going out to tea with her, but had to cancel it.

I am down here on special leave for two days to get my motorcycle, as it will be very handy for getting around. You know how far the camps are from everywhere. I hear that we are all to go on leave as a Battalion, and then come back to Witley, but nothing definite has come up yet.[2]

On Sunday I called at Verites, saw Stokes in the Library and had tea at the Crisps. Only one girl was at home; she had just got back from Abbeville from hospital work.

I expect we will be 6 weeks to two months in the Camp before

The Victory Parade winds its way through Knightsbridge. | *Archival photo*

---

[1] The victory parade.

[2] Witley Camp was south of London, in Surrey, not far from Godalming. This was reportedly a tedious time for many of the 4th Canadian Division troops who lacked Hector's local contacts.

sailing, from the way the other divisions have stuck around.
    Goodbye from
    Your affectionate,
    HECTOR

                                            Witley Camp,
                                            22. 5. 19.

Dear Marg,
    Many thanks for your letter; I should have answered before but
kept on putting it off. We are supposed to get a second leave next week,
but may not. I am putting in for a permanent job on demobilisation. If it
comes off I stay for about two months more so could get down to see you
sometime, as the motorcycle is working well, and I can get anywhere.
    In a great hurry, everything is lovely.[1]
    Your affectionate,
    HECTOR

                                            Witley Camp.
                                            30. 5. 19.

Dear Gerald,
    Glad to get your letter enclosed yesterday; and have decided to get
busy and do a little answering for a change.
    I have decided to stay on here for a few weeks extra and have sent
in my name; so far nothing has happened about it but should hear any day
now. I went up to Town on the Premier[2] for two days and came back
yesterday. Had tea with the Bruntons who seem very nice people, and tried
to see Mr. Pollard, but he was away.[3] The bus behaved very well. I had just
taken it completely down; even taking the engine out of the frame, and
with the help of the D.R., put it together again, so I am satisfied nothing is
wrong. I won't bring a bicycle out with me unless the prices drop
considerably; just now they are simply absurd; everyone wants to buy one

----

[1] Hector was obviously relishing being back in England and not eager to return to the
claustrophobia of the hardscrabble family farm in Aldergrove.
[2] Hector's motorcycle.
[3] Alfred Pollard, the university friend of Moses and Housman from Oxford who lived in
Wimbledon, south London.

at fabulous prices up to £100 for a good second hand. You can't look at anything with speeds[1] under £45.

Glad the parcel arrived safely. The long pistol fits easily into that groove at the end of the case. I got them when two machine gun crews surrendered to us with their guns outside Valenciennes. The telescope sight, I merely picked up. Am bringing over with me two German tin hats; a bayonet and scabbard; a French and German gas mask and a private and N.C.O.'s cloth hat, and a German water bottle. That is the lot. Am having a good time now with plenty of tennis, so see no need to hurry across before Xmas. Oscar should go in July.

R.M.S. Olympic, *sister ship to the* Titanic, *with its First World War dazzle camouflage.* | *Archival photo*

Witley Camp will find me, but perhaps the old address is better.

Your affectionate,
HECTOR

J. Wing,
Witley Camp,
13. 6. 19.

Dear Mamma,

I have definitely decided to stay in England for a few months longer, and this will be my address; though perhaps the London one is really safer.

---

[1] Gears.

Our Battalion sailed a week ago on the Olympic.[1] I was going down to Southampton to see them off but contented myself with the Milford Station[2] at the last minute, as the train was very crowded.

My tennis is improving thanks to plenty of practice, and as I get most afternoons off, I can get out and see people within a ten mile radius very comfortably. The lanes are looking very pretty just now; a little dusty owing to the long drought, but I find I know my way about pretty well. I have got a very nice Wing, several fellows including the O.C. are keen cricketers and we get up games with the local teams. I believe we play a Charterhouse XI next Saturday. They are having a large Pageant again in July like the Centenary in 1911;[3] it ought to be rather good.

I saw Mr. Edward and the girl Rendall on the river yesterday, she is no beauty, seems to have the family nose very pronounced. I saw Jean and Marion Bostock last weekend at their Aunts near Catt Millo and had tennis, also go to the Knowles at Thursley[4] when I feel like it, and generally meet nice people from around.

Heard from Oscar today, he may be able to get down here before he sails.

Must stop,
Your affectionate,
HECTOR

———————

J. Wing,
13. 7. 19.

Dear Mamma,

I am enclosing a letter I wrote to Gerald ages ago and have only just discovered.

We are supposed to finish here the 10th of next month and then the Wing sails as a Unit. Just now we are shipping people through pretty fast, but I hope to get away on a leave at the end of the month. I have not been

---

[1] R.M.S. *Olympic* was the sister ship to the *Titanic* and which acted as a troop ship throughout the First World War. She was fitted with 5″ guns for defence against submarines, but she rammed and sank the only submarine which attacked her. She continued to ply the North Atlantic route until 1935.

[2] The nearest station to Witley Camp.

[3] The tri-centenary of the founding of Charterhouse school and hospital in 1611.

[4] Near Godalming.

away overnight since May except for a conducting tour to Liverpool.[1] But I manage to get plenty of tennis, and last night Mrs. Round asked me up to a dance given by a Mrs. Boyce on Holloway Hill,[2] its ages since I've been to any, the weather has been hopeless for dancing.

Oscar should be sailing any time; I had letter from him from Mr. Ward's a few days ago.

I would have liked to have been in Ottawa and Toronto for the Prince's visit, but may catch up to him in Vancouver or some other place on the way.[3]

The weather here has set fair again once more and I am booked for tennis nine days in the next fortnight, and will probably get about two others filled up before the end: there are some good players here among the girls, and men of course are easy to find.

I was up for Old Carthusian Day last Saturday, and stayed for lunch to the Masque at 10 p.m.[4] There were a quite a few I knew down. Tod is leaving next year and Willet gets the House.

I have finally given up motorcycles and bought a 3-speed Premier. Its good exercise and fast enough for my short journeys. I rather think I shall bring a bicycle out with me if it can be done as kit.

There is some talk of us all getting Demobilisation Pay for staying over here (and incidentally having a good time). If so I should get an extra $100 which is worth taking.

Your affectionate,
HECTOR

———————————

Witley,
22. 7. 19.

My dear Gerald,

Many thanks for your letter and Mamma's; by the time you get this Oscar should be almost back as he sailed a few days ago on the "Winnifredon", I think we sent a lot of men then.

Motorcycles seem cheap enough in Vanc. I'll get one as soon as I reach there and come down to Aldergrove on it, if I can find anything worth while.

———————————

[1] Accompanying a group of departing troops to a troop ship.
[2] Near Godalming
[3] The Prince of Wales (who later became King Edward VIII) visited Canada in 1919 as part of the victory celebrations.
[4] A performance of music and dance held at Charterhouse every four years.

I was to have marched with the Canadians (dismounted) in the Victory March but had been out late for three days before, and on Friday morning I was up at six and up in Town by ten, and back again in time for a dance. I got back to my room at 2.45 A.M. to find a note that I was to leave again at 4.30 A.M. for the march, but it was too much of a good thing, and I got a substitute.

I hope Papa's anaemia is better;[1] as things are I must get back with the Cadre early next month. Otherwise I could find jobs to keep me here till Oct. on Courts-Martial and general cleaning up.

Personally I hate fixed engines, but they are quite serviceable and you should make up to 35 at a pinch on the Yale road as I got that out of very much worse roads in France. But 18-25 is good enough for anything over ten miles. $65 sounded quite reasonable.

I am not getting any more snaps now, haven't taken a photo since I left Belgium.

Was out to tennis at Chilworth Old Manor house yesterday;[2] I met the girls at a Dance at O Wing, we had tennis tea and dinner and finished up with everything from jazzing and singing to a pillow fight. If I could get a job I'd get back to England again so fast that you would not have seen me for dust. Canada is all very well but you don't live.

I hope no one has started talking about the "Capturing of 2 machine gun crews", I simply happened to be at the cellar where they were hiding when they came up to give themselves up. No one knew where the line was just then, and they had hung on waiting for the counter attack.

You were lucky not to get knocked out by the democrat smash;[3] a delivery ford[4] is much more fun, and O and I will see about starting one I think.

I'll write again,
Your affectionate,
HECTOR

---

[1] This was possibly a result of a combination of poor diet, stress and bleeding stomach ulcers, a typical early symptom of stomach cancer which eventually killed him.
[2] A grand Edwardian hotel about six miles north of Southampton.
[3] Gerald was presumably involved in an accident with the family's democrat, a light wagon seating two or more people and drawn by two horses.
[4] A model "T" Ford, the ubiquitous motor vehicle in North America at the time.

[Part letter, undated, but probably end of July 1919.]

51, Chepstow Place
Pembridge Square, W.

. . . to this address, it shows what I am missing, dances, tennis and the river, and I meet new people all the time, like the proverbial snowball; still it will be just the same in Canada when I have settled down a little. I have a programme mapped out right across from Montreal if I can fit it all in.

I had lunch with Marg yesterday, she had thought of going down to Ramsgate but I think has given up the idea now.

I expect Canada had great Peace Celebrations on the 19th.[1] I didn't see anything of them. I felt too beastly tired and went off to bed. Not quite the same as the Armistice time. Much more deliberate but they enjoyed themselves.

Must stop now and do some shopping and exploring. I am having a very quiet time and have let no one know I am up on leave; it saves a lot of trouble.

Expect Oscar is back,
Your affectionate,
HECTOR

51, Chepstow Place,
Pembridge Square, W.
1. 8. 19.

Dear Mamma,

Thanks very much for your letter, and Gerald's also, with the motorcycle enclosures.

Am just up on a sort of last leave that I managed to wangle; don't expect to sail for a week or so yet. Still there is always a chance; as it is now, we have about 80 officers in the mess. They call for about 12 a sailing and then cut it down to four or five at the end, and these are here to get away at once; not on permanent Cadre like myself.

I'll see about the Rosaleen when I get to Godalming. I saw Marg at

---

[1] A temporary Cenotaph was unveiled in Whitehall on June 19, 1919, during a victory parade. Similar celebrations were held elsewhere in the world on the same day, including in Canada. The Vancouver celebrations were held in Stanley Park. Additional observances were held on "Peace Day" – August 4, 1919, the fifth anniversary of the outbreak of the war. Hector's home Township of Langley hosted a "Welcome Home" day for returned soldiers that climaxed with a dinner and ball.

ADMIT BEARER

To the QUADRANGLE, BUCKINGHAM PALACE, on the

occasion of an

INVESTITURE BY H.M. THE KING

(WEATHER PERMITTING)

on the 31 JUL 1918

DEREK KEPPEL,

Master of the Household.

Hector's invitation to Buckingham Palace to receive his Military Cross. There is no mention in his surviving letters of the event, but The Times *of July 31 reports that he received the medal from King George V at 11 o'clock in the Quadrangle of the Palace. Marg accompanied him to the ceremony.* |
Original held by Hugh Jackson

Moreton[1] and came down with her on Wed. Garland was not there, only the children. I had some very good squash, a little tennis, and. some lawn tennis. They have some fine private courts. The house is ugly like Peperharrow Park but very nice inside.[2]

I never see the local papers but I'll look some up if I can get hold of them. Tell Gerald to hang on a bit before he finally decides on a motorcycle, the summer is practically over and then prices of second hand go down pretty badly. The Cleveland looks pretty nice for a two stroke. I don't like the oil mixing with the petrol feed, its never fitted that way on modern English machines; they don't like it. I believe in chain drives but that barrel spring on the front fork is the same as the Triumph and would never stand Aldergrove roads: I used to break them right along in France.

There is a fellow called Levey whom I had in the Pontoons for a while; very decent. I must look him up; he has a garage in Vanc. and will

---

[1] Just northeast of London.
[2] A block-like Georgian stately home, just west of Godalming.

help me in getting hold of a bus at a reasonable price, if he has got back to his job.

I would think that the timing of the magneto would be a bit tricky by the look of things, though they might have some dodge that does not show.

I was going back to Camp today though my leave is not up for four days. I have such a splendid time at the Godalming, Guildford, Haslemere people are very kind and I get invitations everywhere, and as they are sent on . . . [The remainder of this letter is missing]

———————

[Hector's next letter - his last from England - was typewritten]

J. Wing.
Witley
10. 8. 19.

Dear Mamma

We are due to sail on the Belgic as a Wing, most likely on the 16th of this month but it has been put off so many times already that I don't expect to reach Canada much before the beginning of next month.[1]

I am practising typing as there is not much else to do this morning in the Orderly Room, but it is usually hard enough for me to get ideas when I have beastly letters to search for on the keys.

I went up to the Crisps yesterday afternoon for tennis and played several sets, there were only two of the girls at home and a cousin I did not know, but they had a lot of friends as usual and we had quite a good time.

This afternoon I am going over to Seale with one of the fellows in O Wing to play with friends of his; it will be a change after Godalming people all the time. And tomorrow I am playing at Broadwater with a party from all over the area: I think the players around here could hold their own against any district.

I went down to Deal to see Tiger last week at the end of my Leave. The place was absolutely crammed, but I did not see many people there except very ordinary trippers and profiteers. The carriage down from Charing X[2] was packed with a mixture of parcels, hampers and babies with

---

[1] The *S.S. Belgic* was a passenger liner of the White Star Line.
[2] Charing Cross Station, London.

enough grown ups to fill up any air space left over, and most of the babies were violently ill most of the way down. Golf Bungalow is an ideal place for a month's holiday in Summer, but it must be very cold in winter, and of course Tiger finds it hard to get all the fun out of life when she lives there all alone, and has no one to help her in the house.

I got some Rosaleen from Edwards a few days ago and will send it out as it will get there sooner that way than if I bring it myself, as I will be stopping off at various places on the way over: Toronto, Montreal, Ottawa, Altamont[1] anyway, as our ticket is good for a month, it seems a good way to see Canada, especially as I have so many invitations from people I have been with in the last three years. What I want now is a job near Vancouver for the winter and I have letters of introduction to people who may be able to find me what I want. Then I have a scheme for the Spring with another fellow who knows the north country absolutely and we will have a shot at that part of the world; of course very likely nothing will come of it, but it seems worth trying.

I must get busy now and stop this letter,
Your affectionate,
HECTOR

––––––––––

[1] Southwest of Winnipeg, Manitoba. Possibly to see his uncle, Robert Oswald Jackson.

Chapter 12

Shoulder High

Hector sailed from Liverpool on August 16, 1919, on board the S.S. *Belgic* bound for Canada. The ship docked in Halifax a week later, from where he travelled by train to Ottawa. There Hector was discharged from the 10th Battalion Canadian Engineers on August 31, 1919, four years and twelve days after joining the Canadian Expeditionary Force. He returned to Vancouver by train, stopping in various places across Canada to visit friends and relatives.

Hector had left Canada as an impressionable young man, looking for adventure, determined to do something worthwhile but hoping to have fun and excitement while doing it. When he had left Canada in early 1916, Hector already had a strong, resilient character. But nobody could come through the slaughter of that terrible war unchanged. By the time his train finally pulled into the station at Aldergrove and he was reunited with his parents and younger brother, Hector had matured immeasurably. The adventure he had sought had far exceeded any expectations. He had experienced events and seen horrors the like of which he could never have imagined from the patriotic recruiting posters of 1915.

Hector started to rebuild his social life in Vancouver, picking up with the old friends who had survived the war, and starting new friendships. But like many of the soldiers returning home from the war, he must have found civilian life lacking in the raw adrenaline-filled excitement of the Western Front. Any thoughts that he or his father may have had of him taking over the family farm in Aldergrove had long since been washed away by the social whirl of England or vapourised by the shrapnel-filled battles in Flanders. Hector had plans and ideas about getting out and starting something new and exciting in the far north of the province, doing something that would allow him to apply his engineering experience, perhaps in mining.

Rather against his will, and probably at the urging of his father who revered formal education and scientific training, Hector registered as a mature student at the University

Taken after the war, this photo is variously identified as being in either Shastre in Belgium, or back in Canada. | Family album

of British Columbia for a four-year Bachelor of Science programme in mining engineering. Because of the practical experience he had gained in the Canadian Engineers, he was admitted as a third year student. He lived in a house in the Mount Pleasant area (444, West 14th Avenue), just south of False Creek in Vancouver.[1] His parents had rooms in the house whenever they were in the city. The home was conveniently situated, as the temporary buildings that housed the infant University of British Columbia were located nearby.[2]

---

[1] The house on West 14th Avenue is still standing.
[2] The university only moved to its present location on Grey Point in 1922.

Once at university, Hector's natural charm and sense of fun came to the fore again. According to the UBC magazine, within a few months "he was one of the most popular of his class, and always took part in college activities." However, the university's academic environment proved too divorced from reality for someone who had developed his engineering skills through hands-on field experience under battle conditions. A few months after enrolling, Hector wrote to Rupert indicating that he had little intention of sticking out the full two years required to complete the degree, preferring to leave university and apply his engineering experience to mining in the province's north.

Vancouver B.C.
12. 12. 19.

Dear Rupert,[1]

This is to wish you a merry Xmas and a Happy New Year, and I've just heard in a round about way that you are getting married this year. I rather thought from the way you spoke that you intended waiting some time. Anyway the best of luck and my Salaams to Madame.

I am working like a Trojan just now at the University; they put me in as a 3rd. Year Mining. Another year, if I pass gives me a B.Sc., but as I can't possibly make it, thanks to eight years of wasted existence, I'll just get the working knowledge without the honour and glory. Luckily I had enough to look after myself thanks to the war and rather reluctantly I was persuaded to try; but I expect it was the best really.

Exams for the $\frac{1}{2}$ term start tomorrow, and last a week and we get 2 weeks at Xmas. With four months in the summer when I expect to get a job in a mine as experience.

Must stop,
Your affectionate,
HECTOR

What is your title now: Dr. R.W.P. or Major?

---

[1] Rupert was demobilised on August 20, 1919, just eleven days before Hector. He had recently moved to Hartlepoole on the east coast of England to join an established medical practice.

444, 14th Ave.,
4. 1. 20.

Dear Gerald,

Hope by now you have quite recovered.[1] I heard from Oscar just after he got up that you had been pretty bad.

I got up alright and came right up here for lunch as the weather was so beastly foggy, and I felt very dirty and unwashed after the long ride in the jitney.

I had a good time down at Aldergrove and felt ever so much better for it though my hands have not quite recovered yet.[2]

I wonder if you have come across my white comb. I left it upstairs or by the sink, also if you find any of the thumb screws of the trouser press, I wish you would send them along.

I had a quite successful dance Friday night and was dead tired when it began as I had been travelling most of the day, but woke up a little towards the end, and enjoyed myself.

Am going across to N. Vanc. for a walk this afternoon if it keeps fine, and then work again starting with Monday.[3]

Yesterday I saw Noel and Mrs. Buckley, he does not look as ill as people try to make out.

Must stop,
Your affectionate,
HECTOR

Hector on his return to Canada, probably on the farm in Aldergrove. | *Family album*

---

[1] The 1920 Spanish Flu epidemic was sweeping the globe at this time. Some 50,000 people died in Canada alone, and Gerald's respiratory tract infection may have been a mild form of the Spanish Flu.

[2] Hector had apparently spent at least part of his Christmas university vacation working at Aldergrove, helping to restore the farm.

[3] The start of the new university term.

This letter to Gerald was Hector's last. Just two weeks later, on the evening of Sunday January 18, 1920, Hector cycled into downtown Vancouver on the 3-speed bicycle he had bought in England six months earlier, to attend an evening symphony concert. The concert ended at around 10:30 and Hector mounted his bicycle and started his two-mile ride back to the house on 14th Avenue where he was living. It was a typical January night in Vancouver: cold and blustery with rain. As Hector rode across the Connaught Bridge over False Creek at about 11:00 p.m., he was hit by a car driven by a twenty-five-year-old drunken taxi driver. The impact threw him onto the wooden timbers which surfaced the bridge, where he hit his head, inflicting a severe cut above his right eye and causing trauma to the brain. Hector was rushed unconscious to the nearby Vancouver General Hospital but died a week later on January 25, 1920, without regaining consciousness. Ironically, the site of the accident was only a few hundred yards from the D.C.O.R. Drill Hall on Beatty Street, where Hector had first reported for duty after volunteering for military service.

The Connaught Cambie Street Bridge across False Creek in Vancouver, looking north, soon after it opened in 1912. | *Archival photo*

The *Daily Province* newspaper reported on Hector's death:

Hero of War is Victim of Accident.
Tragic Death of Capt. Jackson, M.C., Following Collision on Bridge.

After surviving three years of war in France and Flanders, Capt. Hector John Roderick Jackson, M.C., died at the General Hospital on Sunday night from injuries received in an accident on Cambie Street Bridge the previous Sunday night. While cycling home after attending the symphony concert, he came into collision with a taxi-cab. From the moment of the accident he never recovered consciousness.

The second son of Dr. and Mrs. J. Jackson M.A. (Oxon), of Applegarth, Aldergrove, late principal of Dayaram Jethmal Sind College, Karachi, India, and subsequently director of Scientific Instruction to the State of Baroda, the late Captain Jackson was born in India, but sent home as a small child and educated at Branksome House in Charterhouse School, Godalming, where he proved one of the most prominent of the school athletes, distinguishing himself particularly in football.

Enlisting in the ranks with the North Vancouver Engineers in October 1915, he received a commission upon arriving in England and went to France with the 10th Field Company, remaining with that unit until the close of the war and taking part in the Somme, Vimy, Passchendaele, and the Amiens-Cambrai-Valenciennes advance. He was gassed at the last-named place. After being recommended four times, he was awarded the M.C. Upon returning to British Columbia he proceeded with the third year mining engineering course. His death at the early age of 28 will be much regretted by a large circle of friends here and in Ottawa.[1]

Two brothers served in France, the eldest, Major Rupert Jackson, with the Imperials, and a younger brother, Mr. Oscar Jackson, who is also at the university here, with the Engineers. The funeral took place today, Major the Rev. C.C. Owen officiating.

---

[1] Note that Hector was still 2 months short of turning 28.

Hector's coffin is carried by ex-military friends through driving snow to its final resting place in the military section of Mountain View Cemetery in Vancouver. | *Family album*

Hector was buried in the military section of Mountain View Cemetery in Vancouver. On the day of the funeral, the weather had turned colder, and the rain had changed to wet snow that blew horizontally across the bleak graveyard. The service was conducted by the Reverend C.C. Owen, Dean of Christ Church Cathedral in Vancouver, a family friend. Most of the pallbearers who bore Hector's Union Jack-draped coffin were ex-military friends, including Noel Robinson.

The taxi driver was charged by the attorney general a few days later with manslaughter.

In due course, Hector's grave was marked by a large granite cross and stone bearing his name. As part of the cemetery's reorganization to simplify maintenance, the cross and posts were removed some decades later, leaving only the inscribed marker.

As I write this in 2008, all graves in the military section at Mountain View Cemetery are being renovated to replace existing grave markers with standard Commonwealth War Grave Comission headstones. The original inscription on Hector's headstone will be inscribed on the new headstone. Hector's original granite marker will

Hector's grave soon after his death. | *Family album*

be moved and placed by a maple tree that is to be planted by Langley Township on Jackson Road (24th Avenue), Aldergrove, as a permanent public memorial to Hector.

As is often the case with soldiers returning from extended periods of intense combat, Hector had chosen not to talk much to his family about all he had seen and done on the Western Front, either brushing off events as being of no consequence, or just avoiding talking about them altogether. The period of adjustment that most combat soldiers went through during the transition back to civilian life was never completed before his life was snuffed out by the accident on that miserable dark and wet Vancouver night.

Moses felt he needed to find answers to his unasked questions about his son's wartime work. Eighteen months or so after Hector was killed, he wrote a letter to his son's commanding officer, Colonel Wilgar, asking him about the circumstances of Hector's award of the Military Cross. Colonel Wilgar had returned to civilian life and was with Queens University in Kingston, Ontario.

During the years that Hector had served under his command, Colonel Wilgar had come to know him well and his reply captures the essence of Hector's character; on the one hand his strength of purpose, unshakeable optimism and determination to see a job through, no matter what the personal discomfort or personal risk, and on the other, the sense of humour, enthusiasm and dedication to enjoying himself to the full wherever possible. Colonel Wilgar replied to Moses' letter.

Kingston,
Oct. 24th, 1921

Dear Dr. Jackson:

I am ashamed to have been so long in answering your letter. Everything seems to have conspired to keep me too fully occupied to realise how very remiss I have been. The University term opened with very large classes, very little assistance and no great capacity for work on my part.

Then I undertook the installation of the new heating system for the university and Hospital and the contractors in that work seem to think the main object in their life is the destruction of all references which adds to my spare time jobs.

However all this is only trying to make you think that I have not been negligent. I can't persuade myself of the same. There is really no excuse for me and I am very much ashamed.

Hector received his Military Cross for his work at Passchendaele, as you no doubt know. The circumstances are well impressed on my mind.

The Division asked us, the Engineers, to dig a four line trench to consolidate the position gained, and asked me to send an officer with Major Greville-Gavin to reconnoitre the position.

Hector and Gavin went up about four in the morning - a distance of about seven miles, picked out the ground and returned to Headquarters.

That evening Hector went forward again with two companies of Infantry as his working party, and directed the construction of the trench.[1] All work had to be done at night as the position was most exposed.

Hector's Military Cross is held by Hugh Jackson, his nephew. | *A. Jackson*

---

[1] The unit's war diary reported that the work party that night consisted of 400 men.

During the progress of the work, the Enemy repeatedly shelled the position, and the Infantry, tired out, after their heavy fighting, and exposure of the battles, were only too anxious to take cover and rest.

An Engineer officer in charge of an infantry working party always has to be on the alert. The infantry feel that the foe is near them and their interest is not very warm. So Hector had the usual trouble of keeping them at it and, after every period of shelling, had to personally see that the men got back on the work. That practically meant he had to expose himself continuously to all the shell fire.

In the meantime casualties had been very heavy and wounded had to be evacuated.

The work was completed about daylight. Hector had been continuously on the go since the previous morning, a full 24 hour stretch. He was just about exhausted, but, before coming in, and after he had dismissed the Infantry, he took a look around to see if everything was alright and found two badly wounded Infantry men, who had been missed in the evacuation of the wounded in the dark.

There was your boy left with only one sound sapper to assist him in handling two wounded men out of that mud and muck.

He could easily have given it up – and without criticism – as an impossibility. Daylight was coming on, and the enemy in full view.

He and his sapper runner packed those two wounded boys at least two miles, to a point where ambulance could be got. More than half of the time spent in moving the wounded men was in full view of the Enemy and in broad daylight.

I was getting very anxious that he had not returned and started out to find him, and finally met him, coming off the duck walk, at Kink Dump, near Farabeek.[1]

He never mentioned his difficulties – simply said it was rather a filthy job, admitted being a bit tired and hungry as a horse.

I was quite insistent that he explain why he was so long in returning, and he finally admitted having "helped a couple of chaps" so I gave him up and went for his sapper runner, who told me in no uncertain way of Hector's heroism and devotion.

I attempted to say to Hector something of my appreciation of his action, but he was very much embarrassed, though I know he wasn't displeased.

His recommendation for the M.C. was a brief recital of the above facts.

---

[1] One of the streams that drained from the Passchendaele Ridge.

On two other occasions he was recommended for the M.C., once at Vimy and once in the taking of the outskirts of Lens.

He was never mentioned for the V.C. Such a decoration was almost unattainable in the last war. I think he was mentioned in dispatches after Vimy, but have not the records at hand.

All the time he was cool and reliable under fire, and one of the best little sportsmen I ever knew. Jimmy Wood, one of his brother officers, expressed it well. He said "Jack" is the most loveable little rascal I ever knew.

He was without envy, quite unselfish, and ready for anything – whether mischief or the most dangerous undertaking - at all times, and as far as I could see, with the same cheerful optimism.

I should enjoy more than I could express the privilege of meeting you and telling you a great many things regarding your boy that would interest you.

Very few of his age had made so many real friends, and had seen and done so much. He no doubt had a splendid future, but he had a very complete past. He left his influence on more than is the lot of most men of much greater age. Wherever he is, he is standing square on his feet, without fear and without regrets.

Will you please convey to Mrs. Jackson my very kindest regards.

Yours sincerely,

WILGAR

Hector (back right) with fellow officers from his unit. Major W.P. Wilgar is presumably one of the officers in the centre of the front row. | *Family album*

To an Athlete Dying Young

The time you won your town the race
We chaired you through the market-place;
Man and boy stood cheering by,
And home we brought you shoulder-high.

To-day, the road all runners come,
Shoulder-high we bring you home,
And set you at your threshold down,
Townsman of a stiller town.

Smart lad, to slip betimes away
From fields where glory does not stay
And early though the laurel grows
It withers quicker than the rose.

Eyes the shady night has shut
Cannot see the record cut,
And silence sounds no worse than cheers
After earth has stopped the ears:

Now you will not swell the rout
Of lads that wore their honours out,
Runners whom renown outran
And the name died before the man.

So set, before its echoes fade,
The fleet foot on the sill of shade,
And hold to the low lintel up
The still-defended challenge-cup.

A.E. Housman

Epilogue

Hector's parents never fully recovered from the shock of his unexpected death so soon after they had given thanks for his safe return from the killing fields of the Western Front.

Shortly after Hector's death, the road to the family farm, Applegarth, was officially named Jackson Road in his memory.[1] The road is still marked as that on some road maps today, although it was officially renamed 24th Avenue in 1939 as part of a practical but unimaginative drive to make navigation easier for emergency vehicles.

The war years had taken a severe toll, not only on Hector's parents, but on Applegarth as well. With the absence of three of the family's four sons, and a shortage of hired help, many of whom were also fighting in France, part of the hard-cleared fields had largely reverted to bush. Although Moses was as keen as ever to make Applegarth a model farm, his attempts to keep it going against these odds exhausted him and drained the family coffers. When the wave of ex-servicemen arrived back in Canada at the end of the war, the government subsidized their purchase of new farms and the value of existing farms plummeted. Moses was unable to use Applegarth as collateral for the loans he needed to restore it.

The stress of losing Hector in such a pointless way, the failing farm and financial worries all took their toll. By early 1922, Moses began to succumb to the stomach cancer whose early warning signs of anaemia had manifested themselves while Hector was still in Europe. The accumulated strain had a devastating effect on Hector's mother too, and she suffered a temporary nervous breakdown.

---

[1] Hector was not alone in this honour, and several other roads in Aldergrove were named after servicemen who had been killed.

Housman, hearing of his old friend's decline, hurried to compile his long-awaited volume, *Last Poems*, writing a number of new ones and improving on some that he had drafted many years earlier. Several of the poems in the volume referred obliquely to his love for Moses, although some of the more heartfelt ones were not included and only saw print after both Moses' and Housman's deaths. Housman desperately wanted to finish the collection of verse so Moses could read it and comment before he died. In the introduction to the volume, Housman wrote:

> I publish these poems, few though they are, because it is not likely that I shall ever be impelled to write much more. I can no longer expect to be revisited by the continuous excitement under which in the early months of 1895 I wrote the greater part of my first book, nor indeed could I well sustain it if it came; and it is best that what I have written should be printed while I am here to see it through the press and control its spelling and punctuation.

Housman managed to complete the book just in time and a copy arrived at Applegarth in early November 1922. In that copy, Housman hand wrote a dedication to Moses, accompanied by an artificially cheerful letter in which Housman wrote:

My Dear Mo
    I have been putting off writing so as to be able to send you this precious book, published to-day. The cheerful and exhilarating tone of my verse is so notorious that I feel sure it will do you more good than the doctors; though you do not know, and there are no means of driving the knowledge into your thick head, what a bloody good poet I am. In order to intimidate you and repress your insolence I am enclosing

A.E. Housman, Classical scholar and poet, at Cambridge. | *Archival photo*

the review and leader which the Times devoted to the subject . . . Of this new book there were printed 4000 copies for a first edition, which were all ordered by the booksellers before publication, so there is already a 2nd edition in the press. It is now 11 o'clock in the morning, and I hear that the Cambridge shops are sold out. Please to realize therefore, with fear and respect, that I am an eminent bloke; though I would much rather have followed you around the world and blacked your boots . . . The eminent poet would willingly have exchanged his fame and position for the chance of following his correspondent, in the humblest capacity, to the farthest corners of the earth.

A few days after receiving the book, Moses left Applegarth for the last time; he was admitted to the Vancouver General Hospital in failing health. On November 23, using a blunt pencil, he wrote a final farewell letter to Housman from his hospital bed. In spite of his advanced illness, he remained an astute and boisterous critic, not hesitating to impale his friend with barbs similar to those that Housman frequently used on Moses and others.[1]

Bed 4, Ward T,
General Hospital,
Vancouver, B.C.
23 Nov., 1922

My dear old Hous,
I got your letter and your egregious poems at home about a fortnight ago. I thought of heaping sarcasms on your brain products, as usual, but some of the pieces are good enough to redeem the rest. The *Times* critique was good, and its selections sensible, but the *Observer*, which the faithful Ward sent me, was still better. I hoped to see the *Spectator*, but it has not been sent along. The *Morning Post* is about the only other paper to count. The old woman's *D. Telegraph* and the screamingly radical press, with bosh-writers like that A.G. Gardiner, don't count.[2]
You certainly know how to end the book. But who is going to labour at collecting your Juvenilia from the "Round Table" & elsewhere, and to exploit acute inaccuracies about them in the not far distant future?[3] That

---

[1] The letter is held by the Jackson family and has not previously been published.
[2] A.G. Gardiner was the liberal editor of the *Daily News* from 1902-1919.
[3] *Ye Round Table* was an undergraduate magazine that Housman had helped found at Oxford as a student.

thing that you published in some aesthetic magazine seems to me, in its disregard of all politeness towards possibilities in the unknown future, seems to me to contain nearly half the philosophy of your two books. You will be surprised at my remembering them so nearly, if I am not quite word-perfect.

> Ave atque Vale[1]
> Goodnight. Ensured release,
> Imperishable peace,
> Have these for yours
> While earth's foundations stand
> And sky and sea and land
> And Heaven endures.
> When Earth's foundations flee
> Nor sky, nor land, nor sea
> At all is found
> Content you, let them burn,
> It is not your concern.
> Sleep on, sleep sound!

It wants the poet to punctuate it. It deserved a place in the Shropshire Lad! It was the condensation of so much meaning into a few words – furiously unorthodox though it might be, that struck me.

Your "Mercenary Army" bit is as skilful as anything in the book. It was a good deal quoted out here during the War.

Here is the 30th. No haggis, No whiskey. No nuthink.

The great Ward informs me that your sales had gone up to 17,000 at the time of writing. Your 'Tis little luck that I have had' can have no reference personal to the poet.

I have also seen your portrait in 'Punch'. Ridiculous as it may appear, there is just a faint indication of the shape of your head, and just a hint of an expression that I have seen on your mug once in a way. I suppose your boots are supposed to harmonise with the bucolic heroes you often immortalize, sleeping off their beer in lovely muck.

1 Dec. I am going on fairly well in this hospital, but I will come out of it pretty soon now, well or ill, and finances won't run to these expenses. It is funny to be "land-poor", with severe depression in agricultural values. I have practically all that I originally paid £3,000 for in cash – land and stock etc. with lots of improvements, yet cannot sell or even borrow £200

---

[1] Housman wrote this poem as a belated farewell to his mother who had died when he was a child.

from a bank. The boys all hang together well, but it is an outrage for an older generation to weaken the younger.

We shan't go on at Applegarth as hitherto. The missus dislikes it. I dislike anything else. I will sell the whole or part, or put on a temporary mortgage or something. What I want is a partner, honest and fond of farming. We could easily make the place produce more than it has ever done. There must be lots who would do, if only I knew them.

Land sells worse now than ever. Most of the returned soldiers have gone out of their little lots, and relinquished their land to Govt., with the results that we land-owners have Govt. as

"CURIOSITIES OF LITERATURE."
The Muse. "OH, ALFRED, WE HAVE MISSED YOU! MY LAD! MY SHROPSHIRE LAD!"

The cartoon from Punch magazine referred to by Moses. | *Archival photo*

dealers in ahead of us. Doubtful land will get up again in time, and then everyone will tumble in to buy. The correct thing to do is to wait, if one can. If I were a capitalist I would buy now. The disgusting thing is the way I have let you and Ward down.[1] I will return what I can , when anything comes in, but things shape up for my dying a hopeless bankrupt. Probably the sooner the better as I shall never return to my old self, and at the moment am just a burden to everybody. I apologise in dust and ashes.

I haven't your last letter here, but remember an extraordinary exhibition about blacking boots! My most presentable boots are brown, requiring no blacking, Larry, old chap. At home I wear boots of canvas & rubber composition, known as snagproof, as your choice is for an absolute sinecure. But it would be fine to see you here, though no chance of the old amenities. No 15-mile walks to a good pub to consume old ribs of beef 10"

---

[1] Referring to the unrepaid loans Housman and Ward had made for the initial purchase of Applegarth.

thick, pickled walnuts, and a quart of bitter, with a good tub of cream, & rich cheese to finish. None of that in this beastly land, with their infernal prohibition.[1]

G.W. Ellis stayed with us for some time a year ago.[2] He had farmed in Alberta. He is rather a slacker, but well up in St. John's recollections, so we could talk about many things.

Oscar, Bachelor of Applied Science, is now assaying in the big smelter at Trail, B.C. Gerald ran a motor boat up the coast as an Assistant Fire Ranger for the Forest Dept. in the Summer Vacation. He did so well that they promise him a better job for next summer, but he thinks he will go as a "mucker" or labourer in the Britannia Mine, just for experience.[3] He is going strong at the Univ. That institution has grown wonderfully.

I have seen the *Spectator* review of your emanations. The second paragraph seems to the point, some others less so. The last part of this musical thing from the *Sunday Times* seems largely rot. I did not see the review by Gosse the week before. If you read all the commentaries you must be pretty busy.

I hope your publisher will shoo the Americans off. While lying on my back here I have been exasperated to see how they publish well-known English books, curtailed with only a Yankee publisher's name on the title page, and make their ignorant readers think the author is a Yank. I dislike the arrogant brutes.

Gerald will be up presently & will post this. So here is to continued luck. Printing "Jones of Jesus", "Tennyson in the Moated Grange" etc.[4] may bring you in a fresh fortune at the right time. "First Poems".[5]

Goodbye.

Yours very truly

M.J. Jackson

---

[1] British Columbia along with most of the rest of Canada, banned the sale and consumption of alcohol in late 1917. In 1920 British Columbia became the first Canadian province to repeal prohibition laws, but it required that alcohol be sold through government outlets.

[2] A fellow student at Oxford.

[3] Britannia was a copper mine, twenty-five miles north of Vancouver.

[4] Poems written by Housman in his early years.

[5] Housman never did publish the volume of early poetry as suggested by Moses. However, within a year of Housman's death in 1936, and with Housman's prior approval, his brother Laurence published much of this early work in the volume *More Poems*.

It took almost six weeks for Moses' farewell letter to reach Housman in Cambridge. Later Housman painstakingly traced the weakly penciled words of Moses' last letter to him in ink, faithfully reproducing each letter so as not to lose the handwriting of his lifelong friend.

Housman was horrified by the state of Moses' health and financial circumstances, and replied immediately. Part of his letter reads:[1]

> Trinity College
> Cambridge
> 4 Jan. 1923
>
> My Dear Mo,
>
> I got your letter on New Year's Day. As you threaten to leave the hospital well or ill, I suppose I had better direct this to Applegarth, though I understand it is empty now, rather than to bed 4 . . .
>
> I never was more astounded at anything than at your reproducing my contribution to *Waifs and Strays*. I remember your reading it at Miss Patchett's, and how nervous I felt. If I had known you would recollect it 42 years afterward, my emotions would have been too much for me.
>
> On the copies of the new book already sold in England there will be due to me royalties of about £500. As I cannot be bothered with investments, this will go to swell my already swollen balance at the bank unless you will relieve me of it. Why not rise superior to the natural disagreeableness of your character and behave nicely for once in a way to a fellow who thinks more of you than anything in the world? You are largely responsible for my writing poetry and you ought to take the consequences . . .

Moses stated aim to leave the hospital soon, "well or ill," did not transpire and two weeks later, on January 14, 1923, aged 64, Moses succumbed to the stomach cancer. Housman's letter was still making its laborious way across the Atlantic. Moses never had a chance to read it.

Less than three years after Hector's death, Rosa and Moses' surviving sons gathered in a cemetery once more, for another bleak mid-winter funeral. Moses was buried in the Ocean View Memorial

---

[1] Letter held by the Jackson family.

Park, Vancouver, just a few miles from where Hector had been laid to rest. Once again, family friend the Rev. C.C. Owen led the service. The Hill-Tout and Sprott families were again amongst the mourners.

When he heard of Moses' death, presumably by telegram, Housman wrote to his friend Pollard with whom he and Moses had shared rooms at Oxford:

> Trinity College
> Cambridge
>
> Jan 17 1923
>
> My dear Pollard,
>
> Jackson died peacefully on Sunday night in hospital at Vancouver, where he had gone to be treated for anaemia, with which he had been ailing for some years. I had a letter from him on New Year's Day, which he ended by saying "goodbye". Now I can die myself: I could not have borne to leave him behind me in a world where anything might happen to him.
>
> Yours sincerely,
> A.E. Housman

Housman may well have been thinking of words in his most recent publication that he had penned to mark Moses' marriage forty-seven years before:[1]

> All is quiet, no alarms;
>   Nothing fear of nightly harms.
> Safe you sleep on guarded ground,
>   And in silent circle round
> The thoughts of friends keep watch and ward,
>   Harnessed angels, hand on sword.

The following short poem was probably written soon after Moses' death.[2]

> Now to her lap the incestuous earth
>   The son she bore has ta'en.
> And other sons she brings to birth
>   But not my friend again.

---

[1] *Epithalamium - Last Poems XXIV.*
[2] *A.E.H. Poems VIII*, Ed. Laurence Housman.

Moses' death put the final nail in the coffin of any attempt to revive Applegarth. Oscar and Gerald had been striving to keep Applegarth going when their father's health began to decline badly. However, Gerald was a full-time student at U.B.C., and Oscar, who had completed his degree in Applied Engineering a few months before Moses died, was employed as a metallurgist at Cominco's Sullivan mine at Trail in eastern B.C.

Rosa recovered from her stress-induced breakdown, but with the death of both Moses and Hector, and none of her other sons able to manage the farm full time, it was impractical and unpleasant for her to continue living there alone. Applegarth was put up for sale. But farm prices remained depressed. It was only in the late 1930s that the property was sold and even then, payment was spread out over a lengthy period.

With her sons launched on their careers and the family's meager savings washed by the British Columbian rain into the soils of

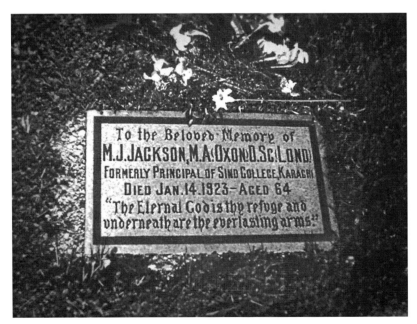

Moses' modest gravestone, partly a reflection of the family's financial straits, still looks the same today. A copy of this photograph hung on Housman's room's wall in Cambridge. | *Family album*

Applegarth, Rosa moved back to England in the mid-1920s. She kept up occasional correspondence with Housman. Ten years after Moses' death she sent his letter opener to Housman. He replied:[1]

> Trinity College
> Cambridge
> 22 Dec. 1932
>
> Dear Mrs Jackson,
>
> I am very grateful for your kindness in giving me the paper knife which belonged to my dear friend, and I shall treasure it to the end of my days.
>
> My advancing age shows itself chiefly in my not taking such long walks as formerly; but otherwise I go on without much change for the worse. That however may soon come, as I have to eat two Christmas dinners on Christmas Eve and a third on the Day itself.
>
> I wish you a happy time among your family, and please convey my best wishes both to those now around you and those whom you are expecting.
>
> I remain yours sincerely
> A.E. Housman

Housman's remark about the paper knife was clearly not meant flippantly. His younger brother, Laurence, visited Housman in his rooms at Trinity College in his later years and enquired about a framed photo portrait that was hanging over the fireplace. Housman is reported to have replied in a "strangely moved voice": "That was my friend Jackson, the man who had more influence on my life than anybody else."

Four months after Rupert had been demobilized at the end of the war, he married Marguerite Marie du Pré de Saint Maur, in Paris. The marriage marked a milestone in a long and happy relationship between Rupert and the Saint Maur family at Saulières, the family home in the Nièvre, southeast of Paris. Rupert was held in great affection by his French brothers-in-law, with whom he shared wartime experiences and a love of the countryside and field sports. The local people always

---

[1] Letter held by the Jackson family.

spoke of him as one of their own, "un chasseur hardi," and enjoyed his soldier's French.

In 1920, Rupert and Marguerite Marie moved to West Hartlepool, County Durham, on the east coast of England, where he joined a medical practice in which he eventually became the senior partner. Although practising as a general practioner, he later became consultant surgeon to the Hartlepool Hospital and the Cameron Hospital and held various honorary appointments with the local police and the National Coal Board. He was an ardent amateur naturalist, a first-class shot, a keen sportsman, and a dedicated musician.

Rupert and Marguerite Marie had a daughter, named Marguerite after her mother, and a son, Hugh (actually christened Alain Hugh).[1] On retirement in 1965, Rupert and Marguerite Marie moved to Five Ashes in Sussex to be near their children. Rupert died in Pembury Hospital, Tunbridge Wells, in 1974 at the age of 84.

Hector's youngest brother, Gerald, had been home schooled at Applegarth as a teen during the war. Although Moses was a very accomplished lecturer at university level, his home schooling of Gerald was less successful, and this and the amount of time that Gerald must have needed to spend doing farm work when his brothers were on the Western Front, meant that he struggled to gain entry to the University of British Columbia soon after the war ended. However, once there, he proved his ability and completed a B.Sc. in Geology and went on to complete his M.Sc. in Mining

Oscar Jackson was awarded a Ph.D. in chemical engineering from the University College of London. | Family album)

---

[1] Much of this information on Rupert comes from Hugh Jackson.

Engineering. Moses died while Gerald was still at university and Gerald put himself through his degree programmes, at least in part, by working during his university vacations.

When Gerald completed his U.B.C. degrees in 1926, he and Oscar, who by then had spent five years in Trail, had little to hold them in Canada and they both moved to Central Africa on the Northern Rhodesian Copperbelt.[1] There Oscar worked as a metallurgist in one of the newly constructed smelters and Gerald carried out geological field mapping as part of an exploration program for additional ore deposits.

Oscar spent eight years in Northern Rhodesia, with two years leave of absence to complete his Ph.D. in metallurgy from Imperial College at the University of London.

Oscar moved to South Africa in 1935 where he joined Union Corporation, one of the major South African mining houses. He was stationed on the gold mines at Springs, a town just east of Johannesburg.

In 1937 Oscar married Jan Fischer, the daughter of a pioneer

Gerald as a young geologist in Northern Rhodesia with an eland, shot to feed his exploration team. | *Family album*

---

[1] Now the Zambian Copperbelt.

farming family from Southern Rhodesia (now Zimbabwe). The couple had two children together, a daughter Geraldine, named after Oscar's brother Gerald, and a son Bruce.

Jan's cousin, Bram Fischer, was a well known anti-apartheid activist who was jailed with Nelson Mandela and eventually died of cancer while under house arrest. Jan was an anti-apartheid campaigner as well, and belonged to the Black Sash organization. This group consisted mainly of liberal white women who held silent solitary anti-apartheid protests and became a thorn in the side of the Afrikaaner Nationalist Government. During a Black Sash protest in Johannesburg in the late 1940s, soon after the Nationalist Party took power, Jan caught pneumonia. Complications set in and she died, leaving Oscar to raise his two young children on his own.

Oscar rose through the ranks of Union Corporation, eventually retiring as the chief metallurgist. In 1949 he was elected the president of the South African Institute of Mining and Metallurgy. He was also an accomplished organist. He died in Johannesburg in 1974, aged 79.

Gerald spent almost three years on the Northern Rhodesian Copperbelt. In 1929, he moved to England to write up his field work as a doctorate at Imperial College, London, and Trinity College, Cambridge. He was awarded his D.Sc. in 1932.

In a masterstroke of mistiming, he completed his doctorate at the depths of the Great Depression and found himself overqualified for a depressed market and unemployable as a geologist. Consequently he emulated his elder brother Rupert, and switched to medicine, a profession he felt would always be in demand. He attended medical school at St. Thomas's Hospital in London. Although Housman had not been able to persuade Gerald's father to accept his £500 in royalties to alleviate the Jackson family's financial hardships, he was able to assist Gerald with student fees and living expenses for medical school in London.

Housman died in April 1936, aged 77. As a student, Gerald had visited his father's friend and his godfather several times during his last illness; he attended Housman's funeral, joining in the hymn that Housman had written many years before in anticipation of the occasion.[1]

---

[1] R.P. Graves, *A.E. Housman; The Scholar-Poet* (1979).

A few months after Housman's death, Rosa travelled to South Africa by mail ship to visit Oscar. There, she fell ill and died on September 22, aged 76. She was buried in the Springs Cemetery near Johannesburg, where Oscar and his daughter Geraldine were later laid to rest beside her.

Gerald completed his internship at St Thomas's, receiving his M.B., B.S. medical degree in 1939 just before the outbreak of the Second World War.

When he qualified, Gerald revisited the land of his birth for a few months as a captain in the Medical Corps of the Indian Army, stationed on the Northwest Frontier between what is now Pakistan and Afghanistan. He returned to England as the Second World War escalated, and joined the RAMC as Hector had advised him to do some twenty-five years previously. The RAMC attached him to the Irish Guards with the initial rank of captain.

In 1943, Gerald met Honor Martin who was working in Combined Operations Headquarters in London where she held a rank junior commander, and was one of Lord Louis Mountbatten's assistants. Gerald and Honor were married in January 1945. Just a week later, Gerald was transferred to Belgium where he spent the last eight months of the war.

At the end of the war, Gerald and Honor decided that a future in grey, exhausted post-war Britain had little appeal. They decided to move to Northern Rhodesia where Gerald had spent three enjoyable years in the bush; there he took up a post as medical officer with the Copperbelt mines which he had

Gerald as a medical officer in the Irish Guards during the Second World War. | Family album

254

helped to develop twenty years earlier as a geologist. Within months of their arrival, however, the couple moved south to Southern Rhodesia where Gerald set up a private medical practice in the capital city, Salisbury.[1] A few years later, Gerald extended his qualifications, again in London, and specialized in anaesthetics while continuing his general practice in Salisbury.

Gerald and Honor raised a family in Salisbury, twins Brian and Martin and a third son, Andrew. Gerald continued to practice general medicine and anaesthesia in Harare until his death at 78. Before his death, he collected and typed the wartime letters written by his brother, Hector, which form the core of this book.

Marg, Hector's aunt, remained in Britain and died in 1939 in Scotland. Her sister, Tiger (Ida Jackson), remained in England and died there the same year. Neither of them ever married.

Agnes and Irene lived in Mission, B.C. for the rest of their lives. Irene continued to work at the Commercial Bank of Canada; she died in 1948. Agnes taught music and died some years after her sister. They too remained unmarried.

---

[1] Now Harare, Zimbabwe.

Selected Bibliography

Aldergrove Heritage Society. *The Place Between*. Aldergrove, B.C.: Aldergrove Heritage Society, 1993.

Brown A., and R. Gimblett. *In the Footsteps of the Canadian Corps: Canada's First World War 1914-1918*. Ottawa: Magic Light Publishing. 2006.

Graves, R.P., *A.E.Housman: The Scholar-Poet*. New York: Charles Scribner's Sons. 1979.

Housman, Laurence, (ed.). *A.E.H., Poems VII*. London: Jonathan Cape. 1937.

Jackson, Moses John. *Personal Diary, 1907-1910*. Unpublished.

Kerry A.J. and W.A. McDill. *The History of the Corps of Canadian Engineers, Vol. 1, 1749-1939*. Ottawa: The Military Engineers Association of Canada. 1962.

Laffin, John. *The Western Front Illustrated 1914-1918*. London: Grange Books. 1997.

Library and Archives Canada, *War Diaries, 10th Battalion, Canadian Engineers*, 1916-1920. , Ottawa. http://www.collectionscanada.gc.ca/archivianet/020152_e.html

Maas, H. (ed.). *The Letters of A.E. Housman*. London: Granada Publishing. 1971.

Naiditch P.G. *Problems in the Life and Writings of A.E. Housman*. Beverly Hills, U.S.A: Krown & Spellman.1995.

BIBLIOGRAPHY

Nicholson, G.W.L. *Official History of the Canadian Army in the First World War: Canadian Expeditionary Force 1914-1919*. Ottawa: Queens Printer and Controller of Stationary. 1962.

Sommer, W. *The Ambitious City*. Canada: Harbour Publishing. 2007.

Todd, R.B. "M.J. Jackson in British Columbia: Some Supplementary Information," *Housman Society Journal*, 26 (2000): 59-61.

Weedon, St.C.E. *A Year with the Gaekwar of Baroda*. Boston: D. Estes & Co. 1911.

Index

About the Author

Andrew Jackson was born in Zimbabwe (formerly Rhodesia) and received a commission in the Rhodesian Corps of Engineers during that country's bush war, which ended in 1979. His background in military engineering allowed him to recognize the value of this unique collection of unpublished letters, written by his uncle, Captain Hector Jackson, as well as others by Hector's father, Dr. Moses Jackson, and Dr. Jackson's lifelong friend, the poet A.E. Housman.

Andrew Jackson is a geologist by profession and an amateur historian by avocation. He spent some years in Vancouver prior to establishing his present home in San Diego, California; he is married with two daughters.